SACREDSPACE

THE
PRAYERBOOK
2024

from the website www.sacredspace.ie
Prayer from the Irish Jesuits

Messenger Publications
www.messenger.ie

ISBN: 9781788126403

Scripture quotations are from New Revised Standard Version Bible,
National Council of the Churches of Christ in the United States of America.
Used by permission. All rights reserved worldwide. www.nrsvbibles.org

Weekly reflections are from books and periodicals published by Messenger Publications.
For more information go to www.messenger.ie

Designed by Messenger Publications Design Department
Typeset in Adobe Caslon Pro & Avant Garde
Printed by Hussar Books

Messenger Publications,
37 Leeson Place,
Dublin D02 E5V0,
Ireland
www.messenger.ie

CONTENTS

Sacred Space Prayer

Bless all who worship you, almighty God,
from the rising of the sun to its setting:
from your goodness enrich us,
by your love inspire us,
by your Spirit guide us,
by your power protect us,
in your mercy receive us,
now and always.

Preface

In 1999 an Irish Jesuit named Alan McGuckian had the simple – but at the time radical – idea of bringing daily prayer to the Internet. No one imagined that his experimental project would grow into a global community with volunteers translating the prayer experience into seventeen different languages.

Millions of people, from numerous Christian traditions, visit www .sacredspace.ie each year, and what they find is an invitation to step away from their busy routines for a few minutes a day to concentrate on what is really important in their lives. Sacred Space offers its visitors the opportunity to grow in prayerful awareness of their friendship with God.

Besides the daily prayer experience, Sacred Space also offers Living Space, with commentaries on the Scripture readings for each day's Catholic Mass. The Chapel of Intentions allows people to add their own prayers, while Pray with the Pope joins the community to the international Apostleship of Prayer. In addition, Sacred Space provides Lenten and Advent retreats, often in partnership with Pray as You Go, and audio prayer service from the British Jesuits.

The contents of this printed edition, first produced in 2004, are taken directly from our Internet site. Despite the increased use of Sacred Space on mobile devices, many people want a book they can hold and carry, and this book has proven especially helpful for prayer groups.

In 2014 the Irish Jesuits entered into an apostolic agreement with the Chicago-Detroit Jesuits, and Sacred Space now operates in partnership with Loyola Press.

I am delighted to bring you the *Sacred Space* book, and I pray that your prayer life will flourish with its help.

Yours in Christ

Paul Campbell SJ

Introduction to

Sacred Space 2024

In preparing this introduction to *Sacred Space*, two friends came to mind; more specifically, two friends, now sadly departed, who taught me life lessons. It struck me that the lessons they taught also give insight into the gift that *Sacred Space* is to all who encounter it.

When asked for his advice on living well, my good friend Monsignor Tom Toner used to say, 'Make sure you take time to stop and smell the roses each day.' I think what he meant was that all of us would do well to recognise that life can be so busy that we get caught up in busyness and miss the real point, which is that there is learning in each moment.

If we stopped to smell the roses each day, we might just tap into those lessons that are out there waiting to be learned. We all have time. Different people have different amounts of it, but we all have some time nonetheless. Each day we have a full twenty-four hours (86,400 seconds) of possibility and are invited to consider how to use that time wisely, in moments of love and learning. *Sacred Space* offers us one way to 'stop and smell the roses each day', giving us a structured way to step out of the busyness of life and into the wonderfully real world of scripture, prayer and reflection. One of the joys of *Sacred Space* is that it accompanies us into and through that world. We are never left alone to our own devices. We are offered guidance and insights to make that time of stopping even more worthwhile.

My second friend was fully alive too. But she wasn't a human being! She was my dog, Jenny. As I was brushing her coat one day, the brush I was using got overloaded with hair. It couldn't take any more and it was becoming ineffective. I needed to change brushes. I needed a deeper brush in order to remove all the excess and dead hair. So I picked up a brush with a rigid, fine comb and it did the job very well indeed. It got deep into Jenny's second (under)coat.

There come times in all of our lives when we need 'a deeper brush'; when life delivers us circumstances or experiences that let us know that we need to go deeper into ourselves, our understanding of the world and our understanding of God in order to grow. Often, but not always, these times are experienced as difficult. For example, they might be times of bereavement that cause us to question the nature of life itself. They might be times of job, health or relationship loss that cause us to feel vulnerable – stripped away. They might also be times of transgressions, when we act in a way that we know goes against what we believe is a good way to be in this world. They also come in the less dramatic, ordinary experiences of life.

A deeper brush for us may be those practices that allow us to shed our excess baggage, those thoughts, feelings and behaviours that hold us back. I wonder if we could perhaps see how we are being invited to find a 'deeper brush'? Some find the 'deeper brush' in solid relationship with others. The sense of having what in Irish is called an 'anam cara' (a soul friend) is often enough for a person to weather the difficulties as well as the joys of life with a framework for understanding it all. If you can find one, an anam cara is a prized gift to receive and to treasure.

Sacred Space is a kind of 'anam cara' in itself. It offers us a 'deeper brush', a way to go to those deeper places; perhaps to shed baggage we no longer need, perhaps to pick up some life-giving luggage for the journey of life. The prospect of going into the deep can make us nervous. *Sacred Space*, though, accompanies us in that experience. It acts as a kind of navigator for the journey, pointing us always, as it does, to the great guide, the greatest 'anam cara' of all – God.

Friends, I am so pleased that you have decided to pick up *Sacred Space*, either for the first time or as part of your regular prayer life. In either circumstance I am sure that it will hold surprising and consoling insights for you. My prayer is that in stopping you will experience sweetness greater than the scent of the sweetest rose, and joy in going to the depths of life's experiences, where we inevitably encounter the Risen Lord.

Jim Deeds

How to Use This Book

During each week of the Liturgical year, begin by reading the 'Something to think and pray about each day this week'. Then proceed through 'The Presence of God', 'Freedom' and 'Consciousness' steps to prepare yourself to hear the word of God in your heart. In the next step, 'The Word', turn to the Scripture reading for each day of the week. Inspiration points are provided if you need them. Then return to the 'Conversation' and 'Conclusion' steps. Use this process every day of the year.

3–9 December 2023

Something to think and pray about each day this week:

If you were to wish people a happy new year today, they would in all probability find it awkward. Nevertheless, we do start a new Christian year with the season of Advent. The changing seasons remind us of different aspects of being Christian, one of which is the conviction that we may always begin again and start new. Last Sunday we looked back and today we look forward: What are *my* hopes for the coming Christian year? How am I now? How would I like to be, as a believer, this time next year? What steps will I take to make that a reality?

Kieran O'Mahony OSA, *Hearers of the Word: Praying &
Exploring the Readings for Advent & Christmas*

The Presence of God

Dear Jesus, I come to you today longing for your presence. I desire to love you as you love me. May nothing ever separate me from you.

Freedom

Lord, grant me the grace to be free from the excesses of this life. Let me not get caught up with the desire for wealth. Keep my heart and mind free to love and serve you.

Consciousness

Where do I sense hope, encouragement and growth in my life? By looking back over the past few months, I may be able to see which activities and occasions have produced rich fruit. If I do notice such areas, I will determine to give those areas both time and space in the future.

The Word

God speaks to each of us individually. I listen attentively, to hear what he is saying to me. Read the text a few times, then listen. *(Please turn to the Scripture on the following pages. Inspiration points are there, should you need them. When you are ready, return here to continue.)*

Conversation

What is stirring in me as I pray? Am I consoled, troubled, left cold? I imagine Jesus standing or sitting at my side, and I share my feelings with him.

Conclusion

Glory be to the Father, and to the Son, and to the Holy Spirit,
As it was in the beginning, is now and ever shall be,
World without end. Amen.

Sunday 3 December
First Sunday of Advent
Mark 13:33–37

Jesus said to his disciples, 'Beware, keep alert; for you do not know when the time will come. It is like a man going on a journey, when he leaves home and puts his slaves in charge, each with his work, and commands the doorkeeper to be on the watch. Therefore, keep awake – for you do not know when the master of the house will come, in the evening, or at midnight, or at cockcrow, or at dawn, or else he may find you asleep when he comes suddenly. And what I say to you I say to all: Keep awake.'

- The Advent season recalls significant events and people to help us to be alert for Christmas. Qualities such as being prepared and staying attentive are highlighted today. May we grow in appreciation of God's greatest gift to us in Jesus and be ready to welcome him on his coming anew to us.
- Good servants await the return of the master. Our master desires to serve us. May our Advent waiting be one that desires to welcome a friend who comes to save, not a thief in the night who is to be feared.

Monday 4 December
Matthew 8:5–11

When he entered Capernaum, a centurion came to him, appealing to him and saying, 'Lord, my servant is lying at home paralysed, in terrible distress.' And he said to him, 'I will come and cure him.' The centurion answered, 'Lord, I am not worthy to have you come under my roof; but only speak the word, and my servant will be healed. For I also am a man under authority, with soldiers under me; and I say to one, "Go", and he goes, and to another, "Come", and he comes, and to my slave, "Do this", and the slave does it.' When Jesus heard him, he was amazed and said to those who followed him, 'Truly I tell you, in no one in Israel have I found such faith. I tell you, many will come from east and west and will eat with Abraham and Isaac and Jacob in the kingdom of heaven.'

- A centurion, an outsider, pleaded with Jesus for his servant who was paralysed and in great distress. In our distress and paralysis we ask for the faith to reach out to you, Lord, and ask you to give us the healing we need.
- The spoken word can be very influential for good or for ill. For the centurion it was sufficient for Jesus to utter it. Lord, your word is one of salvation. May we hear it, respond to it and bring words of comfort to others in turn.

Tuesday 5 December
Luke 10:21–24

At that same hour Jesus rejoiced in the Holy Spirit and said, 'I thank you, Father, Lord of heaven and earth, because you have hidden these things from the wise and the intelligent and have revealed them to infants; yes, Father, for such was your gracious will. All things have been handed over to me by my Father; and no one knows who the Son is except the Father, or who the Father is except the Son and anyone to whom the Son chooses to reveal him.'

Then turning to the disciples, Jesus said to them privately, 'Blessed are the eyes that see what you see! For I tell you that many prophets and kings desired to see what you see, but did not see it, and to hear what you hear, but did not hear it.'

- Jesus who comes is the source of Joy who reveals the Father to us. Intellectuals can fail to grasp the depth of Jesus' message. We are drawn into Jesus' relationship with the Father. May we have childlike faith and trust to accept what Jesus reveals to us, his children.
- Jesus is grateful to the Father for all that was given to him. We are blessed in what we see and hear through what Jesus reveals to us. We pray to rejoice in the Spirit and be prophetic in bringing it to others in Jesus' name.

Wednesday 6 December
Matthew 15:29–37

After Jesus had left that place, he passed along the Sea of Galilee, and he went up the mountain, where he sat down. Great crowds came to him, bringing with them the lame, the maimed, the blind, the mute, and many others. They put them at his feet, and he cured them, so that the crowd was amazed when they saw the mute speaking, the maimed whole, the lame walking, and the blind seeing. And they praised the God of Israel.

Then Jesus called his disciples to him and said, 'I have compassion for the crowd, because they have been with me now for three days and have nothing to eat; and I do not want to send them away hungry, for they might faint on the way.' The disciples said to him, 'Where are we to get enough bread in the desert to feed so great a crowd?' Jesus asked them, 'How many loaves have you?' They said, 'Seven, and a few small fish.' Then ordering the crowd to sit down on the ground, he took the seven loaves and the fish; and after giving thanks he broke them and gave them to the disciples, and the disciples gave them to the crowds. And all of them ate and were filled; and they took up the broken pieces left over, seven baskets full.

- Jesus went up the mountain, but the crowds followed. He cured those in need of healing to the amazement of all. Mountains were places to meet God. Lord, give us a sense of wonder in our meeting with you and heal the scars of life that we carry.
- Jesus had compassion for the people. This was seen in his healing and his provision of food for them. They were hungry for his word and were also physically hungry, having spent three days with him. Lord, may our hunger, inner and outer, lead us to you to satisfy it.

Thursday 7 December
Matthew 7:21.24–27
Jesus said to them, 'Not everyone who says to me, "Lord, Lord", will enter the kingdom of heaven, but only one who does the will of my Father in heaven.

'Everyone then who hears these words of mine and acts on them will be like a wise man who built his house on rock. The rain fell, the floods came, and the winds blew and beat on that house, but it did not fall, because it had been founded on rock. And everyone who hears these words of mine and does not act on them will be like a foolish man who built his house on sand. The rain fell, and the floods came, and the winds blew and beat against that house, and it fell – and great was its fall!'

- The words of Jesus proclaiming the kingdom of God are meant to find a home in the human heart. Calling Jesus 'Lord' needs to be a reality, a lived experience, doing the will of the Father. May we accept you as Lord and live your message in proclaiming your kingdom.
- God's word was lived out by Jesus. We are to build on that solid foundation where our words lead to action. We pray to be houses built on rock that can withstand the storms of life.

Friday 8 December
The Immaculate Conception of the Blessed Virgin Mary
Luke 1:26–38

In the sixth month the angel Gabriel was sent by God to a town in Galilee called Nazareth, to a virgin engaged to a man whose name was Joseph, of the house of David. The virgin's name was Mary. And he came to her and said, 'Greetings, favoured one! The Lord is with you.' But she was much perplexed by his words and pondered what sort of greeting this might be. The angel said to her, 'Do not be afraid, Mary, for you have found favour with God. And now, you will conceive in your womb and bear a son, and you will name him Jesus. He will be great, and will be called the Son of the Most High, and the Lord God will give to him the throne of his ancestor David. He will reign over the house of Jacob for ever, and of his kingdom there will be no end.' Mary said to the angel, 'How can this be, since I am a virgin?' The angel said to her, 'The Holy Spirit will come upon you, and the power of the Most High will overshadow you; therefore the child to be born will be holy; he will be called Son of God. And now, your relative Elizabeth in her old age has also conceived a son; and this is the sixth month for her who was said to be barren. For nothing will be impossible with God.' Then Mary said, 'Here am I, the servant of the Lord; let it be with me according to your word.' Then the angel departed from her.

- Today's feast looks to a new era in God's salvation story. It recalls Mary being prepared for her role as the mother of Jesus, though the reading refers to the conception of Jesus in her womb. Jesus would be born of the family of David, fulfilling God's plan and offering hope for the future. As promised children we pray to continue God's saving story as family members.
- There is the contrast of the greatness of the event of an angel with a surprising message and that of a humble virgin in an obscure village in Galilee. May we have the faith to receive the message of God in the humble settings of our own lives and bring Jesus to birth anew.

Saturday 9 December
Matthew 9:35–10:1.5a.6–8
Then Jesus went about all the cities and villages, teaching in their synagogues, and proclaiming the good news of the kingdom, and curing every disease and every sickness. When he saw the crowds, he had compassion for them, because they were harassed and helpless, like sheep without a shepherd. Then he said to his disciples, 'The harvest is plentiful, but the labourers are few; therefore ask the Lord of the harvest to send out labourers into his harvest.'

Then Jesus summoned his twelve disciples and gave them authority over unclean spirits, to cast them out, and to cure every disease and every sickness.

These twelve Jesus sent out with the following instructions: 'Go nowhere among the Gentiles, and enter no town of the Samaritans, but go rather to the lost sheep of the house of Israel. As you go, proclaim the good news, "The kingdom of heaven has come near." Cure the sick, raise the dead, cleanse the lepers, cast out demons. You received without payment; give without payment.'

- Jesus was the traveller bringing good news of the kingdom and healing. He had compassion for the people as they were 'like sheep without a shepherd'. To facilitate this he desired helpers to gather the harvest. May we have his love and care in reaching out to others, particularly those in most need.

- Jesus took decisive action in spreading the mission in calling the twelve disciples by name and entrusting the same work to them. We are the unlikely ones called at this time and sent out, so we pray for the honesty to respond to his invitation and remain loyal to Jesus.

The Second Week of Advent

10–16 December 2023

Something to think and pray about each day this week:

Advent is the annual season of waiting. We wait for the same reason every year, and we are certain that the One we await – a Person, Jesus, Son of God – will arrive on time. Yet, we find that the waiting is new each year, as Jesus is ever new. Maybe we don't like the waiting, or maybe we enter enthusiastically into Advent, which in some countries now starts in October. Maybe we are happy to wait in patience and quiet.

We wait also to notice where and how God is in our lives. This waiting is often compared to the watchman who waits, noticing all that is happening around him. He's on a height to see the world around him. Advent can be our hill or mountain. Each day we gather something new about God, ourselves and the world.

The way we wait affects how we celebrate and enjoy Christmas. The way we wait may grow in us a new realisation that everything about God, and especially God's Son, is worth our waiting. We wait for the Lord because his day is near. Thanks be to God!

Donal Neary SJ, *The Messenger Advent Booklet: Reflections on the Daily Readings*

The Presence of God

Dear Jesus, as I call on you today, I realise that often I come asking for favours. Today I'd like just to be in your presence. Draw my heart in response to your love.

Freedom

God my creator, you gave me life and the gift of freedom. Through your love I exist in this world. May I never take the gift of life for granted. May I always respect others' right to life.

Consciousness

Dear Lord, help me to remember that you gave me life. Teach me to slow down, to be still and enjoy the pleasures created for me. To be aware of the beauty that surrounds me: the marvel of mountains, the calmness of lakes, the fragility of a flower petal. I need to remember that all these things come from you.

The Word

The word of God comes down to us through the Scriptures. May the Holy Spirit enlighten my mind and my heart to respond to the Gospel teachings. *(Please turn to the Scripture on the following pages. Inspiration points are there, should you need them. When you are ready, return here to continue.)*

Conversation

What feelings are rising in me as I pray and reflect on God's word? I imagine Jesus himself sitting or standing near me, and I open my heart to him.

Conclusion

I thank God for these moments we have spent together and for any insights I have been given concerning the text.

Sunday 10 December
Second Sunday of Advent
Mark 1:1–8

The beginning of the good news of Jesus Christ, the Son of God.
As it is written in the prophet Isaiah,
'See, I am sending my messenger ahead of you,
who will prepare your way;
the voice of one crying out in the wilderness:
"Prepare the way of the Lord,
make his paths straight"',
John the baptiser appeared in the wilderness, proclaiming a baptism of repentance for the forgiveness of sins. And people from the whole Judean countryside and all the people of Jerusalem were going out to him, and were baptised by him in the river Jordan, confessing their sins. Now John was clothed with camel's hair, with a leather belt around his waist, and he ate locusts and wild honey. He proclaimed, 'The one who is more powerful than I is coming after me; I am not worthy to stoop down and untie the thong of his sandals. I have baptised you with water; but he will baptise you with the Holy Spirit.'

- The Gospel is the good news of Jesus, the Son of God. It moves quickly to John the Baptist, who fulfilled the prophecy of Isaiah in introducing Jesus. He proclaimed repentance in the wilderness, drawing crowds. Lord, may we find you in the wilderness of this time and draw inspiration from John in living simply and announcing your presence.

- A good facilitator does not say too much or draw attention to self. John gives a very good example. May we introduce the Lord, show the way and politely step aside when not needed.

Monday 11 December
Luke 5:17–26

One day, while he was teaching, Pharisees and teachers of the law were sitting nearby (they had come from every village of Galilee and Judea and from Jerusalem); and the power of the Lord was with him to heal. Just then some men came, carrying a paralysed man on a bed.

They were trying to bring him in and lay him before Jesus; but finding no way to bring him in because of the crowd, they went up on the roof and let him down with his bed through the tiles into the middle of the crowd in front of Jesus. When he saw their faith, he said, 'Friend, your sins are forgiven you.' Then the scribes and the Pharisees began to question, 'Who is this who is speaking blasphemies? Who can forgive sins but God alone?' When Jesus perceived their questionings, he answered them, 'Why do you raise such questions in your hearts? Which is easier, to say, "Your sins are forgiven you", or to say, "Stand up and walk"? But so that you may know that the Son of Man has authority on earth to forgive sins' – he said to the one who was paralysed – 'I say to you, stand up and take your bed and go to your home.' Immediately he stood up before them, took what he had been lying on, and went to his home, glorifying God. Amazement seized all of them, and they glorified God and were filled with awe, saying, 'We have seen strange things today.'

- The scribes and Pharisees were sitting near to Jesus but were far away from him in their thinking. Others wanted to come near in faith and found a creative way to do so. As your coming draws near, may we have the freedom to bring the paralysed parts of our lives to you for healing.
- This is a story of inner and outer healing, with Jesus indicating priority in his action. As friends of the Lord may we come to him, accepting the help of others in doing so, to receive what he offers.

Tuesday 12 December
Matthew 18:12–14

Jesus asked, 'What do you think? If a shepherd has a hundred sheep, and one of them has gone astray, does he not leave the ninety-nine on the mountains and go in search of the one that went astray? And if he finds it, truly I tell you, he rejoices over it more than over the ninety-nine that never went astray. It is not the will of your Father in heaven that one of these little ones should be lost.'

- Seeking one and leaving ninety-nine could seem foolish or greedy. Our God has a different approach, being compassionate in leaving,

searching, finding and rejoicing. We pray that we may recognise ourselves as lost sheep and allow the Lord find us.
- The shepherd rejoiced in finding the lost sheep. He did not scold it for wandering away. May we appreciate the Lord's joy in finding us and bringing us back from our wandering ways.

Wednesday 13 December
Matthew 11:28–30

At that time Jesus said, 'Come to me, all you that are weary and are carrying heavy burdens, and I will give you rest. Take my yoke upon you, and learn from me; for I am gentle and humble in heart, and you will find rest for your souls. For my yoke is easy, and my burden is light.'
- Come to me, come back, come follow me, come and see, are familiar phrases to us. We are invited into a deeper relationship by our God of welcome, who desires us to live more fully. Lord, open our hearts to hear your message to come to you, to accept your invitation and respond to it, knowing that you want what is best for us.
- Life has its challenges and difficulties, but the Lord offers rest. We are reminded that the Lord is gentle and humble in heart but does not remove all burdens. Let us turn to the Lord for his help in lightening our burdens that we may walk in in greater peace.

Thursday 14 December
Matthew 11:11–15

As they went away, Jesus began to speak to the crowds about John: 'Truly I tell you, among those born of women no one has arisen greater than John the Baptist; yet the least in the kingdom of heaven is greater than he. From the days of John the Baptist until now the kingdom of heaven has suffered violence, and the violent take it by force. For all the prophets and the law prophesied until John came; and if you are willing to accept it, he is Elijah who is to come. Let anyone with ears listen!'
- John the Baptist was a 'child of promise', born of elderly parents and given a distinctive role in preparing the way for Jesus. The prophecies pointed to him. As children of the kingdom of God may we value our privileged position of sharing all that Jesus has given.

- John proclaimed, 'Repent, for the kingdom of heaven has come near.' Jesus brought about a new kingdom. May we learn to live simply as children of Jesus' kingdom, being guided by the example of John amid the violence and trouble of this time.

Friday 15 December
Matthew 11:16–19

Jesus said, 'But to what will I compare this generation? It is like children sitting in the market-places and calling to one another,
   "We played the flute for you, and you did not dance;
   we wailed, and you did not mourn."

For John came neither eating nor drinking, and they say, "He has a demon"; the Son of Man came eating and drinking, and they say, "Look, a glutton and a drunkard, a friend of tax-collectors and sinners!" Yet wisdom is vindicated by her deeds.'

- John the Baptist and Jesus began their mission in a somewhat similar way in calling for repentance. John was an ascetic figure, living in the wilderness and eating what it produced. Jesus went to several parties and associated with tax collectors and sinners. Both took the situation into account in their ministry. In the market-place of this age, we pray that may we have a clear message that is adapted to the situations we encounter, but that holds on to the truth.
- Fasting or feasting can be genuine responses, depending on the situation. Comparing the externals does not do justice to the deeper reality. May we have the wisdom to understand better what is appropriate to each situation and be guided by the inner truth.

Saturday 16 December
Matthew 17:9a.10–13

As they were coming down the mountain, Jesus ordered them, 'Tell no one about the vision until after the Son of Man has been raised from the dead.' And the disciples asked him, 'Why, then, do the scribes say that Elijah must come first?' He replied, 'Elijah is indeed coming and will restore all things; but I tell you that Elijah has already come, and they did not recognise him, but they did to him whatever they pleased. So also the Son of Man is about to suffer at their hands.' Then the disciples understood that he was speaking to them about John the Baptist.

- Elijah was the fiery prophet who proclaimed God's message in very challenging situations. He 'ascended in a whirlwind into heaven' (2 Kings 2:11), and it was believed that he would return before the Messiah was born. John the Baptist was described in similar terms. May we be the new Elijah and be like John with our prophetic voices.

- The prophets had an important place in proclaiming the truth and calling people back from their errant ways. Many, including John the Baptist, suffered for doing so. Jesus saw that the same fate was in store for him. Lord, may we live for you and announce your message, even though it may involve misunderstanding and suffering.

17–23 December 2023

Something to think and pray about each day this week:

Who do you see when you look at Mary – Our Lady? An aunt of mine was once showing a man around her home and in nearly every room she had some picture or other, depicting (as she likes to call her) 'The Blessed Mother'. The man, possibly not overly religious, was a little perturbed and felt he had to comment: 'You have a lot of pictures of Mary,' he said. Without a flinch my aunt replied, 'Oh, but of course, I consider her a personal friend.' No more to be said!

It's a great way to look at Mary – as a 'personal friend' – and in that light you can see why God would dispatch Gabriel to meet her in the kitchen. He knew what sort she was. There was a generosity of spirit there and a kindness that is only truly found in the best of friends. I think that's how she would want us to see her today as we journey with her to Bethlehem in the company of Joseph. She would want us to see her as someone whose door is open to us – no need for formalities or elaborate ritual. The door is open, the light is on and she awaits our approach.

Vincent Sherlock, *Let Advent be Advent*

The Presence of God

'Be still, and know that I am God.' Lord, your words lead us to the calmness and greatness of your presence.

Freedom

I am free. When I look at these words in writing, they seem to create in me a feeling of awe. Yes, a wonderful feeling of freedom. Thank you, God.

Consciousness

At this moment, Lord, I turn my thoughts to you.
I will leave aside my chores and preoccupations.
I will take rest and refreshment in your presence, Lord.

The Word

The word of God comes down to us through the Scriptures. May the Holy Spirit enlighten my mind and my heart to respond to the Gospel teachings. *(Please turn to the Scripture on the following pages. Inspiration points are there, should you need them. When you are ready, return here to continue.)*

Conversation

Begin to talk with Jesus about the Scripture you have just read. What part of it strikes a chord in you? Perhaps the words of a friend – or some story you have heard recently – will slowly rise to the surface of your consciousness. If so, does the story throw light on what the Scripture passage may be trying to say to you?

Conclusion

Glory be to the Father, and to the Son, and to the Holy Spirit,
As it was in the beginning, is now and ever shall be,
World without end. Amen.

Sunday 17 December
Third Sunday of Advent
John 1:6–8.19–28

There was a man sent from God, whose name was John. He came as a witness to testify to the light, so that all might believe through him. He himself was not the light, but he came to testify to the light.

This is the testimony given by John when the Jews sent priests and Levites from Jerusalem to ask him, 'Who are you?' He confessed and did not deny it, but confessed, 'I am not the Messiah.' And they asked him, 'What then? Are you Elijah?' He said, 'I am not.' 'Are you the prophet?' He answered, 'No.' Then they said to him, 'Who are you? Let us have an answer for those who sent us. What do you say about yourself?' He said,

'I am the voice of one crying out in the wilderness,

"Make straight the way of the Lord", '

as the prophet Isaiah said.

Now they had been sent from the Pharisees. They asked him, 'Why then are you baptising if you are neither the Messiah, nor Elijah, nor the prophet?' John answered them, 'I baptise with water. Among you stands one whom you do not know, the one who is coming after me; I am not worthy to untie the thong of his sandal.' This took place in Bethany across the Jordan where John was baptising.

- John the Baptist was a witness and pointed the way to Jesus, the true light. He was clear on his identity and his role, saying he was not the Messiah, or the prophet, but one whose baptism was preparatory. Let us be voices in the wilderness that announce the presence of Jesus, the eternal Word, even if we feel no one is listening.
- John was an object of curiosity, with priests being sent from Jerusalem into the wilderness to investigate. He humbly acknowledged his own role but directed them towards Jesus. In recognising that 'among you stands one you do not know', we may announce Jesus' presence and message in word and in deed.

Monday 18 December
Matthew 1:18–25

Now the birth of Jesus the Messiah took place in this way. When his mother Mary had been engaged to Joseph, but before they lived together, she was found to be with child from the Holy Spirit. Her husband Joseph, being a righteous man and unwilling to expose her to public disgrace, planned to dismiss her quietly. But just when he had resolved to do this, an angel of the Lord appeared to him in a dream and said, 'Joseph, son of David, do not be afraid to take Mary as your wife, for the child conceived in her is from the Holy Spirit. She will bear a son, and you are to name him Jesus, for he will save his people from their sins.' All this took place to fulfil what had been spoken by the Lord through the prophet:

'Look, the virgin shall conceive and bear a son,
   and they shall name him Emmanuel',

which means, 'God is with us.' When Joseph awoke from sleep, he did as the angel of the Lord commanded him; he took her as his wife, but had no marital relations with her until she had borne a son; and he named him Jesus.

- Mary and Joseph were recipients of the mysterious ways of God. Mary was found to be with child from the Holy Spirit and Joseph wondered what to do. He was given direction in a dream, reminding us of Joseph the dreamer in Genesis. Mary would give birth to a son who would be called Jesus, who would save his people from their sins. Lord, as we prepare for your birth, may we be inspired by the faith and example of Mary and Joseph in welcoming you.
- God reassured many who were facing new situations, such as Moses and Jeremiah, with the words 'I will be with you'. May we rely on the fidelity of God and draw strength from Jesus as Emmanuel, God with us, in the challenges of life.

Tuesday 19 December
Luke 1:5–25

In the days of King Herod of Judea, there was a priest named Zechariah, who belonged to the priestly order of Abijah. His wife was a descendant of Aaron, and her name was Elizabeth. Both of them were righteous before God, living blamelessly according to all the commandments and regulations of the Lord. But they had no children, because Elizabeth was barren, and both were getting on in years.

Once when he was serving as priest before God and his section was on duty, he was chosen by lot, according to the custom of the priesthood, to enter the sanctuary of the Lord and offer incense. Now at the time of the incense-offering, the whole assembly of the people was praying outside. Then there appeared to him an angel of the Lord, standing at the right side of the altar of incense. When Zechariah saw him, he was terrified; and fear overwhelmed him. But the angel said to him, 'Do not be afraid, Zechariah, for your prayer has been heard. Your wife Elizabeth will bear you a son, and you will name him John. You will have joy and gladness, and many will rejoice at his birth, for he will be great in the sight of the Lord. He must never drink wine or strong drink; even before his birth he will be filled with the Holy Spirit. He will turn many of the people of Israel to the Lord their God. With the spirit and power of Elijah he will go before him, to turn the hearts of parents to their children, and the disobedient to the wisdom of the righteous, to make ready a people prepared for the Lord.' Zechariah said to the angel, 'How will I know that this is so? For I am an old man, and my wife is getting on in years.' The angel replied, 'I am Gabriel. I stand in the presence of God, and I have been sent to speak to you and to bring you this good news. But now, because you did not believe my words, which will be fulfilled in their time, you will become mute, unable to speak, until the day these things occur.'

Meanwhile, the people were waiting for Zechariah, and wondered at his delay in the sanctuary. When he did come out, he could not speak to them, and they realised that he had seen a vision in the sanctuary. He kept motioning to them and remained unable to speak. When his time of service was ended, he went to his home.

After those days his wife Elizabeth conceived, and for five months she remained in seclusion. She said, 'This is what the Lord has done for me when he looked favourably on me and took away the disgrace I have endured among my people.'

- This is another annunciation story by the angel Gabriel in the more solemn setting of the temple. Zechariah and Elizabeth, both elderly, are promised a child who will be named John and will have the particular mission of bringing people back to the Lord. We pray for openness to the surprising ways of God and recognise that we too have been named for mission.

- The revelation raised questions and doubts of a practical nature for Zechariah, given his age and that of Elizabeth. This is another instance of what God could do. John was going to be the voice but Zechariah lost his voice. Lord, may we turn to you with our doubts so that our tongues do not become mute in revealing God's message.

Wednesday 20 December
Luke 1:26–38

In the sixth month the angel Gabriel was sent by God to a town in Galilee called Nazareth, to a virgin engaged to a man whose name was Joseph, of the house of David. The virgin's name was Mary. And he came to her and said, 'Greetings, favoured one! The Lord is with you.' But she was much perplexed by his words and pondered what sort of greeting this might be. The angel said to her, 'Do not be afraid, Mary, for you have found favour with God. And now, you will conceive in your womb and bear a son, and you will name him Jesus. He will be great, and will be called the Son of the Most High, and the Lord God will give to him the throne of his ancestor David. He will reign over the house of Jacob for ever, and of his kingdom there will be no end.' Mary said to the angel, 'How can this be, since I am a virgin?' The angel said to her, 'The Holy Spirit will come upon you, and the power of the Most High will overshadow you; therefore the child to be born will be holy; he will be called Son of God. And now, your relative Elizabeth in her old age has also conceived a son; and this is the sixth month for her who was said to be barren. For nothing will be impossible with God.' Then Mary said, 'Here am I, the servant of the Lord; let it be with me according to your word.' Then the angel departed from her.

- There was a perplexing message to Mary as favoured by the Lord. Her reaction of wonder, fear and surprise led to a question of how this could be. May we have the openness to hear the message, the freedom to question it and to accept the response, relying on the promise that nothing is impossible to God.
- Perhaps we can note that movement in our own lives – we are asked to do something, which leads us to question why, but then we can be

given a sign that leads us to say 'yes'. This may go on over time. We thank you, Lord, for the surprising ways in which you have entered and guided our lives.

Thursday 21 December
Luke 1:39–45

In those days Mary set out and went with haste to a Judean town in the hill country, where she entered the house of Zechariah and greeted Elizabeth. When Elizabeth heard Mary's greeting, the child leapt in her womb. And Elizabeth was filled with the Holy Spirit and exclaimed with a loud cry, 'Blessed are you among women, and blessed is the fruit of your womb. And why has this happened to me, that the mother of my Lord comes to me? For as soon as I heard the sound of your greeting, the child in my womb leapt for joy. And blessed is she who believed that there would be a fulfilment of what was spoken to her by the Lord.'

- Mary set out on a journey to be with her aged cousin, Elizabeth, in the hill country. It was a meeting of two mothers-to-be, who became pregnant in surprising circumstances. Both could acknowledge God's graciousness to them and be of support to each other. May we have a spirit of gratitude for the new life the Lord has shown us and shared with us.

- This visitation was a meeting of two women of faith who brought joy, comfort and blessing to each other. The presence of their unborn children enhanced the joy of the occasion. May we bring Jesus with us on our visitations, offering hope and promise to those we call to see.

Friday 22 December
Luke 1:46–56

And Mary said,
'My soul magnifies the Lord,
    and my spirit rejoices in God my Saviour,
for he has looked with favour on the lowliness of his servant.
    Surely, from now on all generations will call me blessed;

for the Mighty One has done great things for me,
    and holy is his name.
His mercy is for those who fear him
    from generation to generation.
He has shown strength with his arm;
    he has scattered the proud in the thoughts of their hearts.
He has brought down the powerful from their thrones,
    and lifted up the lowly;
he has filled the hungry with good things,
    and sent the rich away empty.
He has helped his servant Israel,
    in remembrance of his mercy,
according to the promise he made to our ancestors,
    to Abraham and to his descendants for ever.'

And Mary remained with Elizabeth for about three months and then returned to her home.

- Mary's song of praise before the birth of Jesus echoes the song of Hannah after the birth of Samuel (1 Samuel 2:1–10). They were grateful to God, as was Elizabeth, for the gifts given to them in their children. May we have grateful hearts that exude joy and hope in recognising the love and mercy God has shown us. Perhaps we might write our own song of praise.
- We are shown a God of reversals, who has scattered the proud in their thoughts and hearts, brought down the powerful and lifted up the lowly. God looked with favour on Mary, a lowly servant. We pray for humble hearts that can acknowledge the many ways in which God has gifted us in life.

Saturday 23 December
Luke 1:57–66

Now the time came for Elizabeth to give birth, and she bore a son. Her neighbours and relatives heard that the Lord had shown his great mercy to her, and they rejoiced with her.

On the eighth day they came to circumcise the child, and they were going to name him Zechariah after his father. But his mother said, 'No;

he is to be called John.' They said to her, 'None of your relatives has this name.' Then they began motioning to his father to find out what name he wanted to give him. He asked for a writing-tablet and wrote, 'His name is John.' And all of them were amazed. Immediately his mouth was opened and his tongue freed, and he began to speak, praising God. Fear came over all their neighbours, and all these things were talked about throughout the entire hill country of Judea. All who heard them pondered them and said, 'What then will this child become?' For, indeed, the hand of the Lord was with him.

- The birth of John was an important family occasion for Elizabeth and Zechariah. Elizabeth verified the name and Zechariah had to write it on a tablet before his speech returned. We pray that we who are named may have our mouths opened and our tongues freed, so that we can give further praise to God.

- The birth of John was more than a local celebration. Neighbours and relatives rejoiced with Elizabeth and Zechariah, but what happened was talked about throughout the entire hill country of Judea. It heralded a bigger picture in the unfolding of God's story of salvation. We pray that we may have a better sense of community and share good news in our support of each other.

The Fourth Week of Advent/Christmas

24–30 December 2023

Something to think and pray about each day this week:

Many looked forward to the coming of the Messiah, the Christ. He was the hope of the ages to come. But they were dead and gone when he arrived. Jesus praises us that we have seen him. We have seen in him the image of God. As Victor Hugo wrote in *Les Misérables*, if you love, you have seen the face of God. The Jesus we await now is the Jesus we can meet every day – in love, in prayer and in the Eucharist. This is what Pope Francis calls 'social love'. Social love includes our daily relationships, our families and friends, but it also goes beyond them to include a love for the whole world, especially for the poor and those who live in worlds of injustice, war and violence. Our preparation for Christmas puts many challenges to us. The needs of people, both near and far, are great. In Advent we lean into our greatest longings and into the greatest needs of the whole world.

Donal Neary SJ, *The Messenger Advent Booklet:*
Reflections on the Daily Readings

The Presence of God

'Come to me, all you who are weary and are carrying heavy burdens, and I will give you rest.' Here I am, Lord. I come to seek your presence. I long for your healing power.

Freedom

'In these days, God taught me as a schoolteacher teaches a pupil' (St Ignatius). I remind myself that there are things God has to teach me yet, and I ask for the grace to hear those things and let them change me.

Consciousness

Help me, Lord, to be more conscious of your presence. Teach me to recognise your presence in others. Fill my heart with gratitude for the times your love has been shown to me through the care of others.

The Word

God speaks to each of us individually. I listen attentively to hear what he is saying to me. Read the text a few times, then listen. *(Please turn to the Scripture on the following pages. Inspiration points are there, should you need them. When you are ready, return here to continue.)*

Conversation

Conversation requires talking and listening.
As I talk to Jesus, may I also learn to be still and listen.
I picture the gentleness in his eyes and the smile full of love as he gazes on me.
I can be totally honest with Jesus as I tell him of my worries and my cares.
I will open my heart to him as I tell him of my fears and my doubts.
I will ask him to help me place myself fully in his care and to abandon myself to him, knowing that he always wants what is best for me.

Conclusion

I thank God for these moments we have spent together and for any insights I have been given concerning the text.

Sunday 24 December
Fourth Sunday of Advent
Luke 1:26–38

In the sixth month the angel Gabriel was sent by God to a town in Galilee called Nazareth, to a virgin engaged to a man whose name was Joseph, of the house of David. The virgin's name was Mary. And he came to her and said, 'Greetings, favoured one! The Lord is with you.' But she was much perplexed by his words and pondered what sort of greeting this might be. The angel said to her, 'Do not be afraid, Mary, for you have found favour with God. And now, you will conceive in your womb and bear a son, and you will name him Jesus. He will be great, and will be called the Son of the Most High, and the Lord God will give to him the throne of his ancestor David. He will reign over the house of Jacob for ever, and of his kingdom there will be no end.' Mary said to the angel, 'How can this be, since I am a virgin?' The angel said to her, 'The Holy Spirit will come upon you, and the power of the Most High will overshadow you; therefore the child to be born will be holy; he will be called Son of God. And now, your relative Elizabeth in her old age has also conceived a son; and this is the sixth month for her who was said to be barren. For nothing will be impossible with God.' Then Mary said, 'Here am I, the servant of the Lord; let it be with me according to your word.' Then the angel departed from her.

- There is a phrase with a familiar ring to it: 'Do not be afraid, for you have found favour with God.' Being asked to do something different can evoke such a response. However, God's love and fidelity were assured, so it can be said: 'Remember that the power behind you is greater than the task ahead.' May we have the faith to rely on God and not be caught out by our own limited resources.
- Mary was told that all would happen through the action of the Holy Spirit. The name and mission of Jesus as Son of the most High whose kingdom will not end was stated clearly. We pray to imitate Mary in our sharing of that mission.

Monday 25 December
The Nativity of the Lord
John 1:1–18

In the beginning was the Word, and the Word was with God, and the Word was God. He was in the beginning with God. All things came into being through him, and without him not one thing came into being. What has come into being in him was life, and the life was the light of all people. The light shines in the darkness, and the darkness did not overcome it.

There was a man sent from God, whose name was John. He came as a witness to testify to the light, so that all might believe through him. He himself was not the light, but he came to testify to the light. The true light, which enlightens everyone, was coming into the world.

He was in the world, and the world came into being through him; yet the world did not know him. He came to what was his own, and his own people did not accept him. But to all who received him, who believed in his name, he gave power to become children of God, who were born, not of blood or of the will of the flesh or of the will of man, but of God.

And the Word became flesh and lived among us, and we have seen his glory, the glory as of a father's only son, full of grace and truth. (John testified to him and cried out, 'This was he of whom I said, "He who comes after me ranks ahead of me because he was before me."') From his fullness we have all received, grace upon grace. The law indeed was given through Moses; grace and truth came through Jesus Christ. No one has ever seen God. It is God the only Son, who is close to the Father's heart, who has made him known.

- Christmas celebrates the Word made flesh. We share in the divinity of him who shared our humanity. It is a new beginning, re-echoing the creation story in Genesis. The Word was the light of all people. In the darkness of our lives and world we turn to Jesus, the light, and pray that he may help us to overcome the darkness and give witness to his presence.

Tuesday 26 December
St Stephen, Martyr
Matthew 10:17–22
Jesus said to his disciples, 'Beware of them, for they will hand you over to councils and flog you in their synagogues; and you will be dragged before governors and kings because of me, as a testimony to them and the Gentiles. When they hand you over, do not worry about how you are to speak or what you are to say; for what you are to say will be given to you at that time; for it is not you who speak, but the Spirit of your Father speaking through you. Brother will betray brother to death, and a father his child, and children will rise against parents and have them put to death; and you will be hated by all because of my name. But the one who endures to the end will be saved.'

- Stephen relied on God. We are not to worry about what to say as that will be given, with the Spirit of the Father speaking through us. May we have the faith and courage to endure the challenges and temptations of life.

Wednesday 27 December
St John, Apostle and Evangelist
John 20:1a.2–8
Early on the first day of the week, while it was still dark, Mary Magdalene came to the tomb and saw that the stone had been removed from the tomb. So she ran and went to Simon Peter and the other disciple, the one whom Jesus loved, and said to them, 'They have taken the Lord out of the tomb, and we do not know where they have laid him.' Then Peter and the other disciple set out and went towards the tomb. The two were running together, but the other disciple outran Peter and reached the tomb first. He bent down to look in and saw the linen wrappings lying there, but he did not go in. Then Simon Peter came, following him, and went into the tomb. He saw the linen wrappings lying there, and the cloth that had been on Jesus' head, not lying with the linen wrappings but rolled up in a place by itself. Then the other disciple, who reached the tomb first, also went in, and he saw and believed.

- John is understood to be 'the disciple Jesus loved'. He was reclining next to Jesus at the Last Supper when the question of betrayal came up (John 13:24–25); he was present at the foot of the cross and promised to take care of Mary after it (John 19:2–27). We pray, through his intercession, to know, love, welcome and serve Jesus.
- Mary Magdalene ran to tell Peter and John and they ran together to the tomb. John deferred to Peter when they arrived, but he was the more intuitive one in coming to an understanding of and belief in what happened. May we draw strength from his example and be able to slow down so that we can come to a deeper appreciation of the new life Jesus brings.

Thursday 28 December
The Holy Innocents
Matthew 2:13–18
Now after they had left, an angel of the Lord appeared to Joseph in a dream and said, 'Get up, take the child and his mother, and flee to Egypt, and remain there until I tell you; for Herod is about to search for the child, to destroy him.' Then Joseph got up, took the child and his mother by night, and went to Egypt, and remained there until the death of Herod. This was to fulfil what had been spoken by the Lord through the prophet, 'Out of Egypt I have called my son.'

When Herod saw that he had been tricked by the wise men, he was infuriated, and he sent and killed all the children in and around Bethlehem who were two years old or under, according to the time that he had learned from the wise men. Then was fulfilled what had been spoken through the prophet Jeremiah:
'A voice was heard in Ramah,
    wailing and loud lamentation,
Rachel weeping for her children;
    she refused to be consoled, because they are no more.'

- To King Herod, the child Jesus was a threat, a potential opponent. This feast gives some preparation for what lay ahead, when others would seek Jesus' death. May we learn from those who showed love and care for Jesus so that we value all children of God.

- We live at a time when there are many child victims of abuse, of trafficking, of exploitation and wars. May we cherish children as God's gift and learn to maintain a childlike trust in you, Lord, to guide us in our relationships with them, so that they are safe.

Friday 29 December
Luke 2:22–35

When the time came for their purification according to the law of Moses, they brought him up to Jerusalem to present him to the Lord (as it is written in the law of the Lord, 'Every firstborn male shall be designated as holy to the Lord'), and they offered a sacrifice according to what is stated in the law of the Lord, 'a pair of turtle-doves or two young pigeons.'

Now there was a man in Jerusalem whose name was Simeon; this man was righteous and devout, looking forward to the consolation of Israel, and the Holy Spirit rested on him. It had been revealed to him by the Holy Spirit that he would not see death before he had seen the Lord's Messiah. Guided by the Spirit, Simeon came into the temple; and when the parents brought in the child Jesus, to do for him what was customary under the law, Simeon took him in his arms and praised God, saying,

'Master, now you are dismissing your servant in peace,
    according to your word;
for my eyes have seen your salvation,
    which you have prepared in the presence of all peoples,
a light for revelation to the Gentiles
    and for glory to your people Israel.'

And the child's father and mother were amazed at what was being said about him. Then Simeon blessed them and said to his mother Mary, 'This child is destined for the falling and the rising of many in Israel, and to be a sign that will be opposed so that the inner thoughts of many will be revealed – and a sword will pierce your own soul too.'

- Jesus was named eight days after his birth and then, after forty days, he was presented in the Temple. All this was in accordance with Jewish tradition. Jesus was referred to as the promised Messiah, who would redeem Israel. May we draw fruit from that event, recognising the role of the past, but ask for openness to the future the Lord promised.

- Simeon was righteous and devout and looked forward to the consolation of Israel. He was an older person who was familiar with the faith story of his people, but he also knew of the promised Saviour. We pray for that faith vision that helps us to know what is valuable but remain open to what the Lord reveals to us.

Saturday 30 December
Luke 2:36–40

There was also a prophet, Anna the daughter of Phanuel, of the tribe of Asher. She was of a great age, having lived with her husband for seven years after her marriage, then as a widow to the age of eighty-four. She never left the temple but worshipped there with fasting and prayer night and day. At that moment she came, and began to praise God and to speak about the child to all who were looking for the redemption of Jerusalem.

When they had finished everything required by the law of the Lord, they returned to Galilee, to their own town of Nazareth. The child grew and became strong, filled with wisdom; and the favour of God was upon him.

- Anna was an aged woman who was widowed soon after her marriage. She was from a little-known northern tribe. The qualities of her life, her commitment to prayer and to the temple speak eloquently of her. In the ordinariness of our lives, may we have the same faith to wait and to recognise Jesus in the ways he comes into our lives.
- Anna's life could not have been easy, but she had come to terms with it. She was not looking back in self-pity or regret. Rather, she could praise God and speak about Jesus to all who were looking for the redemption of Jerusalem. Lord, you call us beyond the struggles of the past and offer us hope for what lies ahead. May the example of Anna inspire us to live in that spirit.

The First Week of Christmas

31 December 2023–6 January 2024

Something to think and pray about each day this week:

Most cribs have an open door. This is God's door: it is never closed to us. An important message to us today is welcoming and openness. The bonds of Christmas are strong; of memories, love, faith, grief and hope. We remember that with each other we meet and we share life – we grow together.

Bonds can be strong or limited. The bond with a cousin to whom we send a card is not as active a bond as the family we meet regularly and help, support and love. We meet at funerals and weddings. Better that, however, than never meeting at all. Bonds can renew love, even if there are blocks to our relationship. Bonds are made up of love and quarrels, attractions and histories, of all sorts of good and bad things. Even the person who does not go home for Christmas thinks of home these days. Our Christian faith may be a bond. Christmas faith may be a bit like 'we only meet at Christmas'! Isn't it good we meet at Christmas and strengthen these bonds among us? Bonds of love, family, neighbourhood and faith. Something of God, and the community of the Church, binds us this time of year.

We find that God is close and near, and that his word involves us with others – especially with the poor and the migrant, the sinner and the saint. All are called together in him. We visit the poor infant born on the side of the road to make us remember at other times that many are born like that today, that many are poor, and many need the drastic help which Mary and Joseph needed that night.

Give thanks for the good Christmases and ask help for any painful memories to place in the crib. O come let us adore him.

Donal Neary SJ, *Gospel Reflections for Sundays of Year B*

The Presence of God

'I am standing at the door, knocking,' says the Lord. What a wonderful privilege that the Lord of all creation desires to come to me. I welcome his presence.

Freedom

Leave me here freely all alone. / In cell where never sunlight shone. / Should no one ever speak to me. / This golden silence makes me free!

– Part of a poem written by a prisoner at
Dachau concentration camp

Consciousness

How am I really feeling? Lighthearted? Heavy-hearted? I may be very much at peace, happy to be here. Equally, I may be frustrated, worried or angry. I acknowledge how I really am. It is the real me whom the Lord loves.

The Word

I take my time to read the word of God slowly, a few times, allowing myself to dwell on anything that strikes me. *(Please turn to the Scripture on the following pages. Inspiration points are there, should you need them. When you are ready, return here to continue.)*

Conversation

Do I notice myself reacting as I pray with the word of God? Do I feel challenged, comforted, angry? Imagining Jesus sitting or standing by me, I speak out my feelings, as one trusted friend to another.

Conclusion

Glory be to the Father, and to the Son, and to the Holy Spirit,
As it was in the beginning, is now and ever shall be,
World without end. Amen.

Sunday 31 December
The Holy Family
Luke 2:22–40

When the time came for their purification according to the law of Moses, they brought him up to Jerusalem to present him to the Lord (as it is written in the law of the Lord, 'Every firstborn male shall be designated as holy to the Lord'), and they offered a sacrifice according to what is stated in the law of the Lord, 'a pair of turtle-doves or two young pigeons.'

Now there was a man in Jerusalem whose name was Simeon; this man was righteous and devout, looking forward to the consolation of Israel, and the Holy Spirit rested on him. It had been revealed to him by the Holy Spirit that he would not see death before he had seen the Lord's Messiah. Guided by the Spirit, Simeon came into the temple; and when the parents brought in the child Jesus, to do for him what was customary under the law, Simeon took him in his arms and praised God, saying,

'Master, now you are dismissing your servant in peace,
    according to your word;
for my eyes have seen your salvation,
    which you have prepared in the presence of all peoples,
a light for revelation to the Gentiles
    and for glory to your people Israel.'

And the child's father and mother were amazed at what was being said about him. Then Simeon blessed them and said to his mother Mary, 'This child is destined for the falling and the rising of many in Israel, and to be a sign that will be opposed so that the inner thoughts of many will be revealed – and a sword will pierce your own soul too.'

There was also a prophet, Anna the daughter of Phanuel, of the tribe of Asher. She was of a great age, having lived with her husband for seven years after her marriage, then as a widow to the age of eighty-four. She never left the temple but worshipped there with fasting and prayer night and day. At that moment she came, and began to praise

God and to speak about the child to all who were looking for the redemption of Jerusalem.

When they had finished everything required by the law of the Lord, they returned to Galilee, to their own town of Nazareth. The child grew and became strong, filled with wisdom; and the favour of God was upon him.

- We had Zechariah and Elizabeth, Mary and Joseph, and Simeon and Anna, though the latter were not a couple as such. All shared a vision and were open to God's ways. Jesus was central. Mary and Joseph took Jesus to the temple and made their offering as they were a family of faith. We pray for the wisdom to live our faith and present Jesus to others as a guide in life.
- Life in a quiet village such as Nazareth was ordinary in many ways. Jesus grew and became strong. He was maturing in faith as well as humanly, for he was 'filled with wisdom and the favour of God was upon him'. May we continue to grow in maturity, both humanly and spiritually.

Monday 1 January
Mary, Mother of God
Luke 2:16–21

So they went with haste and found Mary and Joseph, and the child lying in the manger. When they saw this, they made known what had been told them about this child; and all who heard it were amazed at what the shepherds told them. But Mary treasured all these words and pondered them in her heart. The shepherds returned, glorifying and praising God for all they had heard and seen, as it had been told them.

After eight days had passed, it was time to circumcise the child; and he was called Jesus, the name given by the angel before he was conceived in the womb.

- Mary said 'yes' to a way of life. What lay ahead had an element of mystery to it. We are told that she was amazed at what was being said about Jesus. She pondered and wondered. Inspired by the shepherds, we ask to be open to God's mysterious ways and to take time to ponder and pray on them.

Tuesday 2 January
John 1:19–28

This is the testimony given by John when the Jews sent priests and Levites from Jerusalem to ask him, 'Who are you?' He confessed and did not deny it, but confessed, 'I am not the Messiah.' And they asked him, 'What then? Are you Elijah?' He said, 'I am not.' 'Are you the prophet?' He answered, 'No.' Then they said to him, 'Who are you? Let us have an answer for those who sent us. What do you say about yourself?' He said,

'I am the voice of one crying out in the wilderness,
"Make straight the way of the Lord",'
as the prophet Isaiah said.

Now they had been sent from the Pharisees. They asked him, 'Why then are you baptising if you are neither the Messiah, nor Elijah, nor the prophet?' John answered them, 'I baptise with water. Among you stands one whom you do not know, the one who is coming after me; I am not worthy to untie the thong of his sandal.' This took place in Bethany across the Jordan where John was baptising.

- Witnesses give evidence. John the Baptist bore testimony by his words and actions. While he was a prophet, he was distinctive in how he lived in the time and setting of his ministry. May our lives bear witness to our faith in Jesus in this time and may our words be in harmony with it.
- Knowing Jesus is at the heart of our call. It looks to a personal relationship, not just information about Jesus. We pray for the humility of John to recognise and accept our role and for the freedom to live it.

Wednesday 3 January
John 1:29–34

The next day he saw Jesus coming towards him and declared, 'Here is the Lamb of God who takes away the sin of the world! This is he of whom I said, "After me comes a man who ranks ahead of me because he was before me." I myself did not know him; but I came baptising with water for this reason, that he might be revealed to Israel.' And John testified, 'I saw the Spirit descending from heaven like a dove, and it remained on him. I myself did not know him, but the one who sent me to baptise with water said to me, "He on whom you see the Spirit descend and remain is the one who baptises with the Holy Spirit." And I myself have seen and have testified that this is the Son of God.'

- John could declare that Jesus was the Lamb of God who takes away the sin of the world. John's mission was preparatory and the focus was now beginning to shift to Jesus and the baptism he offered. Lord, may we draw strength from the example of John and make Jesus the centre of our attention and prayer.
- John desired that Jesus be revealed as the promised one. The presence and action of the Spirit was giving testimony to who Jesus was. We ask for a deeper faith in Jesus as our saviour and desire to bear witness to him as the Lamb of God.

Thursday 4 January
John 1:35–42

The next day John again was standing with two of his disciples, and as he watched Jesus walk by, he exclaimed, 'Look, here is the Lamb of God!' The two disciples heard him say this, and they followed Jesus. When Jesus turned and saw them following, he said to them, 'What are you looking for?' They said to him, 'Rabbi' (which translated means Teacher), 'where are you staying?' He said to them, 'Come and see.' They came and saw where he was staying, and they remained with him that day. It was about four o'clock in the afternoon. One of the two who heard John speak and followed him was Andrew, Simon Peter's brother. He first found his brother Simon and said to him, 'We have found the Messiah' (which is translated Anointed). He brought Simon to Jesus, who looked at him and said, 'You are Simon son of John. You are to be called Cephas' (which is translated Peter).

- Again, John referred to Jesus as the Lamb of God. Two of his disciples decided to follow Jesus who asked them what they wanted. He invited them to 'come and see'. We do not know what they talked about but they spent the rest of the day with Jesus. Lord, let our desires bring us to come and see, to spend time with Jesus, so that we can learn more about him and what he wants for us.
- Word began to spread, with Andrew introducing his brother to the Lord. Jesus gave Simon a new name, for a new mission. We

remember those who introduced us to Jesus in a personal way and we give thanks for them.

Friday 5 January
John 1:43–51

The next day Jesus decided to go to Galilee. He found Philip and said to him, 'Follow me.' Now Philip was from Bethsaida, the city of Andrew and Peter. Philip found Nathanael and said to him, 'We have found him about whom Moses in the law and also the prophets wrote, Jesus son of Joseph from Nazareth.' Nathanael said to him, 'Can anything good come out of Nazareth?' Philip said to him, 'Come and see.' When Jesus saw Nathanael coming towards him, he said of him, 'Here is truly an Israelite in whom there is no deceit!' Nathanael asked him, 'Where did you come to know me?' Jesus answered, 'I saw you under the fig tree before Philip called you.' Nathanael replied, 'Rabbi, you are the Son of God! You are the King of Israel!' Jesus answered, 'Do you believe because I told you that I saw you under the fig tree? You will see greater things than these.' And he said to him, 'Very truly, I tell you, you will see heaven opened and the angels of God ascending and descending upon the Son of Man.'

- More people were introduced to Jesus. There was discussion as to who he was. Human considerations, such as background, could get in the way for some. Lord, you came in the flesh into the ordinary but desire us to embrace the new life you offer.
- Jesus was presenting something at a deeper level, beyond the practical. His message and promise was at a spiritual or faith level. May we grow in openness to 'see greater things' that will reveal the Lord more fully to us.

Saturday 6 January
The Epiphany of Our Lord (IRL)
Matthew 2:1–12

In the time of King Herod, after Jesus was born in Bethlehem of Judea, wise men from the East came to Jerusalem, asking, 'Where is the child who has been born king of the Jews? For we observed his star at its rising, and have come to pay him homage.' When King Herod heard this, he was frightened, and all Jerusalem with him; and calling together all the chief priests and scribes of the people, he inquired of them where the Messiah was to be born. They told him, 'In Bethlehem of Judea; for so it has been written by the prophet:

"And you, Bethlehem, in the land of Judah,
> are by no means least among the rulers of Judah;
for from you shall come a ruler
> who is to shepherd my people Israel."'

Then Herod secretly called for the wise men and learned from them the exact time when the star had appeared. Then he sent them to Bethlehem, saying, 'Go and search diligently for the child; and when you have found him, bring me word so that I may also go and pay him homage.' When they had heard the king, they set out; and there, ahead of them, went the star that they had seen at its rising, until it stopped over the place where the child was. When they saw that the star had stopped, they were overwhelmed with joy. On entering the house, they saw the child with Mary his mother; and they knelt down and paid him homage. Then, opening their treasure-chests, they offered him gifts of gold, frankincense, and myrrh. And having been warned in a dream not to return to Herod, they left for their own country by another road.

- Simeon said Jesus was 'a light for revelation to the Gentiles' (Luke 1:32). The arrival of the wise men was an epiphany, a manifestation of Jesus as Saviour of all. King Herod wanted to safeguard his own interests. Jesus is our star, guiding us to life. May we have the faith to follow him and to manifest him to others.

- A king was afraid of a child. Herod saw Jesus in earthly terms as a potential opponent, thus his search was devious. In his words, may we 'go and search diligently for the child', so that we may offer true homage to him as our king.

The Second Week of Christmas

7–13 January 2024

Something to think and pray about each day this week:

I love wood with a good back story. I made three crosses from wood I rescued from a rubbish tip. They are from a Paper Birch tree that had received a bit of a trim. The tree is in the old Poor Clare Convent in Belfast (I work on the site).

Having rescued the rather nondescript lump of wood I set about sawing it open and saw these wonderful patterns and grain. It really is one of the most beautiful pieces of wood I've ever worked with. And it teaches me a lesson: what is thrown away or discounted as rubbish is often precious.

This applies even more to people than wood. Many people are marginalised, discriminated against and consigned to the rubbish tip of life. And yet all people are precious. Inside all of us we are just as beautiful as and more than the wood my three crosses are made of.

Jesus often hung around with those consigned to the rubbish tip – those seen as 'less than' or on the outside. I think he sends us a powerful lesson down through time – we are all one. No one is on the outside.

Jim Deeds, *The Sacred Heart Messenger*, October 2020

The Presence of God
As I sit here, the beating of my heart,
the ebb and flow of my breathing, the movements of my mind
are all signs of God's ongoing creation of me.
I pause for a moment and become aware
of this presence of God within me.

Freedom
Everything has the potential to draw from me a fuller love and life.
Yet my desires are often fixed, caught, on illusions of fulfilment.
I ask that God, through my freedom, may orchestrate my desires in a
vibrant loving melody rich in harmony.

Consciousness
I ask, how am I within myself today? Am I particularly tired, stressed
or off-form? If any of these characteristics apply, can I try to let go of
the concerns that disturb me?

The Word
I read the word of God slowly, a few times over, and I listen to what
God is saying to me. *(Please turn to the Scripture on the following pages.
Inspiration points are there, should you need them. When you are ready, return
here to continue.)*

Conversation
I begin to talk with Jesus about the Scripture I have just read. What
part of it strikes a chord in me? Perhaps the words of a friend or a story
I have heard recently will slowly rise to the surface of my consciousness.
If so, does the story throw light on what the Scripture passage may be
trying to say to me?

Conclusion
Glory be to the Father, and to the Son, and to the Holy Spirit,
As it was in the beginning, is now and ever shall be,
World without end. Amen.

Sunday 7 January
The Baptism of Our Lord (IRL) The Epiphany of Our Lord (USA)
Mark 1:7–11

He proclaimed, 'The one who is more powerful than I is coming after me; I am not worthy to stoop down and untie the thong of his sandals. I have baptised you with water; but he will baptise you with the Holy Spirit.'

In those days Jesus came from Nazareth of Galilee and was baptised by John in the Jordan. And just as he was coming up out of the water, he saw the heavens torn apart and the Spirit descending like a dove on him. And a voice came from heaven, 'You are my Son, the Beloved; with you I am well pleased.'

- John the Baptist was clear about his identity and his role, which was to prepare the way for Jesus. His baptism was one of repentance. In our baptism, we are immersed in Jesus' mission and given new life. We pray that we may introduce Jesus, help make him known and give him the primary place in our lives.
- In baptism, we are made beloved children; we pray that we may appreciate the gift Jesus shares with us, so that we may live our calling in a generous spirit.

Monday 8 January
The Baptism of Our Lord (USA)
Mark 1:14–20

Now after John was arrested, Jesus came to Galilee, proclaiming the good news of God, and saying, 'The time is fulfilled, and the kingdom of God has come near; repent, and believe in the good news.' As Jesus passed along the Sea of Galilee, he saw Simon and his brother Andrew casting a net into the sea – for they were fishermen. And Jesus said to them, 'Follow me and I will make you fish for people.' And immediately they left their nets and followed him. As he went a little farther, he saw James son of Zebedee and his brother John, who were in their boat mending the nets. Immediately he called them; and they left their father Zebedee in the boat with the hired men, and followed him.

- The beginning of Jesus' mission of proclaiming good news took place at a time and in a context. His call to repentance asked for a change of life, reminding his hearers that the kingdom of God was near. The same invitation is given to us now. May we allow his word and kingdom to find a home in our hearts.
- Ordinary people were called from their places of work and they gave a ready response. May we have that generosity in hearing and responding to the Lord's call to us now.

Tuesday 9 January
Mark 1:21–28
They went to Capernaum; and when the sabbath came, he entered the synagogue and taught. They were astounded at his teaching, for he taught them as one having authority, and not as the scribes. Just then there was in their synagogue a man with an unclean spirit, and he cried out, 'What have you to do with us, Jesus of Nazareth? Have you come to destroy us? I know who you are, the Holy One of God.' But Jesus rebuked him, saying, 'Be silent, and come out of him!' And the unclean spirit, throwing him into convulsions and crying with a loud voice, came out of him. They were all amazed, and they kept on asking one another, 'What is this? A new teaching – with authority! He commands even the unclean spirits, and they obey him.' At once his fame began to spread throughout the surrounding region of Galilee.

- Jesus took sabbath time, going to the synagogue to teach. He made an impression on those present. He was giving example as well as spiritual nourishment to his hearers. Lord, give us ears to hear your word, which is ever new. May it may strengthen us in our following you.
- It was an unclean spirit who recognised Jesus for who he was, calling him the Holy One of God. The power of Jesus was greater and he cast the spirit out. Lord, give us the wisdom to rely on you in the challenges that we face in life, especially when they seem too difficult to deal with.

Wednesday 10 January
Mark 1:29–39

As soon as they left the synagogue, they entered the house of Simon and Andrew, with James and John. Now Simon's mother-in-law was in bed with a fever, and they told him about her at once. He came and took her by the hand and lifted her up. Then the fever left her, and she began to serve them.

That evening, at sunset, they brought to him all who were sick or possessed with demons. And the whole city was gathered around the door. And he cured many who were sick with various diseases, and cast out many demons; and he would not permit the demons to speak, because they knew him.

In the morning, while it was still very dark, he got up and went out to a deserted place, and there he prayed. And Simon and his companions hunted for him. When they found him, they said to him, 'Everyone is searching for you.' He answered, 'Let us go on to the neighbouring towns, so that I may proclaim the message there also; for that is what I came out to do.' And he went throughout Galilee, proclaiming the message in their synagogues and casting out demons.

- Simon's mother-in-law must have been a prominent member of the community, given the promptness with which Jesus was told and the immediacy of his response. It tells us that healing leads to service. May Jesus take us by the hand and raise us up to serve others in his name.
- In a busy life, Jesus took quiet time for prayer. He indicated that he wanted to move on when his companions found him and wanted him to go back. Lord, give us the freedom to see beyond the immediate need, especially when there is something more urgent to do.

Thursday 11 January
Mark 1:40–45

A leper came to him begging him, and kneeling he said to him, 'If you choose, you can make me clean.' Moved with pity, Jesus stretched out his hand and touched him, and said to him, 'I do choose. Be made clean!' Immediately the leprosy left him, and he was made clean. After sternly warning him he sent him away at once, saying to him, 'See that you say nothing to anyone; but go, show yourself to the priest, and offer for your cleansing what Moses commanded, as a testimony to them.' But he went out and began to proclaim it freely, and to spread the word, so that Jesus could no longer go into a town openly, but stayed out in the country; and people came to him from every quarter.

- A leper begged Jesus to be cured. His desire met the desire of Jesus for him. Jesus wanted to be known as more than a miracle worker, so he asked the man to be quiet. May we have the courage and humility to bring our desires to the Lord and allow him to transform them so that they are more in harmony with his desires for us.

Friday 12 January
Mark 2:1–12

When he returned to Capernaum after some days, it was reported that he was at home. So many gathered around that there was no longer room for them, not even in front of the door; and he was speaking the word to them. Then some people came, bringing to him a paralysed man, carried by four of them. And when they could not bring him to Jesus because of the crowd, they removed the roof above him; and after having dug through it, they let down the mat on which the paralytic lay. When Jesus saw their faith, he said to the paralytic, 'Son, your sins are forgiven.' Now some of the scribes were sitting there, questioning in their hearts, 'Why does this fellow speak in this way? It is blasphemy! Who can forgive sins but God alone?' At once Jesus perceived in his spirit that they were discussing these questions among themselves; and he said to them, 'Why do you raise such questions in your hearts? Which is easier, to say to the paralytic, "Your sins are forgiven", or to say, "Stand up and take your mat and walk"? But so that you may know that the Son of Man has authority on earth to forgive sins' – he said to the paralytic – 'I say to you, stand up, take your mat and go to your home.' And he stood up, and immediately took the mat and went out before all of them; so that they were all amazed and glorified God, saying, 'We have never seen anything like this!'

- The return of Jesus attracted a crowd. The paralytic needed help. The people were creative in their approach and were able to place the man in front of Jesus. May we have creativity in coming to Jesus and have the freedom to accept the help of others to facilitate this.
- Jesus had concern for the whole person. He began with interior healing, with the forgiveness of sins. This challenged those present, but then, to the amazement of all, he cured the paralytic. Lord, give us a greater faith in you to accept your healing, internal and external, that we may praise you more fully as our Lord.

Saturday 13 January
Mark 2:13–17
Jesus went out again beside the lake; the whole crowd gathered around him, and he taught them. As he was walking along, he saw Levi son of Alphaeus sitting at the tax booth, and he said to him, 'Follow me.' And he got up and followed him.

And as he sat at dinner in Levi's house, many tax-collectors and sinners were also sitting with Jesus and his disciples – for there were many who followed him. When the scribes of the Pharisees saw that he was eating with sinners and tax-collectors, they said to his disciples, 'Why does he eat with tax-collectors and sinners?' When Jesus heard this, he said to them, 'Those who are well have no need of a physician, but those who are sick; I have come to call not the righteous but sinners.'

- This is a different call, as Levi was summoned from his tax booth to follow Jesus. Another strange choice and an unusual setting, but it was the Lord's choice. Lord, you have called us as other surprising choices. Give us the grace to respond with gratitude so that we may follow you more closely.
- Jesus befriended outsiders and was at home with them. They were people who could recognise their need, in contrast to the scribes and the Pharisees. Lord, we are the tax collectors and sinners whom you have invited to share table with you. Let us accept your invitation with gratitude and grow in openness to what you offer to us.

The Second Week in Ordinary Time

14–20 January 2024

Something to think and pray about each day this week:

The Good Shepherd invites us to rest awhile among the grassy meadows and flowing streams. He wants us to relax in his presence – to be nourished, strengthened and renewed. In this place, we may turn from a closed fist of denial, frustration and turmoil to an open hand of acceptance, relaxation and serenity. After the rest, we may be invited to walk more closely with him, to be freer and more confident and to be better able to navigate the often-hazy path of our lives. It is true that we all need to work on maintaining balance in our lives, but we are not alone. We can learn so much from modern and contemplative wisdom to live life with great richness, and when all is said and done, we can rejoice that we are infinitely loved.

Gavin Thomas Murphy, *Bursting Out in Praise:*
Spirituality and Mental Health

The Presence of God

Dear Jesus, I come to you today longing for your presence. I desire to love you as you love me. May nothing ever separate me from you.

Freedom

Lord, grant me the grace to be free from the excesses of this life. Let me not get caught up with the desire for wealth. Keep my heart and mind free to love and serve you.

Consciousness

Where do I sense hope, encouragement and growth in my life? By looking back over the past few months, I may be able to see which activities and occasions have produced rich fruit. If I do notice such areas, I will determine to give those areas both time and space in the future.

The Word

God speaks to each of us individually. I listen attentively to hear what he is saying to me. Read the text a few times, then listen. *(Please turn to the Scripture on the following pages. Inspiration points are there, should you need them. When you are ready, return here to continue.)*

Conversation

What is stirring in me as I pray? Am I consoled, troubled, left cold? I imagine Jesus standing or sitting at my side, and I share my feelings with him.

Conclusion

Glory be to the Father, and to the Son, and to the Holy Spirit,
As it was in the beginning, is now and ever shall be,
World without end. Amen.

Sunday 14 January
Second Sunday in Ordinary Time
John 1:35–42

The next day John again was standing with two of his disciples, and as he watched Jesus walk by, he exclaimed, 'Look, here is the Lamb of God!' The two disciples heard him say this, and they followed Jesus. When Jesus turned and saw them following, he said to them, 'What are you looking for?' They said to him, 'Rabbi' (which translated means Teacher), 'where are you staying?' He said to them, 'Come and see.' They came and saw where he was staying, and they remained with him that day. It was about four o'clock in the afternoon. One of the two who heard John speak and followed him was Andrew, Simon Peter's brother. He first found his brother Simon and said to him, 'We have found the Messiah' (which is translated Anointed). He brought Simon to Jesus, who looked at him and said, 'You are Simon son of John. You are to be called Cephas' (which is translated Peter).

- John pointed out Jesus as the Lamb of God to two disciples. He is the lamb who would be sacrificed to initiate the new covenant. Jesus asked the two, 'What are you looking for?' They were invited to 'Come and see'. Lord, may we respond to your invitation and your desire for us in finding clearer direction in our lives.

- We are familiar with people introducing others. The two disciples spent the rest of the day with Jesus, although we are not told what they talked about. Andrew went to tell his brother Simon, 'We have found the Messiah.' We pray for a deeper sense of Jesus as Messiah and for the freedom to introduce others to him and him to others with enthusiasm.

Monday 15 January
Mark 2:18–22

Now John's disciples and the Pharisees were fasting; and people came and said to him, 'Why do John's disciples and the disciples of the Pharisees fast, but your disciples do not fast?' Jesus said to them, 'The wedding guests cannot fast while the bridegroom is with them, can they? As long as they have the bridegroom with them, they cannot fast. The days will come when the bridegroom is taken away from them, and then they will fast on that day.

'No one sews a piece of unshrunk cloth on an old cloak; otherwise, the patch pulls away from it, the new from the old, and a worse tear is made. And no one puts new wine into old wineskins; otherwise, the wine will burst the skins, and the wine is lost, and so are the skins; but one puts new wine into fresh wineskins.'

- John the Baptist referred to himself as the friend of the bridegroom (John 3:29). His disciples who fasted asked Jesus why Jesus' disciples did not do so. There will be a time for fasting. Lord, help us to recognise that there is a time and context for feasting and for fasting and give us the freedom to do what is appropriate at the time.
- Jesus spoke of changing times. What he was presenting was new, not a patched-up version of what went before – 'The old law said, but I say to you' (Matthew 5). New wine needed fresh wineskins. Lord, help us to appreciate the gift of the past but help us also to remain open to the new that you reveal to us.

Tuesday 16 January
Mark 2:23–28

One sabbath he was going through the cornfields; and as they made their way his disciples began to pluck heads of grain. The Pharisees said to him, 'Look, why are they doing what is not lawful on the sabbath?' And he said to them, 'Have you never read what David did when he and his companions were hungry and in need of food? He entered the house of God, when Abiathar was high priest, and ate the bread of the Presence, which it is not lawful for any but the priests to eat, and he gave some to his companions.' Then he said to them, 'The sabbath was made for humankind, and not humankind for the sabbath; so the Son of Man is lord even of the sabbath.'

- How the sabbath was observed remained a source of conflict in the life of Jesus. The Pharisees were very conscious of the laws and wanted them to be observed strictly. Jesus had other priorities, and saw the laws as guidelines. Lord, you desire that we may have life to the full and bring life to others – help us to see where you lead and guide us.

- Jesus observed and respected the sabbath, but saw beyond it. He drew on the example of David, who did not keep all the regulations. The sabbath was to offer a time for rest and to give praise to God. Lord, help us to find sabbath time and use it, and thus give glory to the Creator.

Wednesday 17 January
Mark 3:1–6

Again he entered the synagogue, and a man was there who had a withered hand. They watched him to see whether he would cure him on the sabbath, so that they might accuse him. And he said to the man who had the withered hand, 'Come forward.' Then he said to them, 'Is it lawful to do good or to do harm on the sabbath, to save life or to kill?' But they were silent. He looked around at them with anger; he was grieved at their hardness of heart and said to the man, 'Stretch out your hand.' He stretched it out, and his hand was restored. The Pharisees went out and immediately conspired with the Herodians against him, how to destroy him.

- This is another sabbath event where conflict and anger are evident. The action of Jesus in curing the man with the withered hand was not accepted. It led to a conspiracy of the Pharisees and the Herodians to destroy Jesus. Lord, in a world of much blindness, including our own, give us the vision to see what is good to do, and the courage to act on it.
- Jesus had the freedom to notice but the courage to heal. He was grieved at the hardness of heart of the observers, but saw the suffering man as more important than sabbath regulations. Lord, increase our ability to notice and our freedom to bring the withered parts of ourselves to you for healing.

Thursday 18 January
Mark 3:7–12

Jesus departed with his disciples to the lake, and a great multitude from Galilee followed him; hearing all that he was doing, they came to him in great numbers from Judea, Jerusalem, Idumea, beyond the Jordan, and the region around Tyre and Sidon. He told his disciples to have a boat ready for him because of the crowd, so that they would not crush him; for he had cured many, so that all who had diseases pressed upon him to touch him. Whenever the unclean spirits saw him, they fell down before him and shouted, 'You are the Son of God!' But he sternly ordered them not to make him known.

- Jesus' desire for space and quiet time was in marked contrast with the desire of the great multitude that followed him from all the regions around and who continued to follow him wherever he went. Lord, attract us and draw us to yourself, to be more fully part of your company.

- It seems that many in the crowd were slow to believe in who Jesus really was. They were attracted by what he was doing. It is the unclean spirits who were able to recognise him as 'the Son of God'. Lord, may we recognise who you truly are so that we come to you to hear your words and be guided by your example.

Friday 19 January
Mark 3:13–19
He went up the mountain and called to him those whom he wanted, and they came to him. And he appointed twelve, whom he also named apostles, to be with him, and to be sent out to proclaim the message, and to have authority to cast out demons. So he appointed the twelve: Simon (to whom he gave the name Peter); James son of Zebedee and John the brother of James (to whom he gave the name Boanerges, that is, Sons of Thunder); and Andrew, and Philip, and Bartholomew, and Matthew, and Thomas, and James son of Alphaeus, and Thaddaeus, and Simon the Cananaean, and Judas Iscariot, who betrayed him.

- Jesus found time to pray, and it was in that context that he called those he wanted. It was his choice. They were to be with him, companions for mission. Their relationship with Jesus was the core of what they were called to be and do. Lord, draw us closer to you so that we may be good companions to you and your other workers in the continuation of your saving mission.

- The twelve were called by name. They were a varied group with a range of gifts and limits, but they were the ones you chose. You could work through these people and see beyond their limits. Lord, help us to see beyond our own fears and doubts and to rely more fully on you in the mission you have entrusted to us.

Saturday 20 January
Mark 3:20–21

And the crowd came together again, so that they could not even eat. When his family heard it, they went out to restrain him, for people were saying, 'He has gone out of his mind.'

- As is the case with all prophetic people, Jesus provoked a range of reactions. Some were inspired while others saw him as the enemy. Doubtless there were some who were curious, just as there were genuine believers. Lord, give us a deeper faith in you so that you are not crowded out in our lives by noise, or busyness or by other people who do not have time for you.

- Your own people were perplexed by your life. They were concerned with what was happening and felt responsible for rescuing you. Lord, there are times when people in our lives do not understand and think we are out of our minds. Give us the wisdom to understand your ways and the gift of following you amid the misunderstandings of life.

The Third Week in Ordinary Time

21–27 January 2024

Something to think and pray about each day this week:

The image of God as creator is very special. The Bible tells us that God created the heavens and the earth. He also created people in his own image; because of this people have a special relationship with God, their creator.

It's easy to imagine the creator God as very powerful. It's easy to forget that because he created everything, he can very much be found in the people and things around us. Consider a beautiful blue sky on a summer's day. The weather is warm. There are no clouds, and maybe you are relaxing on a beach. As you lie on the beach, you look upwards and the vastness of the blue canvas expands before you. On closer observation, the blue sky meets the azure colour of the sea at the horizon. There is a peace and warmth to be found in such a setting. It is an everyday image created by an everyday God.

Perhaps you have a friend – maybe the friend is your husband, your wife or a good friend you met on life's journey. This person might be described as your 'anam cara'. You can relax in the presence of your soul-mate. You share the ups and downs of life together and solve the problems of the world together. There is the joy of being in the presence of your friend. The companionship that you have with this friend is a mirror of the friendship that you have with God.

Everyday God is just that. He can be found in the ordinary: the hedges in the back garden, the condensation on the window, the joyful laughter of friends and the beauty of a rustic scene. He is the creator God.

Deirdre M. Powell, *God in Every Day: A Whispered Prayer*

The Presence of God

'I am standing at the door, knocking,' says the Lord. What a wonderful privilege that the Lord of all creation desires to come to me. I welcome his presence.

Freedom

I will ask God's help
to be free from my own preoccupations,
to be open to God in this time of prayer,
to come to know, love and serve God more.

Consciousness

In God's loving presence I unwind the past day,
starting from now and looking back, moment by moment.
I gather in all the goodness and light, in gratitude.
I attend to the shadows and what they say to me,
seeking healing, courage, forgiveness.

The Word

Now I turn to the Scripture set out for me this day. I read slowly over the words and see if any sentence or sentiment appeals to me. *(Please turn to the Scripture on the following pages. Inspiration points are there, should you need them. When you are ready, return here to continue.)*

Conversation

Sometimes I wonder what I might say if I were to meet you in person, Lord.
I think I might say, 'Thank you', because you are always there for me.

Conclusion

I thank God for these moments we have spent together and for any insights I have been given concerning the text.

Sunday 21 January
Third Sunday in Ordinary Time
Mark 1:14–20

Now after John was arrested, Jesus came to Galilee, proclaiming the good news of God, and saying, 'The time is fulfilled, and the kingdom of God has come near; repent, and believe in the good news.'

As Jesus passed along the Sea of Galilee, he saw Simon and his brother Andrew casting a net into the lake – for they were fishermen. And Jesus said to them, 'Follow me and I will make you fish for people.' And immediately they left their nets and followed him. As he went a little farther, he saw James son of Zebedee and his brother John, who were in their boat mending the nets. Immediately he called them; and they left their father Zebedee in the boat with the hired men, and followed him.

- Following his baptism Jesus went forth with the good news that the kingdom of God had come near. John had done the preparatory work and the stage was now clear for Jesus as John had been arrested. We pray that we may continue to announce good news – unlike John we know the fruits it has brought.

- Having begun his mission Jesus' first action was to call helpers to him. He invited Simon and Andrew, who were fishermen, to 'follow me and I will make you fish for people'. Jesus cast his net more widely in calling James and John. Lord, you have continued to call people. You call us by name too. May we have the freedom to leave our boats and produce a good catch in your name.

Monday 22 January
Mark 3:22–30

And the scribes who came down from Jerusalem said, 'He has Beelzebul, and by the ruler of the demons he casts out demons.' And he called them to him, and spoke to them in parables, 'How can Satan cast out Satan? If a kingdom is divided against itself, that kingdom cannot stand. And if a house is divided against itself, that house will not be able to stand. And if Satan has risen up against himself and is divided, he cannot stand, but his end has come. But no one can enter a strong man's house and plunder his property without first tying up the strong man; then indeed the house can be plundered.

'Truly I tell you, people will be forgiven for their sins and whatever blasphemies they utter; but whoever blasphemes against the Holy Spirit can never have forgiveness, but is guilty of an eternal sin' – for they had said, 'He has an unclean spirit.'

- The scribes could not accept Jesus' teaching. He was accused of being in league with the forces of evil, though he was clearly on the side of what was good. He reminded them that divided kingdoms do not survive. Lord, give us the wisdom to see you as you truly are and to see that you are strong in protecting us from evil.

- The notion of an unforgiveable sin stops us short as it seems to limit what God can do. It refers to human obstinacy – we can resist and refuse to repent. God can forgive all sins, but we need to ask. Lord, give us the gift of humility to acknowledge the truth and to ask for your forgiveness at all times, knowing that you are stronger than the forces of evil.

Tuesday 23 January
Mark 3:31–35

Then his mother and his brothers came; and standing outside, they sent to him and called him. A crowd was sitting around him; and they said to him, 'Your mother and your brothers and sisters are outside, asking for you.' And he replied, 'Who are my mother and my brothers?' And looking at those who sat around him, he said, 'Here are my mother and my brothers! Whoever does the will of God is my brother and sister and mother.'

- His being surrounded by a crowd made it difficult for Jesus' family to reach him. Jesus availed of the situation to introduce the notion of a wider family that was all-inclusive. Lord, we thank you for including us and giving us a sense of belonging in your family and for sharing your love and life with us as your brothers and sisters.

- At first hearing the response of Jesus could sound like a rebuke or a rejection of his mother and family. In truth he was introducing Mary as a model of discipleship, for who did the will of God better?

For her, as for him, the will of God was at the core of life. Give us the openness to know and carry out your will in the spirit of your family.

Wednesday 24 January
Mark 4:1–20
Again he began to teach beside the lake. Such a very large crowd gathered around him that he got into a boat on the lake and sat there, while the whole crowd was beside the lake on the land. He began to teach them many things in parables, and in his teaching he said to them: 'Listen! A sower went out to sow. And as he sowed, some seed fell on the path, and the birds came and ate it up. Other seed fell on rocky ground, where it did not have much soil, and it sprang up quickly, since it had no depth of soil. And when the sun rose, it was scorched; and since it had no root, it withered away. Other seed fell among thorns, and the thorns grew up and choked it, and it yielded no grain. Other seed fell into good soil and brought forth grain, growing up and increasing and yielding thirty and sixty and a hundredfold.' And he said, 'Let anyone with ears to hear listen!'

When he was alone, those who were around him along with the twelve asked him about the parables. And he said to them, 'To you has been given the secret of the kingdom of God, but for those outside, everything comes in parables; in order that
"they may indeed look, but not perceive,
    and may indeed listen, but not understand;
so that they may not turn again and be forgiven."'
And he said to them, 'Do you not understand this parable? Then how will you understand all the parables? The sower sows the word. These are the ones on the path where the word is sown: when they hear, Satan immediately comes and takes away the word that is sown in them. And these are the ones sown on rocky ground: when they hear the word, they immediately receive it with joy. But they have no root, and endure only for a while; then, when trouble or persecution arises on account of the word, immediately they fall away. And others are those sown among the thorns: these are the ones who hear the word, but the cares

of the world, and the lure of wealth, and the desire for other things come in and choke the word, and it yields nothing. And these are the ones sown on the good soil: they hear the word and accept it and bear fruit, thirty and sixty and a hundredfold.'

- A large crowd gathered when Jesus began to teach. They were on land, while he was in a boat. He used parables to illustrate what he taught about the kingdom, but they needed to be understood. Lord, give us ears to hear your teaching anew and hearts to welcome your message so that we can live it better.

- The parable of the sower illustrates different responses to the word of God. The sowing can seem careless, but it speaks to the reality of life. There was a rich harvest from what fell on good soil. Lord, you desire to plant the word of life in our hearts and call us to prepare for it so that we may bear fruit in your name to the glory of the Father.

Thursday 25 January
The Conversion of St Paul, Apostle
Mark 16:15–18

And he said to them, 'Go into all the world and proclaim the good news to the whole creation. The one who believes and is baptised will be saved; but the one who does not believe will be condemned. And these signs will accompany those who believe: by using my name they will cast out demons; they will speak in new tongues; they will pick up snakes in their hands, and if they drink any deadly thing, it will not hurt them; they will lay their hands on the sick, and they will recover.'

- Paul, as the Apostle to the Gentiles, lived the call to 'go into the whole world and proclaim the good news to the whole creation'. He had the assurance that God was with him on that mission. We pray for unity and that the message of the Lord may be brought to all people.

- Saul become Paul was totally dedicated to what he believed as a Jew and then as a Christian. His life was guided by Jesus and his way. We pray that our energy may be directed to the way of Jesus and that we may live our faith with enthusiasm.

Friday 26 January
Mark 4:26–34

He also said, 'The kingdom of God is as if someone would scatter seed on the ground, and would sleep and rise night and day, and the seed would sprout and grow, he does not know how. The earth produces of itself, first the stalk, then the head, then the full grain in the head. But when the grain is ripe, at once he goes in with his sickle, because the harvest has come.'

He also said, 'With what can we compare the kingdom of God, or what parable will we use for it? It is like a mustard seed, which, when sown upon the ground, is the smallest of all the seeds on earth; yet when it is sown it grows up and becomes the greatest of all shrubs, and puts forth large branches, so that the birds of the air can make nests in its shade.'

With many such parables he spoke the word to them, as they were able to hear it; he did not speak to them except in parables, but he explained everything in private to his disciples.

- Much growth in life happens quietly and becomes evident with the passing of time. A seed takes time to grow. It is God's desire that the word of life may grow in us. Lord, give us the patience to wait for the gradual change and growth that is to occur, so that it may bring a rich harvest in your name.

- Many things in life begin small and may seem insignificant to begin with, but they can grow into something bigger. God plants seeds in the heart that have the potential to produce good fruit. Lord, help us to understand the story of our lives as parables written by you that will provide shelter and comfort to others.

Saturday 27 January
Mark 4:35–41

On that day, when evening had come, he said to them, 'Let us go across to the other side.' And leaving the crowd behind, they took him with them in the boat, just as he was. Other boats were with him. A great gale arose, and the waves beat into the boat, so that the boat was already being swamped. But he was in the stern, asleep on the cushion; and they woke him up and said to him, 'Teacher, do you not care that we are perishing?' He woke up and rebuked the wind, and said to the sea, 'Peace! Be still!' Then the wind ceased, and there was a dead calm. He said to them, 'Why are you afraid? Have you still no faith?' And they were filled with great awe and said to one another, 'Who then is this, that even the wind and the sea obey him?'

- There are many storms in our lives and in our world. They can arise suddenly and disturb our peace and quiet. Sometimes the storms are more internal, when we fall prey to self-doubt and fear. Lord, you are always present. Wake us from the sleep that can overtake us so that we can be alert and ready to turn to you for what we need at the time.

- Those facing new situations were fearful and doubted their own ability to deal with the situation, whether we think of Jeremiah when he was called (Jeremiah 1) or Mary at the annunciation (Luke 1), but you, Lord, assured them that you would be with them. Like them, may we come to trust you for what we need when we encounter the storms of life.

28 January–3 February 2024

Something to think and pray about each day this week:

Sometimes when I'm out and about I do a bit of 'anger spotting'. There's a lot of it about, and when you've tuned in to anger you notice it more – just like the trained plane-spotter, train-spotter or bird watcher, whose trained eye and ear see and hear more than the ordinary passer-by.

Anyway, what got me started on this anger thing … well, I was conducting a penance service in a parish. Rather than talk about forgiveness, I talked about the gift of healing, and I gave a little reflection on how much anger there was in the world today. I asked people to reflect on anger in their lives. I can't break the seal of confession but the flood gates opened. It was as if people were given a chance to name something that they kept hidden and that hidden thing was destroying them.

Don't get me wrong. Not all anger is bad, sometimes anger is justified. In the face of wrong-doing righteous anger can have a place, but it can't last for ever. It is given to you to alert you to something that has to be faced up to and acted upon. Righteous anger has some very nasty first cousins. They are plain old anger, jealous anger, vindictive anger or self-righteous anger. Put these guys together in the one room and there is some family battle. If your anger isn't righteous but is one of these nasty first cousins, well then, let go of it as it will only drag you down.

Alan Hilliard, *Dipping into Life: 40 Reflections for a Fragile Faith*

The Presence of God
At any time of the day or night we can call on Jesus.
He is always waiting, listening for our call.
What a wonderful blessing.
No phone needed, no e-mails, just a whisper.

Freedom
If God were trying to tell me something, would I know?
If God were reassuring me or challenging me, would I notice?
I ask for the grace to be free of my own preoccupations
and open to what God may be saying to me.

Consciousness
Help me, Lord, become more conscious of your presence. Teach me to recognise your presence in others. Fill my heart with gratitude for the times your love has been shown to me through the care of others.

The Word
In this expectant state of mind, please turn to the text for the day with confidence. Believe that the Holy Spirit is present and may reveal whatever the passage has to say to you. Read reflectively, listening with a third ear to what may be going on in your heart. *(Please turn to the Scripture on the following pages. Inspiration points are there, should you need them. When you are ready, return here to continue.)*

Conversation
Conversation requires talking and listening. As I talk to Jesus, may I also learn to pause and listen. I picture the gentleness in his eyes and the love in his smile. I can be totally honest with Jesus as I tell him my worries and cares. I will open my heart to Jesus as I tell him my fears and doubts. I will ask him to help me place myself fully in his care, knowing that he always desires good for me.

Conclusion
I thank God for these moments we have spent together and for any insights I have been given concerning the text.

Sunday 28 January
Fourth Sunday in Ordinary Time
Mark 1:21–28

They went to Capernaum; and when the sabbath came, he entered the synagogue and taught. They were astounded at his teaching, for he taught them as one having authority, and not as the scribes. Just then there was in their synagogue a man with an unclean spirit, and he cried out, 'What have you to do with us, Jesus of Nazareth? Have you come to destroy us? I know who you are, the Holy One of God.' But Jesus rebuked him, saying, 'Be silent, and come out of him!' And the unclean spirit, throwing him into convulsions and crying with a loud voice, came out of him. They were all amazed, and they kept on asking one another, 'What is this? A new teaching – with authority! He commands even the unclean spirits, and they obey him.' At once his fame began to spread throughout the surrounding region of Galilee.

- Jesus was in the synagogue on the sabbath. He was teaching, so his prophetic lifestyle was emerging. He taught with authority, not like the scribes. He had something fresh and new to share and could do so in a convincing way. Lord, we pray that we might be prophetic in sharing your message in an authoritative way.

Monday 29 January
Mark 5:1–20

They came to the other side of the lake, to the country of the Gerasenes. And when he had stepped out of the boat, immediately a man out of the tombs with an unclean spirit met him. He lived among the tombs; and no one could restrain him any more, even with a chain; for he had often been restrained with shackles and chains, but the chains he wrenched apart, and the shackles he broke in pieces; and no one had the strength to subdue him. Night and day among the tombs and on the mountains he was always howling and bruising himself with stones. When he saw Jesus from a distance, he ran and bowed down before him; and he shouted at the top of his voice, 'What have you to do with me, Jesus, Son of the Most High God? I adjure you by God, do not torment me.' For he had said to him, 'Come out of the man, you unclean spirit!' Then Jesus asked him, 'What is your name?' He replied, 'My name is Legion; for we are many.' He begged him earnestly not to send them out of the country. Now there on the hillside a great herd of swine was feeding; and the unclean spirits begged him, 'Send us into the swine; let us enter them.' So he gave them permission. And the unclean spirits came out and entered the swine; and the herd, numbering about two thousand, rushed down the steep bank into the lake, and were drowned in the lake.

The swineherds ran off and told it in the city and in the country. Then people came to see what it was that had happened. They came to Jesus and saw the demoniac sitting there, clothed and in his right mind, the very man who had had the legion; and they were afraid. Those who had seen what had happened to the demoniac and to the swine reported it. Then they began to beg Jesus to leave their neighbourhood. As he was getting into the boat, the man who had been possessed by demons begged him that he might be with him. But Jesus refused, and said to him, 'Go home to your friends, and tell them how much the Lord has done for you, and what mercy he has shown you.' And he went away and began to proclaim in the Decapolis how much Jesus had done for him; and everyone was amazed.

- This was an unusual event in that swine do not have much importance for the Jewish people. The core of the story is about the power of evil and that of Jesus being greater. Attention is to be drawn to Jesus and what he did to set the demoniac free. Lord, help us to focus on the essentials, noting your power and compassion, that it may set us free to counteract the evil we encounter.

- There were different reactions to Jesus and what he did. The demoniac who had been cured wanted to stay with Jesus, but Jesus sent him home with the mission of proclaiming what he had done for him. Lord, what you did caused amazement. Help us to keep focused on you amid the varied opinions and distractions of life, for it is in you that we will find true freedom.

Tuesday 30 January
Mark 5:21–43

When Jesus had crossed again in the boat to the other side, a great crowd gathered round him; and he was by the lake. Then one of the leaders of the synagogue named Jairus came and, when he saw him, fell at his feet and begged him repeatedly, 'My little daughter is at the point of death. Come and lay your hands on her, so that she may be made well, and live.' So he went with him.

And a large crowd followed him and pressed in on him. Now there was a woman who had been suffering from haemorrhages for twelve years. She had endured much under many physicians, and had spent all that she had; and she was no better, but rather grew worse. She had heard about Jesus, and came up behind him in the crowd and touched his cloak, for she said, 'If I but touch his clothes, I will be made well.' Immediately her haemorrhage stopped; and she felt in her body that she was healed of her disease. Immediately aware that power had gone forth from him, Jesus turned about in the crowd and said, 'Who touched my clothes?' And his disciples said to him, 'You see the crowd pressing in on you; how can you say, "Who touched me?"' He looked all round to see who had done it. But the woman, knowing what had happened to her, came in fear and trembling, fell down before him, and told him the whole truth. He said to her, 'Daughter, your faith has made you well; go in peace, and be healed of your disease.'

While he was still speaking, some people came from the leader's house to say, 'Your daughter is dead. Why trouble the teacher any further?' But overhearing what they said, Jesus said to the leader of the synagogue, 'Do not fear, only believe.' He allowed no one to follow him except Peter, James, and John, the brother of James. When they came to the house of the leader of the synagogue, he saw a commotion, people weeping and wailing loudly. When he had entered, he said to them, 'Why do you make a commotion and weep? The child is not dead but sleeping.' And they laughed at him. Then he put them all outside, and took the child's father and mother and those who were with him, and went in where the child was. He took her by the hand and said to her, 'Talitha cum', which means, 'Little girl, get up!' And immediately the girl got up and began to walk about (she was twelve years of age). At this they were overcome with amazement. He strictly ordered them that no one should know this, and told them to give her something to eat.

- There was a twelve-year-old girl and a woman afflicted with an infirmity for twelve years. A leader of the synagogue pleaded with Jesus to heal his daughter. Jesus responded but was interrupted by the woman. The leader had to wait. Lord, help us to come to a fuller faith in you and have the wisdom to recognise what has priority in what is asked of us.

- The woman with the haemorrhages took the initiative in approaching Jesus. Her situation was somewhat desperate. She had faith, believing that touching his cloak would make her better. Lord, help us to realise where we lose life and energy, where we need to touch you and be touched by you to find true life.

Wednesday 31 January
Mark 6:1–6

He left that place and came to his home town, and his disciples followed him. On the sabbath he began to teach in the synagogue, and many who heard him were astounded. They said, 'Where did this man get all this? What is this wisdom that has been given to him? What deeds of power are being done by his hands! Is not this the carpenter, the son of Mary and brother of James and Joses and Judas and Simon, and are not his sisters here with us?' And they took offence at him. Then Jesus said to them, 'Prophets are not without honour, except in their home town, and among their own kin, and in their own house.' And he could do no deed of power there, except that he laid his hands on a few sick people and cured them. And he was amazed at their unbelief.

- Jesus' going home to teach in the synagogue on the sabbath brought different reactions. At first, those present were astounded, but soon Jesus became too much for them. Lord, there are times when we do not want people to be different and to challenge us, so it is easier to dismiss them. Give us the freedom to let people be and to help change us for the better.

- Frequently we hear questions about people, about their backgrounds and where they come from. Prophets are not without honour except in their home towns. We live in a world of many prejudices, with a tendency to put labels on people. Lord, open up our narrow world and give us a wider horizon for life.

Thursday 1 February
Mark 6:7–13

He called the twelve and began to send them out two by two, and gave them authority over the unclean spirits. He ordered them to take nothing for their journey except a staff; no bread, no bag, no money in their belts; but to wear sandals and not to put on two tunics. He said to them, 'Wherever you enter a house, stay there until you leave the place. If any place will not welcome you and they refuse to hear you, as you leave, shake off the dust that is on your feet as a testimony against them.' So they went out and proclaimed that all should repent. They cast out many demons, and anointed with oil many who were sick and cured them.

- Setting out on a journey, beginning a mission, meant doing some preparation, both in keeping a focus and assessing what to take. Jesus called the twelve and gave them authority over unclean spirits. Help us to understand more fully what you ask of us so that we may respond with generosity.
- There is much encouragement to travel lightly now. Jesus wanted the twelve to have a clear focus, so he instructed them to take necessities only and to rely on others for hospitality. We ask for a clearer sense of mission so that we are not overburdened by non-essentials but trust you for what we need to do your work.

Friday 2 February
The Presentation of the Lord
Luke 2:22–40

When the time came for their purification according to the law of Moses, they brought him up to Jerusalem to present him to the Lord (as it is written in the law of the Lord, 'Every firstborn male shall be designated as holy to the Lord'), and they offered a sacrifice according to what is stated in the law of the Lord, 'a pair of turtle-doves or two young pigeons.'

Now there was a man in Jerusalem whose name was Simeon; this man was righteous and devout, looking forward to the consolation of Israel, and the Holy Spirit rested on him. It had been revealed to him by the Holy Spirit that he would not see death before he had seen the Lord's Messiah. Guided by the Spirit, Simeon came into the temple; and when the parents brought in the child Jesus, to do for him what was customary under the law, Simeon took him in his arms and praised God, saying,

'Master, now you are dismissing your servant in peace,
    according to your word;
for my eyes have seen your salvation,
    which you have prepared in the presence of all peoples,
a light for revelation to the Gentiles
    and for glory to your people Israel.'

And the child's father and mother were amazed at what was being said about him. Then Simeon blessed them and said to his mother Mary, 'This child is destined for the falling and the rising of many in Israel, and to be a sign that will be opposed so that the inner thoughts of many will be revealed – and a sword will pierce your own soul too.'

There was also a prophet, Anna the daughter of Phanuel, of the tribe of Asher. She was of a great age, having lived with her husband for seven years after her marriage, then as a widow to the age of eighty-four. She never left the temple but worshipped there with fasting and prayer night and day. At that moment she came, and began to praise God and to speak about the child to all who were looking for the redemption of Jerusalem.

When they had finished everything required by the law of the Lord, they returned to Galilee, to their own town of Nazareth. The child grew and became strong, filled with wisdom; and the favour of God was upon him.

- A child is a gift of God. There was a special place for the first-born. Presentation in the temple in Jerusalem was a spiritual occasion in a solemn setting. References to the guidance of the Holy Spirit in the life of Simeon highlight this. May we treasure those special occasions in our lives when we encountered people of faith who were supportive.
- Mary and Joseph were amazed at what was being said about Jesus. The shadow of the cross loomed in the background, with Simeon's reference to 'a sign that will be opposed', and that Mary would have a sword of sorrow. Lord, as children presented to you in the temple, may we recognise that your way to glory was through suffering.

Saturday 3 February
Mark 6:30–34

The apostles gathered around Jesus, and told him all that they had done and taught. He said to them, 'Come away to a deserted place all by yourselves and rest a while.' For many were coming and going, and they had no leisure even to eat. And they went away in the boat to a deserted place by themselves. Now many saw them going and recognised them, and they hurried there on foot from all the towns and arrived ahead of them. As he went ashore, he saw a great crowd; and he had compassion for them, because they were like sheep without a shepherd; and he began to teach them many things.

- In a busy life, with many people around, there was little opportunity to take a break or even to eat. Jesus saw the need for rest, for some quiet time, and he invited the apostles to a deserted place for a rest. It remains a good message to all who have busy lives. May we have the wisdom to step back and not let work dominate us to the point of exhaustion.
- The people observed where Jesus and the apostles were going and hurried there. Jesus assessed the situation, recognised their need and was able to forego his time of rest to reach out to them. Lord, help us to recognise when we are selfish and when there is a genuine call to respond, so that we may be guided by you in our relationships with others.

4–10 February 2024

Something to think and pray about each day this week:

The popularity of the Lord's Prayer may today partly spring from the perception that it has a universal application and can be shared by all who believe in a common creator God. For Christians, however, the prayer is above all a series of petitions addressed to the Father of Our Lord and Saviour Jesus Christ. And in saying the Our Father we are reminding ourselves that we together form a pilgrim Church. The idea of the Church as a people on pilgrimage to the promised land of heaven was a favourite one of Augustine in the fourth and fifth centuries. In modern times it has been given a powerful place in Christian thinking by the Second Vatican Council's stressing that the Catholic Church is much more than a multinational institution with its head office in Rome. Above all, it is God's new People, a fulfilment of Israel, which the Council described as 'making its pilgrim way in hope towards its goal, the heavenly fatherland' (*Decree on Ecumenism*, 2). The Council confirmed this in a striking quotation from Augustine when it pronounced that 'the Church, "like a pilgrim in a foreign land, presses forward amid the persecutions of the world and the consolations of God", announcing the cross and death of the Lord until He comes (1 Corinthians 11:26)' (*Decree on the Church*, 8). As such, just like ancient Israel in the desert, we need our daily bread.

Jack Mahoney SJ, *Glimpses of the Gospels:*
Theological, Spiritual & Practical Reflections

The Presence of God

As I sit here, the beating of my heart, the ebb and flow of my breathing, the movements of my mind are all signs of God's ongoing creation of me. I pause for a moment and become aware of this presence of God within me.

Freedom

It is so easy to get caught up with the trappings of wealth in this life. Grant, O Lord, that I may be free from greed and selfishness. Remind me that the best things in life are free: Love, laughter, caring and sharing.

Consciousness

Knowing that God loves me unconditionally, I can afford to be honest about how I am. How has the day been, and how do I feel now? I share my feelings openly with the Lord.

The Word

Lord Jesus, you became human to communicate with me. You walked and worked on this earth. You endured the heat and struggled with the cold. All your time on this earth was spent in caring for humanity.You healed the sick, you raised the dead. Most important of all, you saved me from death. *(Please turn to the Scripture on the following pages. Inspiration points are there, should you need them. When you are ready, return here to continue.)*

Conversation

Sometimes I wonder what I might say if I were to meet you in person, Lord.I think I might say, 'Thank you', because you are always there for me.

Conclusion

I thank God for these moments we have spent together and for any insights I have been given concerning the text.

Sunday 4 February
Fifth Sunday in Ordinary Time
Mark 1:29–39

As soon as they left the synagogue, they entered the house of Simon and Andrew, with James and John. Now Simon's mother-in-law was in bed with a fever, and they told him about her at once. He came and took her by the hand and lifted her up. Then the fever left her, and she began to serve them.

That evening, at sunset, they brought to him all who were sick or possessed with demons. And the whole city was gathered around the door. And he cured many who were sick with various diseases, and cast out many demons; and he would not permit the demons to speak, because they knew him.

In the morning, while it was still very dark, he got up and went out to a deserted place, and there he prayed. And Simon and his companions hunted for him. When they found him, they said to him, 'Everyone is searching for you.' He answered, 'Let us go on to the neighbouring towns, so that I may proclaim the message there also; for that is what I came out to do.' And he went throughout Galilee, proclaiming the message in their synagogues and casting out demons.

- There was a sense of immediacy in the action of Jesus in this situation. Lord, help us to understand better the difference between the immediate and the urgent so that we might make good decisions in the service of your people.
- Jesus attracted the whole city who came to the door. He cured many and then we are told 'he would not permit the demon to speak because they knew him'. Lord, we need your healing but we want to know you as Lord with deeper faith so that we can make you known to others as Messiah.

Monday 5 February
Mark 6:53–56

When they had crossed over, they came to land at Gennesaret and moored the boat. When they got out of the boat, people at once recognised him, and rushed about that whole region and began to bring the sick on mats to wherever they heard he was. And wherever he went, into villages or cities or farms, they laid the sick in the market-places, and begged him that they might touch even the fringe of his cloak; and all who touched it were healed.

- Coming to recognise, know, love and follow Jesus are significant aspects of life and of our relationship with him. May we grow in our capacity to recognise Jesus under the many guises in which he reveals himself so that we live a more meaningful relationship with him, as this is our heart's desire.
- Many sought healing and rushed to Jesus. Touching him was important, for even the fringe of his cloak was believed to bring healing. Lord, you desire to touch our lives in many ways to bring healing and comfort. Let us touch your garment to bring greater healing of the past.

Tuesday 6 February
Mark 7:1–13
Now when the Pharisees and some of the scribes who had come from Jerusalem gathered around him, they noticed that some of his disciples were eating with defiled hands, that is, without washing them. (For the Pharisees, and all the Jews, do not eat unless they thoroughly wash their hands, thus observing the tradition of the elders; and they do not eat anything from the market unless they wash it; and there are also many other traditions that they observe, the washing of cups, pots, and bronze kettles.) So the Pharisees and the scribes asked him, 'Why do your disciples not live according to the tradition of the elders, but eat with defiled hands?' He said to them, 'Isaiah prophesied rightly about you hypocrites, as it is written,
      "This people honours me with their lips,
         but their hearts are far from me;
      in vain do they worship me,
         teaching human precepts as doctrines."
You abandon the commandment of God and hold to human tradition.'

Then he said to them, 'You have a fine way of rejecting the commandment of God in order to keep your tradition! For Moses said, "Honour your father and your mother"; and, "Whoever speaks evil of father or mother must surely die." But you say that if anyone tells father or mother, "Whatever support you might have had from me is Corban" (that is, an offering to God) – then you no longer permit doing anything for a father or mother, thus making void the word of God through your tradition that you have handed on. And you do many things like this.'

- Jesus challenged the external rituals that were used in a protective or self-centred way rather than giving glory to God. The actions did not harmonise with a heart that was in tune with the Lord. Lord, give us a living faith that respects the past but remains open to the new as you reveal it.

Wednesday 7 February
Mark 7:14–23

Then he called the crowd again and said to them, 'Listen to me, all of you, and understand: there is nothing outside a person that by going in can defile, but the things that come out are what defile.'

When he had left the crowd and entered the house, his disciples asked him about the parable. He said to them, 'Then do you also fail to understand? Do you not see that whatever goes into a person from outside cannot defile, since it enters, not the heart but the stomach, and goes out into the sewer?' (Thus he declared all foods clean.) And he said, 'It is what comes out of a person that defiles. For it is from within, from the human heart, that evil intentions come: fornication, theft, murder, adultery, avarice, wickedness, deceit, licentiousness, envy, slander, pride, folly. All these evil things come from within, and they defile a person.'

- To listen and understand requires realism to have ears and minds that are open, that can entertain and embrace the new, that can let go of what is no longer useful, that do not presuppose ready answers. Lord, give us the freedom to listen anew and minds that can embrace change for the better.

Thursday 8 February
Mark 7:24–30
From there he set out and went away to the region of Tyre. He entered a house and did not want anyone to know he was there. Yet he could not escape notice, but a woman whose little daughter had an unclean spirit immediately heard about him, and she came and bowed down at his feet. Now the woman was a Gentile, of Syrophoenician origin. She begged him to cast the demon out of her daughter. He said to her, 'Let the children be fed first, for it is not fair to take the children's food and throw it to the dogs.' But she answered him, 'Sir, even the dogs under the table eat the children's crumbs.' Then he said to her, 'For saying that, you may go – the demon has left your daughter.' So she went home, found the child lying on the bed, and the demon gone.

- The Gentile woman had the courage to intercede when others would have hesitated. Being an outsider and a woman did not inhibit her. We ask for the faith of the woman to request what we want from the Lord.
- Jesus' initial response was not very encouraging; it might even seem off-putting. Was he trying to put her off or challenge her faith? May we have the courage to persist, and the wisdom to respond when we encounter challenging situations on our faith journeys.

Friday 9 February
Mark 7:31–37
Then he returned from the region of Tyre, and went by way of Sidon towards the Sea of Galilee, in the region of the Decapolis. They brought to him a deaf man who had an impediment in his speech; and they begged him to lay his hand on him. He took him aside in private, away from the crowd, and put his fingers into his ears, and he spat and touched his tongue. Then looking up to heaven, he sighed and said to him, 'Ephphatha', that is, 'Be opened.' And immediately his ears were opened, his tongue was released, and he spoke plainly. Then Jesus ordered them to tell no one; but the more he ordered them, the more zealously they proclaimed it. They were astounded beyond

measure, saying, 'He has done everything well; he even makes the deaf to hear and the mute to speak.'

- Most of the time we take the gifts of hearing and speaking for granted, until we encounter someone who has them in a limited way. They seem so significant for communication until we observe what someone without them can do. Lord, help us to appreciate the gifts we have and be less focused on what we do not have as abundantly as we would like.

Saturday 10 February
Mark 8:1–10

In those days when there was again a great crowd without anything to eat, he called his disciples and said to them, 'I have compassion for the crowd, because they have been with me now for three days and have nothing to eat. If I send them away hungry to their homes, they will faint on the way – and some of them have come from a great distance.' His disciples replied, 'How can one feed these people with bread here in the desert?' He asked them, 'How many loaves do you have?' They said, 'Seven.' Then he ordered the crowd to sit down on the ground; and he took the seven loaves, and after giving thanks he broke them and gave them to his disciples to distribute; and they distributed them to the crowd. They had also a few small fish; and after blessing them, he ordered that these too should be distributed. They ate and were filled; and they took up the broken pieces left over, seven baskets full. Now there were about four thousand people. And he sent them away. And immediately he got into the boat with his disciples and went to the district of Dalmanutha.

- Jesus had nourished the crowd with his word. Now his attention turned to the practical. Lord, too often we begin with the practical and fail to get to the deeper gift. Help us to notice and learn from you.
- Jesus, you appreciated life and all of creation. Give us compassionate hearts to feed the hungry and not be judgemental about what they eat and what they leave behind. May we value all that you have given us.

The Sixth Week in Ordinary Time

11–17 February 2024

Something to think and pray about each day this week:

Archbishop Joe Cassidy, late of Tuam, often said that 'Prayer is the oxygen of our faith.' The language of the liturgy becomes a foundation to help our ongoing spiritual development as well as conversion, because faith-beliefs anchor as well as guide us in the way we live.

The short Latin prepositions of the Eucharistic doxology – *'per'*, *'cum'*, *'in'* – give us a significant script for our daily lives as Christians: through Christ, with Christ and in Christ. Whatever we do or say, wherever we live, we do all through, with and in Christ. After all, he is Emmanuel, God-with-us.

Pope Francis has offered us a celebrated maxim that the Eucharist, 'although it is the fullness of sacramental life, is not a prize for the perfect, but a powerful medicine and nourishment for the weak'. The people of God include all those who accept Jesus' invitation to sit at the table of communion and community to celebrate his real presence at the 'supper of the Lamb'.

As we pray this doxology at Mass or silently in the depths of our hearts in our quieter moments, may it be the core of our beliefs about ourselves and all our relationships.

John Cullen, *The Sacred Heart Messenger*, September 2022

The Presence of God
'Come to me, all you who are weary and are carrying heavy burdens, and I will give you rest.' Here I am, Lord. I come to seek your presence. I long for your healing power.

Freedom
God is not foreign to my freedom. The Spirit breathes life into my most intimate desires, gently nudging me towards all that is good. I ask for the grace to let myself be enfolded by the Spirit.

Consciousness
I remind myself that I am in the presence of the Lord. I will take refuge in his loving heart. He is my strength in times of weakness. He is my comforter in times of sorrow.

The Word
I take my time to read the word of God slowly, a few times, allowing myself to dwell on anything that strikes me. *(Please turn to the Scripture on the following pages. Inspiration points are there, should you need them. When you are ready, return here to continue.)*

Conversation
Jesus, you always welcomed little children when you walked on this earth. Teach me to have a childlike trust in you. Teach me to live in the knowledge that you will never abandon me.

Conclusion
Glory be to the Father, and to the Son, and to the Holy Spirit,
As it was in the beginning, is now and ever shall be,
World without end. Amen.

Sunday 11 February
Sixth Sunday in Ordinary Time
Mark 1:40–45

A leper came to him begging him, and kneeling he said to him, 'If you choose, you can make me clean.' Moved with pity, Jesus stretched out his hand and touched him, and said to him, 'I do choose. Be made clean!' Immediately the leprosy left him, and he was made clean. After sternly warning him he sent him away at once, saying to him, 'See that you say nothing to anyone; but go, show yourself to the priest, and offer for your cleansing what Moses commanded, as a testimony to them.' But he went out and began to proclaim it freely, and to spread the word, so that Jesus could no longer go into a town openly, but stayed out in the country; and people came to him from every quarter.

- Desire is important in life as it gives direction and momentum. The leper knew what he wanted and believed that Jesus had the power to grant it. He came in humility, begging from a kneeling position. Jesus met him with a compassionate response. Lord, we come to you in our need and ask healing for the leprosy in our lives.
- This is a story of healing and touching. Strictly speaking, Jesus should not have touched a leper. Neither should the leper have approached Jesus, as lepers had to isolate themselves and call out 'unclean, unclean' to anyone who approached. Lord, help us to realise where we isolate ourselves from others so that we may become more community-minded in life.

Monday 12 February
Mark 8:11–13

The Pharisees came and began to argue with him, asking him for a sign from heaven, to test him. And he sighed deeply in his spirit and said, 'Why does this generation ask for a sign? Truly I tell you, no sign will be given to this generation.' And he left them, and getting into the boat again, he went across to the other side.

- Looking for signs is a familiar theme in the gospels. Many found it difficult to accept Jesus' teaching and actions without looking for something more. In our age, people look for scientific evidence in many situations. Lord, help us to move beyond the rational and logical, to the quality of our relationship with you, and to give witness to our faith in you.

- Jesus did not comply with the request for a sign. That would have been to cheat his listeners from moving on in faith that was more solidly based. Jesus was giving signs but the people seemed unable to interpret them as they were looking in the wrong direction. Lord, we pray that we may see and appreciate what you offer, for it is enduring and satisfies our true needs.

Tuesday 13 February
Mark 8:14–21

Now the disciples had forgotten to bring any bread; and they had only one loaf with them in the boat. And he cautioned them, saying, 'Watch out – beware of the yeast of the Pharisees and the yeast of Herod.' They said to one another, 'It is because we have no bread.' And becoming aware of it, Jesus said to them, 'Why are you talking about having no bread? Do you still not perceive or understand? Are your hearts hardened? Do you have eyes, and fail to see? Do you have ears, and fail to hear? And do you not remember? When I broke the five loaves for the five thousand, how many baskets full of broken pieces did you collect?' They said to him, 'Twelve.' 'And the seven for the four thousand, how many baskets full of broken pieces did you collect?' And they said to him, 'Seven.' Then he said to them, 'Do you not yet understand?'

- The disciples did not understand the deeper meaning of Jesus providing bread for the crowd. When we pray for our daily bread, we are looking for more than material food. Yeast ferments the dough but the Lord desires the yeast that ferments life. We ask for freedom that we may be changed internally and be a better influence in society.
- Jesus was inviting his disciples to the fuller and richer meaning of what he offered. Their perception was limited, their hearts were hardened, their eyes did not see, their ears did not hear and their memory was not accurate. Lord, give us the insight to hunger for the bread that gives life for ever, so that we are not lost in the material aspects of life.

Wednesday 14 February
Ash Wednesday
Matthew 6:1–6.16–18

'Beware of practising your piety before others in order to be seen by them; for then you have no reward from your Father in heaven.

'So whenever you give alms, do not sound a trumpet before you, as the hypocrites do in the synagogues and in the streets, so that they may be praised by others. Truly I tell you, they have received their reward. But when you give alms, do not let your left hand know what your right hand is doing, so that your alms may be done in secret; and your Father who sees in secret will reward you.

'And whenever you pray, do not be like the hypocrites; for they love to stand and pray in the synagogues and at the street corners, so that they may be seen by others. Truly I tell you, they have received their reward. But whenever you pray, go into your room and shut the door and pray to your Father who is in secret; and your Father who sees in secret will reward you.

'And whenever you fast, do not look dismal, like the hypocrites, for they disfigure their faces so as to show others that they are fasting. Truly I tell you, they have received their reward. But when you fast, put oil on your head and wash your face, so that your fasting may be seen not by others but by your Father who is in secret; and your Father who sees in secret will reward you.'

- The invitation in Lent is to turn towards God in true worship. Attention is drawn to some possible pitfalls, to areas where we can be too centred on ourselves and our own glory. We pray for the freedom to turn to the Lord for direction that will keep us focused, as we need guidance to travel the road that the Lord has taken.
- Almsgiving, prayer and fasting are significant aspects of our lives and of our relationship with the Lord and others. We are called to give glory to God, bringing us beyond selfish interests that can dominate. Lord, we desire to walk with you, but we need your help to do so, strengthened by your example and teaching.

Thursday 15 February
Luke 9:22–25
Jesus said to them, 'The Son of Man must undergo great suffering, and be rejected by the elders, chief priests, and scribes, and be killed, and on the third day be raised.'

Then he said to them all, 'If any want to become my followers, let them deny themselves and take up their cross daily and follow me. For those who want to save their life will lose it, and those who lose their life for my sake will save it. What does it profit them if they gain the whole world, but lose or forfeit themselves?'

- We have begun our journey towards Jerusalem with Jesus and we are reminded about what it entails. Jesus' teaching and way of life would challenge the existing system and be too much for the religious leaders. Lord, we tend to shy away from suffering – give us the strength and courage to stay with you, knowing that your death is the way to life.

- Jesus reminds us that his call involves self-denial and foregoing our own way. We follow his way and are asked to respond as he did. Being asked to take up one's cross means living like Jesus and for him. Lord, show us what is of lasting value and where true profit is to be found.

Friday 16 February
Matthew 9:14–15
Then the disciples of John came to him, saying, 'Why do we and the Pharisees fast often, but your disciples do not fast?' And Jesus said to them, 'The wedding-guests cannot mourn as long as the bridegroom is with them, can they? The days will come when the bridegroom is taken away from them, and then they will fast.'

- John the Baptist's life was ascetic. He lived in the wilderness and ate locusts and wild honey, advocating a similar life-style for his followers. It was very different from the reports they were hearing about Jesus attending dinners. This Lent, help us fast from all that is divisive and critical in our relationships with others.

- Jesus reminded his hearers that he would not be with them always from an earthly perspective. They were to be glad and to celebrate while he was with them in a physical and personal way. Lord, you are the bridegroom, our friend, who invites us to rejoice with you. Give us the strength to continue to do what is right at all times.

Saturday 17 February
Luke 5:27–32

After this he went out and saw a tax-collector named Levi, sitting at the tax booth; and he said to him, 'Follow me.' And he got up, left everything, and followed him.

Then Levi gave a great banquet for him in his house; and there was a large crowd of tax-collectors and others sitting at the table with them. The Pharisees and their scribes were complaining to his disciples, saying, 'Why do you eat and drink with tax-collectors and sinners?' Jesus answered, 'Those who are well have no need of a physician, but those who are sick; I have come to call not the righteous but sinners to repentance.'

- Jesus called Levi, a tax collector, as a disciple. Caravaggio depicts Levi caught in a dilemma, with one hand pointing to himself as if to say, 'You are calling me?', his other hand on the money he had collected. Lord, we also are unlikely choices but you call us. Help us to let go of what we cling to so readily so that we are freer to follow you.
- A range of people interacted with Jesus who reached out to all. To let Jesus lead seemed to be too much for the Pharisees, who were critical of his teaching and his actions in befriending tax collectors and sinners. Give us what we need to hear your call afresh and to respond with generosity.

The First Week of Lent

18–24 February 2024

Something to think and pray about each day this week:

Too often we think of Lent as a time to give things up, rather than time to take on something new. Ask yourself how you can respond to Christ's call in a more proactive way this Lent. To do so it might be good to make a regular examination of conscience, something St Ignatius encouraged. Think about:

1. The gifts I have received from God during the day that I can be thankful for.
2. Where I have cooperated with God during the day. Where I have not worked with God but given in to sinful elements within me, neglecting what God wants of me.
3. The forgiveness God offers me for the times when I have not responded to his presence and love in my life.
4. How God's help will guide me through things to come and how the Holy Spirit will be with me.

Do this daily examination of conscience daily during Lent and see how it draws you closer to an awareness of God's presence in your life and of the kind of life God is calling you to lead.

Pat Corkery, *The Sacred Heart Messenger*, March 2022

The Presence of God

What is present to me is what has a hold on my becoming.
I reflect on the presence of God always there in love,
amidst the many things that have a hold on me.
I pause and pray that I may let God
affect my becoming in this precise moment.

Freedom

By God's grace I was born to live in freedom. Free to enjoy the pleasures he created for me. Dear Lord, grant that I may live as you intended, with complete confidence in your loving care.

Consciousness

I exist in a web of relationships: links to nature, people, God. I trace out these links, giving thanks for the life that flows through them. Some links are twisted or broken; I may feel regret, anger, disappointment. I pray for the gift of acceptance and forgiveness.

The Word

God speaks to each of us individually. I listen attentively to hear what he is saying to me. Read the text a few times, then listen. *(Please turn to the Scripture on the following pages. Inspiration points are there, should you need them. When you are ready, return here to continue.)*

Conversation

I begin to talk with Jesus about the Scripture I have just read. What part of it strikes a chord in me? Perhaps the words of a friend – or some story I have heard recently – will rise to the surface in my consciousness. If so, does the story throw light on what the Scripture passage may be saying to me?

Conclusion

Glory be to the Father, and to the Son, and to the Holy Spirit,
As it was in the beginning, is now and ever shall be,
World without end. Amen.

Sunday 18 February
First Sunday of Lent
Mark 1:12–15

And the Spirit immediately drove him out into the wilderness. He was in the wilderness for forty days, tempted by Satan; and he was with the wild beasts; and the angels waited on him.

Now after John was arrested, Jesus came to Galilee, proclaiming the good news of God, and saying, 'The time is fulfilled, and the kingdom of God has come near; repent, and believe in the good news.'

- Immediately after his baptism and the affirmation of his mission 'the Spirit drove Jesus' into the wilderness. It was seen as a place of testing, but it was also where God could be found. Lord, give us the Spirit to help us to recognise the challenging aspects of living out our baptism, so that we are not complacent.

Monday 19 February
Matthew 25:31–46

'When the Son of Man comes in his glory, and all the angels with him, then he will sit on the throne of his glory. All the nations will be gathered before him, and he will separate people one from another as a shepherd separates the sheep from the goats, and he will put the sheep at his right hand and the goats at the left. Then the king will say to those at his right hand, "Come, you that are blessed by my Father, inherit the kingdom prepared for you from the foundation of the world; for I was hungry and you gave me food, I was thirsty and you gave me something to drink, I was a stranger and you welcomed me, I was naked and you gave me clothing, I was sick and you took care of me, I was in prison and you visited me." Then the righteous will answer him, "Lord, when was it that we saw you hungry and gave you food, or thirsty and gave you something to drink? And when was it that we saw you a stranger and welcomed you, or naked and gave you clothing? And when was it that we saw you sick or in prison and visited you?" And the king will answer them, "Truly I tell you, just as you did it to one of the least of these who are members of my family, you did it to me." Then he will say to those at his left hand, "You that are accursed, depart from me into the eternal fire prepared for the devil and his angels; for I was hungry and you gave me no food, I was thirsty and you gave me nothing to drink, I was a stranger and you did not welcome me, naked and you did not give me clothing, sick and in prison and you did not visit me." Then they also will answer, "Lord, when was it that we saw you hungry or thirsty or a stranger or naked or sick or in prison, and did not take care of you?" Then he will answer them, "Truly I tell you, just as you did not do it to one of the least of these, you did not do it to me." And these will go away into eternal punishment, but the righteous into eternal life.'

- The qualities desired are those of the 'corporal works of mercy', which deal with genuine concern for those on the margins of life. Jesus cared for the most vulnerable and reminds us that we are to do the same. Lord, give us the freedom to move beyond our comfort zones to reach out to those in need, for you are present in them.

- The reading speaks about more than passing actions as it calls for converted hearts. Ultimately, we will be judged on love, or perhaps we will judge ourselves on how we respond to those in need. Lord, give us compassionate hearts and heal us of the prejudices that can blind us to their presence in life.

Tuesday 20 February
Matthew 6:7–15
'When you are praying, do not heap up empty phrases as the Gentiles do; for they think that they will be heard because of their many words. Do not be like them, for your Father knows what you need before you ask him.

'Pray then in this way:
Our Father in heaven,
    hallowed be your name.
    Your kingdom come.
    Your will be done,
        on earth as it is in heaven.

Give us this day our daily bread.
And forgive us our debts,
as we also have forgiven our debtors.
And do not bring us to the time of trial,
but rescue us from the evil one.

For if you forgive others their trespasses, your heavenly Father will also forgive you; but if you do not forgive others, neither will your Father forgive your trespasses.'

- We pray 'Our Father', not 'my Father'. We are on a journey together. Forgiveness is central to good relationships. We pray to the Lord for his forgiveness, to be able to forgive ourselves and each other, knowing that the Lord is bigger than our failures.

Wednesday 21 February
Luke 11:29–32

When the crowds were increasing, he began to say, 'This generation is an evil generation; it asks for a sign, but no sign will be given to it except the sign of Jonah. For just as Jonah became a sign to the people of Nineveh, so the Son of Man will be to this generation. The queen of the South will rise at the judgement with the people of this generation and condemn them, because she came from the ends of the earth to listen to the wisdom of Solomon, and see, something greater than Solomon is here! The people of Nineveh will rise up at the judgement with this generation and condemn it, because they repented at the proclamation of Jonah, and see, something greater than Jonah is here!'

- Jonah was the reluctant prophet to the Ninevites. When he did go and proclaim the message, the people repented and changed their evil ways. Jesus drew on the story of Jonah to teach. Lord, touch our hearts that we may be converted to you and your message.
- Prophets proclaimed the truth of God's message and prepared the way for Jesus. They announced the good news that was to be fulfilled in Jesus, who was greater than the prophets, being the Son of God, the word incarnate. We ask that we may come to deeper repentance so that we might strengthen our relationship with Jesus.

Thursday 22 February
The Chair of St Peter
Matthew 16:13–19
Now when Jesus came into the district of Caesarea Philippi, he asked his disciples, 'Who do people say that the Son of Man is?' And they said, 'Some say John the Baptist, but others Elijah, and still others Jeremiah or one of the prophets.' He said to them, 'But who do you say that I am?' Simon Peter answered, 'You are the Messiah, the Son of the living God.' And Jesus answered him, 'Blessed are you, Simon son of Jonah! For flesh and blood has not revealed this to you, but my Father in heaven. And I tell you, you are Peter, and on this rock I will build my church, and the gates of Hades will not prevail against it. I will give you the keys of the kingdom of heaven, and whatever you bind on earth will be bound in heaven, and whatever you loose on earth will be loosed in heaven.'

- This is not about a chair, but about its occupant, who is a source of unity among believers. Authority is meant to be for service. May our relationship with Jesus be a source of strength to us that we can grow more fully into the unity he desires.
- This gospel is not simply information about Jesus, but is about a prophetic call to a personal relationship. Lord, you reassure us of your support. May we live it out in a personal and prophetic way.

Friday 23 February
Matthew 5:20–26
Jesus said to them, 'For I tell you, unless your righteousness exceeds that of the scribes and Pharisees, you will never enter the kingdom of heaven.

'You have heard that it was said to those of ancient times, "You shall not murder"; and "whoever murders shall be liable to judgement." But I say to you that if you are angry with a brother or sister, you will be liable to judgement; and if you insult a brother or sister, you will be liable to the council; and if you say, "You fool", you will be liable to the hell of fire. So when you are offering your gift at the altar, if you remember that your brother or sister has something against you, leave your gift there before the altar and go; first be reconciled to your brother or sister, and then come and offer your gift. Come to terms quickly with your accuser while you are on the way to court with him, or your accuser may hand you over to the judge, and the judge to the guard, and you will be thrown into prison. Truly I tell you, you will never get out until you have paid the last penny.'

- Jesus' kingdom was in marked contrast to the kingdoms of the world. The scribes and Pharisees were trapped by externals and by their role in society. We pray to recognise where external factors have too much importance for us, so that we can choose to look to the Lord and his kingdom of justice, love and peace.

Saturday 24 February
Matthew 5:43–48

Jesus said, 'You have heard that it was said, "You shall love your neighbour and hate your enemy." But I say to you, Love your enemies and pray for those who persecute you, so that you may be children of your Father in heaven; for he makes his sun rise on the evil and on the good, and sends rain on the righteous and on the unrighteous. For if you love those who love you, what reward do you have? Do not even the tax-collectors do the same? And if you greet only your brothers and sisters, what more are you doing than others? Do not even the Gentiles do the same? Be perfect, therefore, as your heavenly Father is perfect.'

- God loves all that God has made (Wisdom 11:24), and all that God has created is good (Genesis 1:12, 25, 31). That provides a lens through which to look at life and relationships. Human factors, such as jealousy and envy, can get in the way of the harmony God desires. May we have a vision that is inclusive, open to all.
- There is a clear tendency in our time to label people and make that label stick for ever. One failure can be allowed to categorise someone for life. Living by selfish human categories does not respect the inherent dignity of each person. Lord, we pray to see beyond the externals to the dignity of each person as loved into existence by you.

25 February–2 March 2024

Something to think and pray about each day this week:

Jesus heard at the Transfiguration that he was beloved! We all want to know that someone would say that they love us.

We are God's favoured ones. We live in the big wide world of God's love, and Jesus on Tabor was allowing himself to be loved in the radiant light of God, shining even in the cloud.

Together we are loved as Peter, James and John were loved in community. Light is caught from one to the other. We are the light of Tabor Mountain for each other – all are loved. Those whom I like and those I like less! The radiant body of Christ was hammered and killed later by ourselves. Love killed at Calvary rose again. Love cannot die.

We can transfigure or disfigure each other. We can bring out the light and the hope and the joy in our belonging to God!

We can transfigure a school, a parish, a community or any group by first of all our being loved by God and letting love emit from ourselves. If we really believe we are loved by God, then the world we live in is transfigured – changed utterly.

Donal Neary SJ, *Gospel Reflections for Sundays of Year B*

The Presence of God
'Be still, and know that I am God!' Lord, your words lead us to the calmness and greatness of your presence.

Freedom
'In these days, God taught me as a schoolteacher teaches a pupil' (St Ignatius). I remind myself that there are things God has to teach me yet, and I ask for the grace to hear them and let them change me.

Consciousness
How am I really feeling? Lighthearted? Heavyhearted? I may be very much at peace, happy to be here.
Equally, I may be frustrated, worried or angry.
I acknowledge how I really am. It is the real me whom the Lord loves.

The Word
God speaks to each of us individually. I listen attentively to hear what he is saying to me. Read the text a few times, then listen. *(Please turn to the Scripture on the following pages. Inspiration points are there, should you need them. When you are ready, return here to continue.)*

Conversation
Do I notice myself reacting as I pray with the word of God? Do I feel challenged, comforted, angry? Imagining Jesus sitting or standing by me, I speak out my feelings, as one trusted friend to another.

Conclusion
I thank God for these moments we have spent together and for any insights I have been given concerning the text.

Sunday 25 February
Second Sunday of Lent
Mark 9:2–10

Six days later, Jesus took with him Peter and James and John, and led them up a high mountain apart, by themselves. And he was transfigured before them, and his clothes became dazzling white, such as no one on earth could bleach them. And there appeared to them Elijah with Moses, who were talking with Jesus. Then Peter said to Jesus, 'Rabbi, it is good for us to be here; let us make three dwellings, one for you, one for Moses, and one for Elijah.' He did not know what to say, for they were terrified. Then a cloud overshadowed them, and from the cloud there came a voice, 'This is my Son, the Beloved; listen to him!' Suddenly when they looked around, they saw no one with them any more, but only Jesus.

As they were coming down the mountain, he ordered them to tell no one about what they had seen, until after the Son of Man had risen from the dead. So they kept the matter to themselves, questioning what this rising from the dead could mean.

- The transfiguration, which reveals something further of Jesus' identity, comes immediately after the first prediction of his passion. Jesus was fulfilling both the Law and the prophets, but bringing them to a new place. We pray that we may be transformed and see beyond the suffering to the glory that Jesus promised.
- The reaction of Peter, James and John was one of attraction and terror. There was the reassuring voice of the Father: 'This is my Son, the Beloved, listen to him!' Lord, you remind us of the glory you desire to share with us. May we have the faith to come down the mountain and continue the journey with you.

Monday 26 February
Luke 6:36–38

'Do not judge, and you will not be judged; do not condemn, and you will not be condemned. Forgive, and you will be forgiven; give, and it will be given to you. A good measure, pressed down, shaken together, running over, will be put into your lap; for the measure you give will be the measure you get back.'

- These days have been naming qualities of discipleship. Luke can be called the gospel of mercy, revealing a compassionate God who wants us to have the same care in our relationships. Lord, you are merciful to us and we pray that we may be tolerant and patient with the failings of others, as you are with ours.
- It is easy to fall into judgement and condemnation of those who seem to fall short of our standards. We are prone to fall into judgement of the personal aspects. May we have a humble stance that acknowledges our own limits so that we are more understanding of others.

Tuesday 27 February
Matthew 23:1–12

Then Jesus said to the crowds and to his disciples, 'The scribes and the Pharisees sit on Moses' seat; therefore, do whatever they teach you and follow it; but do not do as they do, for they do not practise what they teach. They tie up heavy burdens, hard to bear, and lay them on the shoulders of others; but they themselves are unwilling to lift a finger to move them. They do all their deeds to be seen by others; for they make their phylacteries broad and their fringes long. They love to have the place of honour at banquets and the best seats in the synagogues, and to be greeted with respect in the market-places, and to have people call them rabbi. But you are not to be called rabbi, for you have one teacher, and you are all students. And call no one your father on earth, for you have one Father – the one in heaven. Nor are you to be called instructors, for you have one instructor, the Messiah. The greatest among you will be your servant. All who exalt themselves will be humbled, and all who humble themselves will be exalted.'

- Moses had a prominent place in the faith story of the Israelites, as a teacher of the law. Those who succeeded him in that role, the Scribes and the Pharisees, seemed to have lost perspective. Their outward behaviour was at odds with the spirit of the law. Lord, may we not be held bound by our own importance, but allow your teaching to show us the way.
- We live in a world where honours can take on much importance. Lord, your way is one of humility and truth. You bring down the

powerful and raise up the lowly (Luke 1:52). Help us to transform our hearts to be more like yours, so that poverty, simplicity and truth are to the fore in our lives and in our relationships.

Wednesday 28 February
Matthew 20:17–28

While Jesus was going up to Jerusalem, he took the twelve disciples aside by themselves, and said to them on the way, 'See, we are going up to Jerusalem, and the Son of Man will be handed over to the chief priests and scribes, and they will condemn him to death; then they will hand him over to the Gentiles to be mocked and flogged and crucified; and on the third day he will be raised.'

Then the mother of the sons of Zebedee came to him with her sons, and kneeling before him, she asked a favour of him. And he said to her, 'What do you want?' She said to him, 'Declare that these two sons of mine will sit, one at your right hand and one at your left, in your kingdom.' But Jesus answered, 'You do not know what you are asking. Are you able to drink the cup that I am about to drink?' They said to him, 'We are able.' He said to them, 'You will indeed drink my cup, but to sit at my right hand and at my left, this is not mine to grant, but it is for those for whom it has been prepared by my Father.'

When the ten heard it, they were angry with the two brothers. But Jesus called them to him and said, 'You know that the rulers of the Gentiles lord it over them, and their great ones are tyrants over them. It will not be so among you; but whoever wishes to be great among you must be your servant, and whoever wishes to be first among you must be your slave; just as the Son of Man came not to be served but to serve, and to give his life a ransom for many.'

- Jesus made the journey to Jerusalem, foretelling what awaited him there. He would be 'handed over' to others. He wanted to do the Father's will. Lord, we desire to go to Jerusalem with you but are fearful of the cost and pain involved. Give us the strength to stay with you, for it is you we want, not suffering.
- This is another instance of the disciples not getting Jesus' message. The mother of James and John wanted some prominence for her

sons. The other disciples had similar designs but were slower to take action. Jesus, give us your spirit of humility and service in our lives.

Thursday 29 February
Luke 16:19–31

Jesus said to them, 'There was a rich man who was dressed in purple and fine linen and who feasted sumptuously every day. And at his gate lay a poor man named Lazarus, covered with sores, who longed to satisfy his hunger with what fell from the rich man's table; even the dogs would come and lick his sores. The poor man died and was carried away by the angels to be with Abraham. The rich man also died and was buried. In Hades, where he was being tormented, he looked up and saw Abraham far away with Lazarus by his side. He called out, "Father Abraham, have mercy on me, and send Lazarus to dip the tip of his finger in water and cool my tongue; for I am in agony in these flames." But Abraham said, "Child, remember that during your lifetime you received your good things, and Lazarus in like manner evil things; but now he is comforted here, and you are in agony. Besides all this, between you and us a great chasm has been fixed, so that those who might want to pass from here to you cannot do so, and no one can cross from there to us." He said, "Then, father, I beg you to send him to my father's house – for I have five brothers – that he may warn them, so that they will not also come into this place of torment." Abraham replied, "They have Moses and the prophets; they should listen to them." He said, "No, father Abraham; but if someone goes to them from the dead, they will repent." He said to him, "If they do not listen to Moses and the prophets, neither will they be convinced even if someone rises from the dead."'

- Another story of contrast, between a rich and a poor man. For Jesus, no one was excluded; he sought to nourish all with food that endured. It is an invitation to change our attitudes. May our poverty and a lack of inclusion not impede us in being voices for justice, seeking to bring about change.
- It is a world with unequal distribution of resources. While some dine well, others lack food. Jesus had a hunger for justice. This asks

for action, not pious words. We pray that we may hunger for what is right and not remain silent at the gate of life.

Friday 1 March
Matthew 21:33–43.45–46

Jesus said to them, 'Listen to another parable. There was a landowner who planted a vineyard, put a fence around it, dug a wine press in it, and built a watch-tower. Then he leased it to tenants and went to another country. When the harvest time had come, he sent his slaves to the tenants to collect his produce. But the tenants seized his slaves and beat one, killed another, and stoned another. Again he sent other slaves, more than the first; and they treated them in the same way. Finally he sent his son to them, saying, "They will respect my son." But when the tenants saw the son, they said to themselves, "This is the heir; come, let us kill him and get his inheritance." So they seized him, threw him out of the vineyard, and killed him. Now when the owner of the vineyard comes, what will he do to those tenants?' They said to him, 'He will put those wretches to a miserable death, and lease the vineyard to other tenants who will give him the produce at the harvest time.'

Jesus said to them, 'Have you never read in the scriptures:
"The stone that the builders rejected
    has become the cornerstone;
this was the Lord's doing,
    and it is amazing in our eyes"?

Therefore I tell you, the kingdom of God will be taken away from you and given to a people that produces the fruits of the kingdom.'

When the chief priests and the Pharisees heard his parables, they realised that he was speaking about them. They wanted to arrest him, but they feared the crowds, because they regarded him as a prophet.

- Having made careful preparations, the landowner expected a good return. The self-interest of the tenants became apparent over time. Lord, help us to be responsible with the gifts given to us so that we produce a good harvest in your name
- The owner sent his son, expecting that he would be given better treatment, but the tenants saw it as an opportunity. The story tells

of the tenants coming to a miserable end, but could a compassionate God surprise us by acting differently? Lord, show us your compassion for the ways we have misused what you have entrusted to us.

Saturday 2 March
Luke 15:1–3.11–32

Now all the tax-collectors and sinners were coming near to listen to him. And the Pharisees and the scribes were grumbling and saying, 'This fellow welcomes sinners and eats with them.'

So he told them this parable:

'There was a man who had two sons. The younger of them said to his father, "Father, give me the share of the property that will belong to me." So he divided his property between them. A few days later the younger son gathered all he had and travelled to a distant country, and there he squandered his property in dissolute living. When he had spent everything, a severe famine took place throughout that country, and he began to be in need. So he went and hired himself out to one of the citizens of that country, who sent him to his fields to feed the pigs. He would gladly have filled himself with the pods that the pigs were eating; and no one gave him anything. But when he came to himself he said, "How many of my father's hired hands have bread enough and to spare, but here I am dying of hunger! I will get up and go to my father, and I will say to him, 'Father, I have sinned against heaven and before you; I am no longer worthy to be called your son; treat me like one of your hired hands.'" So he set off and went to his father. But while he was still far off, his father saw him and was filled with compassion; he ran and put his arms around him and kissed him. Then the son said to him, "Father, I have sinned against heaven and before you; I am no longer worthy to be called your son." But the father said to his slaves, "Quickly, bring out a robe – the best one – and put it on him; put a ring on his finger and sandals on his feet. And get the fatted calf and kill it, and let us eat and celebrate; for this son of mine was dead and is alive again; he was lost and is found!" And they began to celebrate.

'Now his elder son was in the field; and when he came and approached the house, he heard music and dancing. He called one of the slaves and asked what was going on. He replied, "Your brother has come, and your father has killed the fatted calf, because he has got him back safe and sound." Then he became angry and refused to go in. His father came out and began to plead with him. But he answered his father, "Listen! For all these years I have been working like a slave for you, and I have never disobeyed your command; yet you have never given me even a young goat so that I might celebrate with my friends. But when this son of yours came back, who has devoured your property with prostitutes, you killed the fatted calf for him!" Then the father said to him, "Son, you are always with me, and all that is mine is yours. But we had to celebrate and rejoice, because this brother of yours was dead and has come to life; he was lost and has been found."'

- A familiar parable of contrasts. The younger son asked for freedom and went far away to get distance from home. In time, he 'came to himself' and decided to return. May we recognise when we wander away so that we may come to our senses and return home to you.
- This is one of the great stories of compassion, which means being moved to the depth of one's being. The father reached out to his errant son, restoring him to full family membership. We pray that we may recognise our need and welcome the extravagant, forgiving love of the Father.

The Third Week of Lent

3–9 March 2024

Something to think and pray about each day this week:

In Italian, Lent is *quaresima* or forty (days). In German, it is *Fastenzeit*, literally 'fasting time', or time for bodily restraint. Our English word comes from an older Anglo-Saxon word for spring – len(c)ten – whence our word Lent, as the days are lengthening. Thus, Italian tells us *how long it will last* (with its symbolic overtones). German tells us *what we are supposed to do* in that season. But English tells us *what is supposed to happen*, that is, we hope to experience a springtime of faith, a time of growth and new life.

Ask the LORD for rain in the season of the late spring rains – the LORD who causes thunderstorms – and he will give everyone showers of rain and green growth in the field. (Zechariah 10:1)

Kieran J. O'Mahony OSA, *Hearers of the Word: Praying and Exploring the Readings for Lent and Holy Week*

The Presence of God

I remind myself that, as I sit here now, God is gazing on me with love and holding me in being. I pause for a moment and think of this.

Freedom

'There are very few people who realise what God would make of them if they abandoned themselves into his hands, and let themselves be formed by his grace' (St Ignatius). I ask for the grace to trust myself totally to God's love.

Consciousness

Where do I sense hope, encouragement and growth in my life? By looking back over the past few months, I may be able to see which activities and occasions have produced rich fruit. If I do notice such areas, I will determine to give those areas both time and space in the future.

The Word

Lord Jesus, you became human to communicate with me. You walked and worked on this earth. You endured the heat and struggled with the cold. All your time on this earth was spent in caring for humanity. You healed the sick, you raised the dead. Most important of all, you saved me from death. *(Please turn to the Scripture on the following pages. Inspiration points are there, should you need them. When you are ready, return here to continue.)*

Conversation

What is stirring in me as I pray? Am I consoled, troubled, left cold? I imagine Jesus standing or sitting at my side, and I share my feelings with him.

Conclusion

Glory be to the Father, and to the Son, and to the Holy Spirit,
As it was in the beginning, is now and ever shall be,
World without end. Amen.

Sunday 3 March
Third Sunday of Lent
John 2:13–25

The Passover of the Jews was near, and Jesus went up to Jerusalem. In the temple he found people selling cattle, sheep, and doves, and the money-changers seated at their tables. Making a whip of cords, he drove all of them out of the temple, both the sheep and the cattle. He also poured out the coins of the money-changers and overturned their tables. He told those who were selling the doves, 'Take these things out of here! Stop making my Father's house a market-place!' His disciples remembered that it was written, 'Zeal for your house will consume me.' The Jews then said to him, 'What sign can you show us for doing this?' Jesus answered them, 'Destroy this temple, and in three days I will raise it up.' The Jews then said, 'This temple has been under construction for forty-six years, and will you raise it up in three days?' But he was speaking of the temple of his body. After he was raised from the dead, his disciples remembered that he had said this; and they believed the scripture and the word that Jesus had spoken.

When he was in Jerusalem during the Passover festival, many believed in his name because they saw the signs that he was doing. But Jesus on his part would not entrust himself to them, because he knew all people and needed no one to testify about anyone; for he himself knew what was in everyone.

- The Gospel of John is attentive to the Jewish festivals and their place in the lives of the people. What Jesus observed was at variance with what he believed about his Father's house. May we who live in the market-place that has become a temple for many, have the courage and zeal to stand for the truth.
- Jesus declared a different mission in the sacred environment of the Temple. He spoke of himself as the new temple. Lord, help us to see beyond structures and buildings to the person of Jesus as the cornerstone of our faith.

Monday 4 March
Luke 4:24-30

And he said, 'Truly I tell you, no prophet is accepted in the prophet's hometown. But the truth is, there were many widows in Israel in the time of Elijah, when the heaven was shut up three years and six months, and there was a severe famine over all the land; yet Elijah was sent to none of them except to a widow at Zarephath in Sidon. There were also many lepers in Israel in the time of the prophet Elisha, and none of them was cleansed except Naaman the Syrian.' When they heard this, all in the synagogue were filled with rage. They got up, drove him out of the town, and led him to the brow of the hill on which their town was built, so that they might hurl him off the cliff. But he passed through the midst of them and went on his way.

- Jesus' reputation had grown when he returned home. His personal approach evoked a strong reaction. The local people thought he was to blame for their discomfort. Help us to realise when we fall into the trap of confusing the message with the messenger, so that we may allow the truth to change us.
- Jesus drew on the example of outsiders, who responded to the message of the prophets. He was calling his hearers to faith in him. Lord, help us to recognise that we are the locals who are slow to accept you, as our prejudices can blind us to the reality of who you really are.

Tuesday 5 March
Matthew 18:21-35

Then Peter came and said to him, 'Lord, if another member of the church sins against me, how often should I forgive? As many as seven times?' Jesus said to him, 'Not seven times, but, I tell you, seventy-seven times.

'For this reason the kingdom of heaven may be compared to a king who wished to settle accounts with his slaves. When he began the reckoning, one who owed him ten thousand talents was brought to him; and, as he could not pay, his lord ordered him to be sold, together with his wife and children and all his possessions, and payment to be made. So the slave fell on his knees before him, saying, "Have patience with me, and I will pay you everything." And out of pity for him, the lord of that slave released him and forgave him the debt. But that same slave, as he went out, came upon one of his fellow-slaves who owed him a hundred denarii; and seizing him by the throat, he said, "Pay what you owe." Then his fellow-slave fell down and pleaded with him, "Have patience with me, and I will pay you." But he refused; then he went and threw him into prison until he should pay the debt. When his fellow-slaves saw what had happened, they were greatly distressed, and they went and reported to their lord all that had taken place. Then his lord summoned him and said to him, "You wicked slave! I forgave you all that debt because you pleaded with me. Should you not have had mercy on your fellow-slave, as I had mercy on you?" And in anger his lord handed him over to be tortured until he should pay his entire debt. So my heavenly Father will also do to every one of you, if you do not forgive your brother or sister from your heart.'

- Peter asked Jesus a practical question about the number of times to forgive. Jesus was thinking of more than limited numbers. Jesus, you reveal a merciful God of love who forgives without limit; open our hearts to have a similar disposition when we feel hurt or overlooked.
- Jesus taught and lived forgiveness. In life, small-mindedness and a lack of perspective can prevail. Forgiveness is key to the quality of family and community life. Lord, help us to appreciate your forgiveness so that we can have larger hearts in the situations of conflict that we encounter in life.

Wednesday 6 March
Matthew 5:17–19
Jesus said to them, 'Do not think that I have come to abolish the law or the prophets; I have come not to abolish but to fulfil. For truly I tell you, until heaven and earth pass away, not one letter, not one stroke of a letter, will pass from the law until all is accomplished. Therefore, whoever breaks one of the least of these commandments, and teaches others to do the same, will be called least in the kingdom of heaven; but whoever does them and teaches them will be called great in the kingdom of heaven.'

- The law of God, given to Moses, and the teaching of the prophets were important aspects of the lives of the Israelites as people of the covenant. Lord, as people of the new covenant, may we be guided by your law of love in living as your disciples.
- Jesus came to fulfil the law and the prophets, bringing the people to a new place in a relationship of love with him. The law is to be written on our hearts, not on stone tablets. May we grow in freedom to live out our relationship with Jesus and to be prophetic voices for the truth he reveals to us.

Thursday 7 March
Luke 11:14–23

Now he was casting out a demon that was mute; when the demon had gone out, the one who had been mute spoke, and the crowds were amazed. But some of them said, 'He casts out demons by Beelzebul, the ruler of the demons.' Others, to test him, kept demanding from him a sign from heaven. But he knew what they were thinking and said to them, 'Every kingdom divided against itself becomes a desert, and house falls on house. If Satan also is divided against himself, how will his kingdom stand? – for you say that I cast out the demons by Beelzebul. Now if I cast out the demons by Beelzebul, by whom do your exorcists cast them out? Therefore they will be your judges. But if it is by the finger of God that I cast out the demons, then the kingdom of God has come to you. When a strong man, fully armed, guards his castle, his property is safe. But when one stronger than he attacks him and overpowers him, he takes away his armour in which he trusted and divides his plunder. Whoever is not with me is against me, and whoever does not gather with me scatters.'

- Jesus preached and taught. Healing added a further dimension to his ministry of transformation. We sometimes seem to lack the power of speech when we meet an inhospitable audience. May we have the courage to proclaim Jesus and bring his healing to the broken people of our time.
- Jesus cast out demons by the power of God. His kingdom is one of justice, love and peace. We are called as his companions to stand by

him, being a source of unity. Lord, may we draw strength from you, knowing that your power is greater than the voices of dissent and the forces of evil.

Friday 8 March
Mark 12:28–34

One of the scribes came near and heard them disputing with one another, and seeing that he answered them well, he asked him, 'Which commandment is the first of all?' Jesus answered, 'The first is, "Hear, O Israel: the Lord our God, the Lord is one; you shall love the Lord your God with all your heart, and with all your soul, and with all your mind, and with all your strength." The second is this, "You shall love your neighbour as yourself." There is no other commandment greater than these.' Then the scribe said to him, 'You are right, Teacher; you have truly said that "he is one, and besides him there is no other"; and "to love him with all the heart, and with all the understanding, and with all the strength", and "to love one's neighbour as oneself", – this is much more important than all whole burnt-offerings and sacrifices.' When Jesus saw that he answered wisely, he said to him, 'You are not far from the kingdom of God.' After that no one dared to ask him any question.

- The Ten Commandments are far more than a series of negative prescriptions, of 'Thou shalt not'. They provide a way of life, founded on love, to right relationships with God and others. May we value more fully the guidance that God gives us and allow it to enrich our lives and our relationships.
- In responding to the scribe, Jesus gave a nice summary in saying that loving God was first and loving others followed from it. Love was at the heart of God's way. Lord, give us hearts that love you and others as our brothers and sisters whom you love unconditionally.

Saturday 9 March
Luke 18:9–14

He also told this parable to some who trusted in themselves that they were righteous and regarded others with contempt: 'Two men went up to the temple to pray, one a Pharisee and the other a tax-collector. The

Pharisee, standing by himself, was praying thus, "God, I thank you that I am not like other people: thieves, rogues, adulterers, or even like this tax-collector. I fast twice a week; I give a tenth of all my income." But the tax-collector, standing far off, would not even look up to heaven, but was beating his breast and saying, "God, be merciful to me, a sinner!" I tell you, this man went down to his home justified rather than the other; for all who exalt themselves will be humbled, but all who humble themselves will be exalted.'

- This is another story of contrasting attitudes. How the Pharisee and tax collector saw themselves and God influenced how they prayed. May we have the freedom to acknowledge the truth about God and ourselves so that we may pray in humility for mercy.

- We are halfway through Lent and this is a time to check how we are doing. We began centred on God, but that may have shifted. Perhaps we are proud of how well we are doing or critical of our shortcomings. Lord, help us to renew our focus and to keep our eyes on you as we continue our Lenten journey.

The Fourth Week of Lent

10–16 March 2024

Something to think and pray about each day this week:

In preparing for Lent, Pope Francis quotes Hosea (6:6): 'What I want is mercy, not sacrifice'. This is a shift of emphasis away from what I do, to what God does in me.

Yet people may still get caught up in Lent as simply a time of self-sacrifice, a giving up of stuff through self-discipline or willpower. There's nothing wrong with that, but just notice the emphasis on the self and what 'I' am doing. It seems almost to cut God out of the picture.

The quote from Hosea is inviting us to act in a merciful or loving way, which is subtly different. For example, a person may be called to go the extra mile with someone, to mend a fractured relationship, to ask forgiveness for a hurt caused, to turn away from vice and reform their life.

Obviously there is sacrifice involved here, and there is always a cost in changing for the better, but the goal is not sacrifice, it's trying to do the right thing, the loving thing, and it can be hard … doing what God wants, though, brings its own courage, hidden strength and grace, which allows us to go beyond our normal selves.

Brendan McManus SJ, *The Sacred Heart Messenger*, February 2021

The Presence of God
I pause for a moment
and reflect on God's life-giving presence
in every part of my body,
in everything around me,
in the whole of my life.

Freedom
Many countries are at this moment suffering the agonies of war. I bow my head in thanksgiving for my freedom. I pray for all prisoners and captives.

Consciousness
Knowing that God loves me unconditionally, I look honestly over the past day, its events and my feelings. Do I have something to be grateful for? Then I give thanks. Is there something I am sorry for? Then I ask forgiveness.

The Word
Now I turn to the Scripture set out for me this day. I read slowly over the words and see if any sentence or sentiment appeals to me. *(Please turn to the Scripture on the following pages. Inspiration points are there, should you need them. When you are ready, return here to continue.)*

Conversation
I know with certainty that there were times when you carried me, Lord. There were times when it was through your strength that I got through the dark times in my life.

Conclusion
Glory be to the Father, and to the Son, and to the Holy Spirit,
As it was in the beginning, is now and ever shall be,
World without end. Amen.

Sunday 10 March
Fourth Sunday of Lent
John 3:14–21

And just as Moses lifted up the serpent in the wilderness, so must the Son of Man be lifted up, that whoever believes in him may have eternal life.

'For God so loved the world that he gave his only Son, so that everyone who believes in him may not perish but may have eternal life.

'Indeed, God did not send the Son into the world to condemn the world, but in order that the world might be saved through him. Those who believe in him are not condemned; but those who do not believe are condemned already, because they have not believed in the name of the only Son of God. And this is the judgement, that the light has come into the world, and people loved darkness rather than light because their deeds were evil. For all who do evil hate the light and do not come to the light, so that their deeds may not be exposed. But those who do what is true come to the light, so that it may be clearly seen that their deeds have been done in God.'

- Jesus was sent into the world to bring salvation. The world is ambivalent to Jesus, though God's desire is clear – for us to have eternal life though Jesus. We pray to recognise the gift and the desire of God so that we are not captivated and drawn off course by the attractions of the world.
- The lifting up of the serpent brought liberation to the Israelites from its poisonous effects (Numbers 21:9). Jesus was to be lifted up on the cross, offering his life for our salvation. As children of light may we have hearts that believe in Jesus and respond in love, raising up people who are caught in the darkness.

Monday 11 March
John 4:43-54

When the two days were over, he went from that place to Galilee (for Jesus himself had testified that a prophet has no honour in the prophet's own country). When he came to Galilee, the Galileans welcomed him, since they had seen all that he had done in Jerusalem at the festival; for they too had gone to the festival.

Then he came again to Cana in Galilee where he had changed the water into wine. Now there was a royal official whose son lay ill in Capernaum. When he heard that Jesus had come from Judea to Galilee, he went and begged him to come down and heal his son, for he was at the point of death. Then Jesus said to him, 'Unless you see signs and wonders you will not believe.' The official said to him, 'Sir, come down before my little boy dies.' Jesus said to him, 'Go; your son will live.' The man believed the word that Jesus spoke to him and started on his way. As he was going down, his slaves met him and told him that his child was alive. So he asked them the hour when he began to recover, and they said to him, 'Yesterday at one in the afternoon the fever left him.' The father realised that this was the hour when Jesus had said to him, 'Your son will live.' So he himself believed, along with his whole household. Now this was the second sign that Jesus did after coming from Judea to Galilee.

- Jesus, as a prophet, was welcomed in Galilee by the people who had seen what he had done in Jerusalem at the festival. Evidence had been provided to enable them to move on. Lord, may we have the faith to accept the evidence you give and to value others as your people.
- A royal official, believing Jesus could heal his son, begged for it. Jesus challenged the official's faith before responding. We pray to recognise the wonders the Lord performs so that our faith is deepened and our response is more wholehearted.

Tuesday 12 March
John 5:1–16

After this there was a festival of the Jews, and Jesus went up to Jerusalem.

Now in Jerusalem by the Sheep Gate there is a pool, called in Hebrew Beth-zatha, which has five porticoes. In these lay many invalids – blind, lame, and paralysed. One man was there who had been ill for thirty-eight years. When Jesus saw him lying there and knew that he had been there a long time, he said to him, 'Do you want to be made well?' The sick man answered him, 'Sir, I have no one to put me into the pool when the water is stirred up; and while I am making my way, someone else steps down ahead of me.' Jesus said to him, 'Stand up, take your mat and walk.' At once the man was made well, and he took up his mat and began to walk.

Now that day was a sabbath. So the Jews said to the man who had been cured, 'It is the sabbath; it is not lawful for you to carry your mat.' But he answered them, 'The man who made me well said to me, "Take up your mat and walk."' They asked him, 'Who is the man who said to you, "Take it up and walk"?' Now the man who had been healed did not know who it was, for Jesus had disappeared in the crowd that was there. Later Jesus found him in the temple and said to him, 'See, you have been made well! Do not sin any more, so that nothing worse happens to you.' The man went away and told the Jews that it was Jesus who had made him well. Therefore the Jews started persecuting Jesus, because he was doing such things on the sabbath.

- Jesus was present at another festival and healed on the sabbath. He was Lord of the sabbath as well as being the new temple. Lord, help us to appreciate external places and occasions of worship, that we may develop the interior dimensions that enhance them.
- Jesus healed the man who had been ill for a long time. The Jews seemed to be more concerned about externals, such as carrying a mat, whereas Jesus was compassionate and personal. Doing God's work aroused opposition on this occasion. May we be guided by the spirit and not the letter of the law in helping others.

Wednesday 13 March
John 5:17–30

But Jesus answered them, 'My Father is still working, and I also am working.' For this reason the Jews were seeking all the more to kill him, because he was not only breaking the sabbath, but was also calling God his own Father, thereby making himself equal to God.

Jesus said to them, 'Very truly, I tell you, the Son can do nothing on his own, but only what he sees the Father doing; for whatever the Father does, the Son does likewise. The Father loves the Son and shows him all that he himself is doing; and he will show him greater works than these, so that you will be astonished. Indeed, just as the Father raises the dead and gives them life, so also the Son gives life to whomsoever he wishes. The Father judges no one but has given all judgement to the Son, so that all may honour the Son just as they honour the Father. Anyone who does not honour the Son does not honour the Father who sent him. Very truly, I tell you, anyone who hears my word and believes him who sent me has eternal life, and does not come under judgement, but has passed from death to life.

'Very truly, I tell you, the hour is coming, and is now here, when the dead will hear the voice of the Son of God, and those who hear will live. For just as the Father has life in himself, so he has granted the Son also to have life in himself; and he has given him authority to execute judgement, because he is the Son of Man. Do not be astonished at this; for the hour is coming when all who are in their graves will hear his voice and will come out – those who have done good, to the resurrection of life, and those who have done evil, to the resurrection of condemnation.

'I can do nothing on my own. As I hear, I judge; and my judgement is just, because I seek to do not my own will but the will of him who sent me.'

- Our God is active and close to us. Jesus said, 'My Father is still working and I also am working.' Jesus is Emmanuel, God with us. In the joys and struggles of life may we draw strength and comfort from the presence of Jesus and the work he has done for us.
- Jesus was one with the Father in his life and mission. He draws us into this relationship of love. Having eternal life speaks of life now and not just in the future. Lord, help us to come to a deeper faith in your presence with us and within us, that we may share your glory.

Thursday 14 March
John 5:31–47

Jesus said to them, 'If I testify about myself, my testimony is not true. There is another who testifies on my behalf, and I know that his testimony to me is true. You sent messengers to John, and he testified to the truth. Not that I accept such human testimony, but I say these things so that you may be saved. He was a burning and shining lamp, and you were willing to rejoice for a while in his light. But I have a testimony greater than John's. The works that the Father has given me to complete, the very works that I am doing, testify on my behalf that the Father has sent me. And the Father who sent me has himself testified on my behalf. You have never heard his voice or seen his form, and you do not have his word abiding in you, because you do not believe him whom he has sent.

'You search the scriptures because you think that in them you have eternal life; and it is they that testify on my behalf. Yet you refuse to come to me to have life. I do not accept glory from human beings. But I know that you do not have the love of God in you. I have come in my Father's name, and you do not accept me; if another comes in his own name, you will accept him. How can you believe when you accept glory from one another and do not seek the glory that comes from the one who alone is God? Do not think that I will accuse you before the Father; your accuser is Moses, on whom you have set your hope. If you believed Moses, you would believe me, for he wrote about me. But if you do not believe what he wrote, how will you believe what I say?'

- The will of the Father and being sent was of central importance in the life and mission of Jesus. He said, 'I seek not to do my own will but the will of him who sent me.' May we who are sent by him have the freedom to carry out what the Lord wants in our lives of service.
- The identity of Jesus was becoming clearer over time. Jesus called on witnesses to testify to his identity – John the Baptist, the Father, the works he did, scripture and Moses. We pray that we may have the faith and wisdom to notice the many signs that Jesus shares with us so that we are more effective witnesses for him.

Friday 15 March
John 7:1–2.10.25–30

After this Jesus went about in Galilee. He did not wish to go about in Judea because the Jews were looking for an opportunity to kill him. Now the Jewish festival of Booths was near.

But after his brothers had gone to the festival, then he also went, not publicly but as it were in secret.

Now some of the people of Jerusalem were saying, 'Is not this the man whom they are trying to kill? And here he is, speaking openly, but they say nothing to him! Can it be that the authorities really know that this is the Messiah? Yet we know where this man is from; but when the Messiah comes, no one will know where he is from.' Then Jesus cried out as he was teaching in the temple, 'You know me, and you know where I am from. I have not come on my own. But the one who sent me is true, and you do not know him. I know him, because I am from him, and he sent me.' Then they tried to arrest him, but no one laid hands on him, because his hour had not yet come.

- Jesus went back to Galilee, but he went to Jerusalem secretly for the festival, which gave thanks for the harvest as well as recalling a time when the chosen people lived in tents. Lord, may we draw strength from you and honour your festivals on the journey of life.

- There was conflict between knowing Jesus and knowing about him. His background and teaching led to divided opinions. Lord, we live at a time when many do not believe in you or see you as relevant. We pray that we may know you better and give more personal testimony to you.

Saturday 16 March
John 7:40–53

When they heard these words, some in the crowd said, 'This is really the prophet.' Others said, 'This is the Messiah.' But some asked, 'Surely the Messiah does not come from Galilee, does he? Has not the scripture said that the Messiah is descended from David and comes from Bethlehem, the village where David lived?' So there was a division in the crowd because of him. Some of them wanted to arrest him, but no one laid hands on him.

Then the temple police went back to the chief priests and Pharisees, who asked them, 'Why did you not arrest him?' The police answered, 'Never has anyone spoken like this!' Then the Pharisees replied, 'Surely you have not been deceived too, have you? Has any one of the authorities or of the Pharisees believed in him? But this crowd, which does not know the law – they are accursed.' Nicodemus, who had gone to Jesus before, and who was one of them, asked, 'Our law does not judge people without first giving them a hearing to find out what they are doing, does it?' They replied, 'Surely you are not also from Galilee, are you? Search and you will see that no prophet is to arise from Galilee.'

- There were more disputes about who Jesus was. Concerns at the practical level about his background blinded the crowd to the true message of Jesus. May we have a deeper sense of who Jesus is and a closer relationship with him so that we can make him known.

- There were divided opinions on Jesus. The temple police failed to arrest him, to the unhappiness of the chief priests and the Pharisees. Nicodemus, who had first come to Jesus by night (John 3:2), said Jesus was entitled to a fair hearing. Lord, you present reliable credentials. May we have the courage to declare this.

17–23 March 2024

Something to think and pray about each day this week:

Our stories of St Patrick are varied. Legend puts him in the corner of countless fields the length and breadth of Ireland. It puts him on top of Croagh Patrick, in the stillness of Lough Derg and at numerous holy wells. Was he in these places? The answer may very well be yes – he was there insofar as his name and the flame from Slane reflected the Gospel and shone in the hearts and souls of Irish people.

Is he in parades, marching bands or floats? Is he in greened rivers or landmarks across the globe that are, for the day, illuminated in green? He could and should be, but he might struggle to be found in many of the practices associated with him today.

It is about keeping the flame alive and burning and finding him again, in the corner of a field, in the lovely church with its towering steeple, in the quiet home where the 'Rosary is told', in the holy water font inside the front door of a house where blessing is made possible as we come and go.

Vincent Sherlock, *The Sacred Heart Messenger*, March 2022

The Presence of God

I pause for a moment and think of the love and the grace that God showers on me. I am created in the image and likeness of God, I am God's dwelling place.

Freedom

Lord, you granted me the great gift of freedom. In these times, O Lord, grant that I may be free from any form of racism or intolerance. Remind me that we are all equal in your loving eyes.

Consciousness

Knowing that God loves me unconditionally, I can afford to be honest about how I am.

How has the day been, and how do I feel now? I share my feelings openly with the Lord.

The Word

I take my time to read the word of God slowly, a few times, allowing myself to dwell on anything that strikes me. *(Please turn to the Scripture on the following pages. Inspiration points are there, should you need them. When you are ready, return here to continue.)*

Conversation

Sometimes I wonder what I might say if I were to meet you in person, Lord. I think I might say, 'Thank you', because you are always there for me.

Conclusion

I thank God for these moments we have spent together and for any insights I have been given concerning the text.

Sunday 17 March
Fifth Sunday of Lent
St Patrick, Patron of Ireland (IRL)
Mark 16:15–20

And he said to them, 'Go into all the world and proclaim the good news to the whole creation. The one who believes and is baptised will be saved; but the one who does not believe will be condemned. And these signs will accompany those who believe: by using my name they will cast out demons; they will speak in new tongues; they will pick up snakes in their hands, and if they drink any deadly thing, it will not hurt them; they will lay their hands on the sick, and they will recover.'

So then the Lord Jesus, after he had spoken to them, was taken up into heaven and sat down at the right hand of God. And they went out and proclaimed the good news everywhere, while the Lord worked with them and confirmed the message by the signs that accompanied it.

- Jesus drew Patrick to himself and sent him on mission to Ireland. It meant returning to a place where he had been enslaved and had suffered. Help us to recognise where we are enslaved now so that we might be free to announce the good news as Patrick did.
- The surprising ways of God bore fruit through the labours of St Patrick, who came to a pagan nation. There is need of a renewed vision to declare that mission in a changed country. May we value the gifts of the past and be strengthened by them in facing the future.

Monday 18 March
John 8:1–11

Early in the morning he came again to the temple. All the people came to him and he sat down and began to teach them. The scribes and the Pharisees brought a woman who had been caught in adultery; and making her stand before all of them, they said to him, 'Teacher, this woman was caught in the very act of committing adultery. Now in the law Moses commanded us to stone such women. Now what do you say?' They said this to test him, so that they might have some charge to bring against him. Jesus bent down and wrote with his finger on the ground. When they kept on questioning him, he straightened up and said to them, 'Let anyone among you who is without sin be the first to throw a stone at her.' And once again he bent down and wrote on the ground. When they heard it, they went away, one by one, beginning with the elders; and Jesus was left alone with the woman standing before him. Jesus straightened up and said to her, 'Woman, where are they? Has no one condemned you?' She said, 'No one, sir.' And Jesus said, 'Neither do I condemn you. Go your way, and from now on do not sin again.'

- In the sacred setting of the temple, the Pharisees challenged Jesus. A woman was accused of adultery. The Pharisees were asked to look into their own hearts, at the hidden stones they were carrying. Lord, help us to appreciate the dignity of all sinners, knowing that we are included.

- The Pharisees asked a practical question about the law. Jesus saw beyond the law to a person. He did not focus on the past, but offered a new future. Lord, may we be able to straighten up, look you in the eye and accept your forgiveness.

Tuesday 19 March
St Joseph, Husband of the Blessed Virgin Mary
Luke 2:41–51a

Now every year his parents went to Jerusalem for the festival of the Passover. And when he was twelve years old, they went up as usual for the festival. When the festival was ended and they started to return, the boy Jesus stayed behind in Jerusalem, but his parents did not know it. Assuming that he was in the group of travellers, they went a day's journey. Then they started to look for him among their relatives and friends. When they did not find him, they returned to Jerusalem to search for him. After three days they found him in the temple, sitting among the teachers, listening to them and asking them questions. And all who heard him were amazed at his understanding and his answers. When his parents saw him they were astonished; and his mother said to him, 'Child, why have you treated us like this? Look, your father and I have been searching for you in great anxiety.' He said to them, 'Why were you searching for me? Did you not know that I must be in my Father's house?' But they did not understand what he said to them. Then he went down with them and came to Nazareth, and was obedient to them. His mother treasured all these things in her heart.

- Joseph was described as 'righteous' (Matthew 1:19). He went with Mary and Jesus to the Temple in Jerusalem for the Passover. Faith and trust in God were evident in his life. May we imitate him by manifesting our faith in the ordinary and the everyday.
- With Mary, Joseph searched for Jesus when he was lost. It was challenging for Joseph to understand Jesus' reply about being in the Father's house. Lord, may we draw strength from Joseph's searching, that we may take Jesus home with us.

Wednesday 20 March
John 8:31–42
Then Jesus said to the Jews who had believed in him, 'If you continue in my word, you are truly my disciples; and you will know the truth, and the truth will make you free.' They answered him, 'We are descendants of Abraham and have never been slaves to anyone. What do you mean by saying, "You will be made free"?'

Jesus answered them, 'Very truly, I tell you, everyone who commits sin is a slave to sin. The slave does not have a permanent place in the household; the son has a place there for ever. So if the Son makes you free, you will be free indeed. I know that you are descendants of Abraham; yet you look for an opportunity to kill me, because there is no place in you for my word. I declare what I have seen in the Father's presence; as for you, you should do what you have heard from the Father.'

They answered him, 'Abraham is our father.' Jesus said to them, 'If you were Abraham's children, you would be doing what Abraham did, but now you are trying to kill me, a man who has told you the truth that I heard from God. This is not what Abraham did. You are indeed doing what your father does.' They said to him, 'We are not illegitimate children; we have one father, God himself.' Jesus said to them, 'If God were your Father, you would love me, for I came from God and now I am here. I did not come on my own, but he sent me.'

- Jesus told and lived the truth of who he was and shared the Father's message with us. The truth liberates, taking away all disguises and pretence. Lord, help us to acknowledge and accept the truth of who you are and who we are, so that our relationship with you is more real.
- Jesus is the Son who sets us free and desires us to respond to that gift. He came into the world to testify to the truth and those who belong to the truth listen to his voice. Lord, may we have the freedom to hear your truth and let it guide our lives.

Thursday 21 March
John 8:51–59

Jesus said to them, 'Very truly, I tell you, whoever keeps my word will never see death.' The Jews said to him, 'Now we know that you have a demon. Abraham died, and so did the prophets; yet you say, "Whoever keeps my word will never taste death." Are you greater than our father Abraham, who died? The prophets also died. Who do you claim to be?' Jesus answered, 'If I glorify myself, my glory is nothing. It is my Father who glorifies me, he of whom you say, "He is our God", though you do not know him. But I know him; if I were to say that I do not know him, I would be a liar like you. But I do know him and I keep his word. Your ancestor Abraham rejoiced that he would see my day; he saw it and was glad.' Then the Jews said to him, 'You are not yet fifty years old, and have you seen Abraham?' Jesus said to them, 'Very truly, I tell you, before Abraham was, I am.' So they picked up stones to throw at him, but Jesus hid himself and went out of the temple.

- Jesus' word was life-giving. His hearers were trapped at the surface level so they could not hear it. Lord, help us to retain your vision amid the many voices that clamour for attention, being focused more on the immediate than the enduring.
- Jesus' claim of knowing and being at one with the Father brought much confusion and downright opposition, with a desire to kill him. We pray to be drawn more fully into that love relationship with the Father that will guide us through the discordant voices of this age.

Friday 22 March
John 10:31–42

The Jews took up stones again to stone him. Jesus replied, 'I have shown you many good works from the Father. For which of these are you going to stone me?' The Jews answered, 'It is not for a good work that we are going to stone you, but for blasphemy, because you, though only a human being, are making yourself God.' Jesus answered, 'Is it not written in your law, "I said, you are gods"? If those to whom the word of God came were called "gods" – and the scripture cannot be annulled – can you say that the one whom the Father has sanctified and sent into the world is blaspheming because I said, "I am God's Son"? If I am not doing the works of my Father, then do not believe me. But if I do them, even though you do not believe me, believe the works, so that you may know and understand that the Father is in me and I am in the Father.' Then they tried to arrest him again, but he escaped from their hands.

He went away again across the Jordan to the place where John had been baptising earlier, and he remained there. Many came to him, and they were saying, 'John performed no sign, but everything that John said about this man was true.' And many believed in him there.

- The build-up of opposition became more evident, with Jesus seen as the problem. He was accused of making himself God. We ask that we may appreciate him more fully, being invited to share in his divinity as he shared in our humanity.
- They tried to arrest Jesus but he escaped their hands. Some came to believe in him as they were able to interpret the signs. May we have that facility and the freedom to recognise and to declare that we believe in him.

Saturday 23 March
John 11:45–56

Many of the Jews therefore, who had come with Mary and had seen what Jesus did, believed in him. But some of them went to the Pharisees and told them what he had done. So the chief priests and the Pharisees called a meeting of the council, and said, 'What are we to do? This man is performing many signs. If we let him go on like this, everyone will believe in him, and the Romans will come and destroy both our holy place and our nation.' But one of them, Caiaphas, who was high priest that year, said to them, 'You know nothing at all! You do not understand that it is better for you to have one man die for the people than to have the whole nation destroyed.' He did not say this on his own, but being high priest that year he prophesied that Jesus was about to die for the nation, and not for the nation only, but to gather into one the dispersed children of God. So from that day on they planned to put him to death.

Jesus therefore no longer walked about openly among the Jews, but went from there to a town called Ephraim in the region near the wilderness; and he remained there with the disciples.

Now the Passover of the Jews was near, and many went up from the country to Jerusalem before the Passover to purify themselves. They were looking for Jesus and were asking one another as they stood in the temple, 'What do you think? Surely he will not come to the festival, will he?'

- The religious leaders were becoming more perturbed by reports about Jesus. Caiaphas said it was better to have one man die for the people than to have the whole nation destroyed. Lord, deepen our faith to see your death as the way to life and the formation of a new nation.

- The Passover was near, but Jesus was about to initiate a new Passover that would bring deliverance from internal slavery. He did not go about openly because of the opposition. Lord, give us the freedom to tell where you are to be found, as we need your help to bring people to you, the source of life.

Holy Week

24–30 March 2024

Something to think and pray about each day this week:

On Palm Sunday the Teacher says, 'I am to celebrate the Passover with you.' He enters each of our homes and turns them into churches; and, even more, present in each place, lifted on the cross of his own human life – 'and I, if I be lifted up, will draw all things to myself' (John 12:32, cf. 3:14, 5:21). He unites us all together in one body. It is this body of Christ, each other and the world, that we receive on Palm Sunday – this is our global eucharist: bearing each other's burdens, aware of the world's suffering.

Palm Sunday also takes us to the cross. Symbols give us our identity, self-image, our way of explaining ourselves to ourselves and to others. Symbols determine the kind of history we tell and retell. In the Christian tradition the cross is the ultimate symbol. Today this cross remains as a poignant, and appropriate, reminder of a man who embodied the Christian virtue of loving without counting the cost, and who tragically paid the ultimate price. Through this cross a man long dead lives again, somehow speaking to ears that belong to people not yet born.

John Scally, *The Sacred Heart Messenger*, April 2021

The Presence of God

Dear Jesus, today I call on you, but not to ask for anything. I'd like only to dwell in your presence. May my heart respond to your love.

Freedom

God, my creator, you gave me life and the gift of freedom. Through your love I exist in this world. May I never take the gift of life for granted. May I always respect others' right to life.

Consciousness

I ask how I am today. Am I particularly tired, stressed or anxious? If any of these characteristics apply, can I try to let go of the concerns that disturb me?

The Word

The word of God comes down to us through the Scriptures. May the Holy Spirit enlighten my mind and my heart to respond to the Gospel teachings. *(Please turn to the Scripture on the following pages. Inspiration points are there, should you need them. When you are ready, return here to continue.)*

Conversation

I begin to talk with Jesus about the Scripture I have just read. What part of it strikes a chord in me? Perhaps the words of a friend – or some story I have heard recently – will rise to the surface in my consciousness. If so, does the story throw light on what the Scripture passage may be saying to me?

Conclusion

Glory be to the Father, and to the Son, and to the Holy Spirit,
As it was in the beginning, is now and ever shall be,
World without end. Amen.

Sunday 24 March
Palm Sunday of the Passion of the Lord
Mark 14:1–15:47
It was two days before the Passover and the festival of Unleavened Bread. The chief priests and the scribes were looking for a way to arrest Jesus by stealth and kill him; for they said, 'Not during the festival, or there may be a riot among the people.'

While he was at Bethany in the house of Simon the leper, as he sat at the table, a woman came with an alabaster jar of very costly ointment of nard, and she broke open the jar and poured the ointment on his head. But some were there who said to one another in anger, 'Why was the ointment wasted in this way? For this ointment could have been sold for more than three hundred denarii, and the money given to the poor.' And they scolded her. But Jesus said, 'Let her alone; why do you trouble her? She has performed a good service for me. For you always have the poor with you, and you can show kindness to them whenever you wish; but you will not always have me. She has done what she could; she has anointed my body beforehand for its burial. Truly I tell you, wherever the good news is proclaimed in the whole world, what she has done will be told in remembrance of her.'

Then Judas Iscariot, who was one of the twelve, went to the chief priests in order to betray him to them. When they heard it, they were greatly pleased, and promised to give him money. So he began to look for an opportunity to betray him.

On the first day of Unleavened Bread, when the Passover lamb is sacrificed, his disciples said to him, 'Where do you want us to go and make the preparations for you to eat the Passover?' So he sent two of his disciples, saying to them, 'Go into the city, and a man carrying a jar of water will meet you; follow him, and wherever he enters, say to the owner of the house, "The Teacher asks, Where is my guest room where I may eat the Passover with my disciples?" He will show you a large room upstairs, furnished and ready. Make preparations for us there.' So the disciples set out and went to the city, and found everything as he had told them; and they prepared the Passover meal.

When it was evening, he came with the twelve. And when they had taken their places and were eating, Jesus said, 'Truly I tell you, one of you will betray me, one who is eating with me.' They began to be distressed and to say to him one after another, 'Surely, not I?' He said to them, 'It is one of the twelve, one who is dipping bread into the bowl with me. For the Son of Man goes as it is written of him, but woe to that one by whom the Son of Man is betrayed! It would have been better for that one not to have been born.'

While they were eating, he took a loaf of bread, and after blessing it he broke it, gave it to them, and said, 'Take; this is my body.' Then he took a cup, and after giving thanks he gave it to them, and all of them drank from it. He said to them, 'This is my blood of the covenant, which is poured out for many. Truly I tell you, I will never again drink of the fruit of the vine until that day when I drink it new in the kingdom of God.'

When they had sung the hymn, they went out to the Mount of Olives. And Jesus said to them, 'You will all become deserters; for it is written,

"I will strike the shepherd,
    and the sheep will be scattered."

But after I am raised up, I will go before you to Galilee.' Peter said to him, 'Even though all become deserters, I will not.' Jesus said to him, 'Truly I tell you, this day, this very night, before the cock crows twice, you will deny me three times.' But he said vehemently, 'Even though I must die with you, I will not deny you.' And all of them said the same.

They went to a place called Gethsemane; and he said to his disciples, 'Sit here while I pray.' He took with him Peter and James and John, and began to be distressed and agitated. And he said to them, 'I am deeply grieved, even to death; remain here, and keep awake.' And going a little farther, he threw himself on the ground and prayed that, if it were possible, the hour might pass from him. He said, 'Abba, Father, for you all things are possible; remove this cup from me; yet, not what I want, but what you want.' He came and found them sleeping; and he said to Peter, 'Simon, are you asleep? Could you not keep awake one hour? Keep awake and pray that you may not come into the time of trial; the spirit indeed is willing, but the flesh is weak.' And again he went away and prayed, saying the same words. And once more he came and found them sleeping, for their eyes were very heavy; and they did not know what to say to him. He came a third time and said to them, 'Are you still sleeping and taking your rest? Enough! The hour has come; the Son of Man is betrayed into the hands of sinners. Get up, let us be going. See, my betrayer is at hand.'

Immediately, while he was still speaking, Judas, one of the twelve, arrived; and with him there was a crowd with swords and clubs, from the chief priests, the scribes, and the elders. Now the betrayer had given them a sign, saying, 'The one I will kiss is the man; arrest him and lead him away under guard.' So when he came, he went up to him at once and said, 'Rabbi!' and kissed him. Then they laid hands on him and arrested him. But one of those who stood near drew his sword and struck the slave of the high priest, cutting off his ear. Then Jesus said to them, 'Have you come out with swords and clubs to arrest me as though I were a bandit? Day after day I was with you in the temple teaching, and you did not arrest me. But let the scriptures be fulfilled.' All of them deserted him and fled.

A certain young man was following him, wearing nothing but a linen cloth. They caught hold of him, but he left the linen cloth and ran off naked.

They took Jesus to the high priest; and all the chief priests, the elders, and the scribes were assembled. Peter had followed him at a distance, right into the courtyard of the high priest; and he was sitting with the guards, warming himself at the fire. Now the chief priests and the whole council were looking for testimony against Jesus to put him to death; but they found none. For many gave false testimony against him, and their testimony did not agree. Some stood up and gave false testimony against him, saying, 'We heard him say, "I will destroy this temple that is made with hands, and in three days I will build another, not made with hands."' But even on this point their testimony did not agree. Then the high priest stood up before them and asked Jesus, 'Have you no answer? What is it that they testify against you?' But he was silent and did not answer. Again the high priest asked him, 'Are you the Messiah, the Son of the Blessed One?' Jesus said, 'I am; and

"you will see the Son of Man
seated at the right hand of the Power",

and "coming with the clouds of heaven."'

Then the high priest tore his clothes and said, 'Why do we still need witnesses? You have heard his blasphemy! What is your decision?' All of them condemned him as deserving death. Some began to spit on him, to blindfold him, and to strike him, saying to him, 'Prophesy!' The guards also took him over and beat him.

While Peter was below in the courtyard, one of the servant-girls of the high priest came by. When she saw Peter warming himself, she stared at him and said, 'You also were with Jesus, the man from Nazareth.' But he denied it, saying, 'I do not know or understand what you are talking about.' And he went out into the forecourt. Then the cock crowed. And the servant-girl, on seeing him, began again to say to the bystanders, 'This man is one of them.' But again he denied it. Then after a little while the bystanders again said to Peter, 'Certainly you are one of them; for you are a Galilean.' But he began to curse, and he swore an oath, 'I do not know this man you are talking about.' At that moment the cock crowed for the second time. Then Peter remembered that Jesus had said to him, 'Before the cock crows twice, you will deny me three times.' And he broke down and wept.

As soon as it was morning, the chief priests held a consultation with the elders and scribes and the whole council. They bound Jesus, led him away, and handed him over to Pilate. Pilate asked him, 'Are you the King of the Jews?' He answered him, 'You say so.' Then the chief priests accused him of many things. Pilate asked him again, 'Have you no answer? See how many charges they bring against you.' But Jesus made no further reply, so that Pilate was amazed.

Now at the festival he used to release a prisoner for them, anyone for whom they asked. Now a man called Barabbas was in prison with the rebels who had committed murder during the insurrection. So the crowd came and began to ask Pilate to do for them according to his custom. Then he answered them, 'Do you want me to release for you the King of the Jews?' For he realized that it was out of jealousy that the chief priests had handed him over. But the chief priests stirred up the crowd to have him release Barabbas for them instead. Pilate spoke to them again, 'Then what do you wish me to do with the man you call the

King of the Jews?' They shouted back, 'Crucify him!' Pilate asked them, 'Why, what evil has he done?' But they shouted all the more, 'Crucify him!' So Pilate, wishing to satisfy the crowd, released Barabbas for them; and after flogging Jesus, he handed him over to be crucified.

Then the soldiers led him into the courtyard of the palace (that is, the governor's headquarters); and they called together the whole cohort. And they clothed him in a purple cloak; and after twisting some thorns into a crown, they put it on him. And they began saluting him, 'Hail, King of the Jews!' They struck his head with a reed, spat upon him, and knelt down in homage to him. After mocking him, they stripped him of the purple cloak and put his own clothes on him. Then they led him out to crucify him.

They compelled a passer-by, who was coming in from the country, to carry his cross; it was Simon of Cyrene, the father of Alexander and Rufus. Then they brought Jesus to the place called Golgotha (which means the place of a skull). And they offered him wine mixed with myrrh; but he did not take it. And they crucified him, and divided his clothes among them, casting lots to decide what each should take.

It was nine o'clock in the morning when they crucified him. The inscription of the charge against him read, 'The King of the Jews.' And with him they crucified two bandits, one on his right and one on his left. Those who passed by derided him, shaking their heads and saying, 'Aha! You who would destroy the temple and build it in three days, save yourself, and come down from the cross!' In the same way the chief priests, along with the scribes, were also mocking him among themselves and saying, 'He saved others; he cannot save himself. Let the Messiah, the King of Israel, come down from the cross now, so that we may see and believe.' Those who were crucified with him also taunted him.

When it was noon, darkness came over the whole land until three in the afternoon. At three o'clock Jesus cried out with a loud voice, 'Eloi, Eloi, lama sabachthani?' which means, 'My God, my God, why have you forsaken me?' When some of the bystanders heard it, they said, 'Listen, he is calling for Elijah.' And someone ran, filled a sponge with sour wine, put it on a stick, and gave it to him to drink, saying, 'Wait, let us see whether Elijah will come to take him down.' Then Jesus gave a loud cry and breathed his last. And the curtain of the temple was torn in two, from top to bottom. Now when the centurion, who stood facing him, saw that in this way he breathed his last, he said, 'Truly this man was God's Son!'

There were also women looking on from a distance; among them were Mary Magdalene, and Mary the mother of James the younger and of Joses, and Salome. These used to follow him and provided for him when he was in Galilee; and there were many other women who had come up with him to Jerusalem.

When evening had come, and since it was the day of Preparation, that is, the day before the sabbath, Joseph of Arimathea, a respected member of the council, who was also himself waiting expectantly for the kingdom of God, went boldly to Pilate and asked for the body of Jesus. Then Pilate wondered if he were already dead; and summoning the centurion, he asked him whether he had been dead for some time. When he learned from the centurion that he was dead, he granted the body to Joseph. Then Joseph bought a linen cloth, and taking down the body, wrapped it in the linen cloth, and laid it in a tomb that had been hewn out of the rock. He then rolled a stone against the door of the tomb. Mary Magdalene and Mary the mother of Joses saw where the body was laid.

- Jesus could be described as the suffering servant in Mark's Gospel. There is the challenge of staying with him to understand suffering as we tend to struggle to find meaning in it. We pray to be strengthened by the passion, remembering that it is Jesus we want, not suffering.
- The welcome of Jesus to Jerusalem was in marked contrast to the events of the following days. Spending time with key people in the drama helps us to enter more fully into the passion of Jesus and of the world. We pray that we may be able to stay with you, Lord, amid the trials you endured.

Monday 25 March
John 12:1–11

Six days before the Passover Jesus came to Bethany, the home of Lazarus, whom he had raised from the dead. There they gave a dinner for him. Martha served, and Lazarus was one of those at the table with him. Mary took a pound of costly perfume made of pure nard, anointed Jesus' feet, and wiped them with her hair. The house was filled with the fragrance of the perfume. But Judas Iscariot, one of his disciples (the one who was about to betray him), said, 'Why was this perfume not sold for three hundred denarii and the money given to the poor?' (He said this not because he cared about the poor, but because he was a thief; he kept the common purse and used to steal what was put into it.) Jesus said, 'Leave her alone. She bought it so that she might keep it for the day of my burial. You always have the poor with you, but you do not always have me.'

When the great crowd of the Jews learned that he was there, they came not only because of Jesus but also to see Lazarus, whom he had raised from the dead. So the chief priests planned to put Lazarus to death as well, since it was on account of him that many of the Jews were deserting and were believing in Jesus.

- The context was a dinner in the home of Lazarus with the apostles shortly before Passover. Jesus accepted the welcome. Meanwhile, the chief priests were planning to kill him and Lazarus. May we gather with you as your friends and be willing to live as your anointed ones.

- Mary's generosity in pouring out costly perfume contrasted with the miserly attitude of Judas. She portrayed the self-giving of Jesus. Lord, give us generous hearts that can give without counting the cost, that seek to serve you in the poor of our time.

Tuesday 26 March
John 13:21–33, 36–38

After saying this Jesus was troubled in spirit, and declared, 'Very truly, I tell you, one of you will betray me.' The disciples looked at one another, uncertain of whom he was speaking. One of his disciples – the one whom Jesus loved – was reclining next to him; Simon Peter therefore motioned to him to ask Jesus of whom he was speaking. So while reclining next to Jesus, he asked him, 'Lord, who is it?' Jesus answered, 'It is the one to whom I give this piece of bread when I have dipped it in the dish.' So when he had dipped the piece of bread, he gave it to Judas son of Simon Iscariot. After he received the piece of bread, Satan entered into him. Jesus said to him, 'Do quickly what you are going to do.' Now no one at the table knew why he said this to him. Some thought that, because Judas had the common purse, Jesus was telling him, 'Buy what we need for the festival'; or, that he should give something to the poor. So, after receiving the piece of bread, he immediately went out. And it was night.

When he had gone out, Jesus said, 'Now the Son of Man has been glorified, and God has been glorified in him. If God has been glorified in him, God will also glorify him in himself and will glorify him at once. Little children, I am with you only a little longer. You will look for me; and as I said to the Jews so now I say to you, "Where I am going, you cannot come."

Simon Peter said to him, 'Lord, where are you going?' Jesus answered, 'Where I am going, you cannot follow me now; but you will follow afterwards.' Peter said to him, 'Lord, why can I not follow you now? I will lay down my life for you.' Jesus answered, 'Will you lay down your life for me? Very truly, I tell you, before the cock crows, you will have denied me three times.'

- Jesus told the disciples that one of them would betray him. Peter's curiosity was aroused and he sought the answer through the beloved disciple. This was supposed to be a table of union, with a bond between those who shared it. Lord, make us aware of the times we have betrayed loyalty and not been faithful to your covenant with us.
- Judas, having taken the bread, went out. It was night. That symbolised the internal darkness that that taken over. Lord, help us to recognise when darkness prevails in our lives, when we become negative and pessimistic, so that we may turn back to you, the true light.

Wednesday 27 March
Matthew 26:14–25

Then one of the twelve, who was called Judas Iscariot, went to the chief priests and said, 'What will you give me if I betray him to you?' They paid him thirty pieces of silver. And from that moment he began to look for an opportunity to betray him.

On the first day of Unleavened Bread the disciples came to Jesus, saying, 'Where do you want us to make the preparations for you to eat the Passover?' He said, 'Go into the city to a certain man, and say to him, "The Teacher says, My time is near; I will keep the Passover at your house with my disciples."' So the disciples did as Jesus had directed them, and they prepared the Passover meal.

When it was evening, he took his place with the twelve; and while they were eating, he said, 'Truly I tell you, one of you will betray me.' And they became greatly distressed and began to say to him one after another, 'Surely not I, Lord?' He answered, 'The one who has dipped his hand into the bowl with me will betray me. The Son of Man goes as it is written of him, but woe to that one by whom the Son of Man is betrayed! It would have been better for that one not to have been born.' Judas, who betrayed him, said, 'Surely not I, Rabbi?' He replied, 'You have said so.'

- Joseph was sold by his own brothers for twenty pieces of silver and ended up being their saviour (Genesis 37:25–28). Judas, who was not known for his honesty (John 12:6), betrayed Jesus for thirty pieces of silver. May we acknowledge our greed and self-interest so that we are more free to serve you in your people.
- Jesus indicated that his time was near and asked the disciples to prepare the Passover meal. He knew that Judas would betray him. Lord, may we be honest in bringing our struggles to you as we recognise our capacity to deny and betray you.

Thursday 28 March
Holy Thursday
John 13:1–15
Now before the festival of the Passover, Jesus knew that his hour had come to depart from this world and go to the Father. Having loved his own who were in the world, he loved them to the end. The devil had already put it into the heart of Judas son of Simon Iscariot to betray him. And during supper Jesus, knowing that the Father had given all

things into his hands, and that he had come from God and was going to God, got up from the table, took off his outer robe, and tied a towel around himself. Then he poured water into a basin and began to wash the disciples' feet and to wipe them with the towel that was tied around him. He came to Simon Peter, who said to him, 'Lord, are you going to wash my feet?' Jesus answered, 'You do not know now what I am doing, but later you will understand.' Peter said to him, 'You will never wash my feet.' Jesus answered, 'Unless I wash you, you have no share with me.' Simon Peter said to him, 'Lord, not my feet only but also my hands and my head!' Jesus said to him, 'One who has bathed does not need to wash, except for the feet, but is entirely clean. And you are clean, though not all of you.' For he knew who was to betray him; for this reason he said, 'Not all of you are clean.'

After he had washed their feet, had put on his robe, and had returned to the table, he said to them, 'Do you know what I have done to you? You call me Teacher and Lord – and you are right, for that is what I am. So if I, your Lord and Teacher, have washed your feet, you also ought to wash one another's feet. For I have set you an example, that you also should do as I have done to you.'

- Jesus knew that his hour had come to depart this world. Having loved his own, he loved them to the end. Jesus had clarity on what was happening, but the disciples were confused. We pray for the freedom to listen to Jesus and to be less concerned about our own interests.
- It was servants who washed the master's feet (Luke 12:35–40). Jesus reversed the process. He set an example for us. Lord, like Peter, we tend to protest at you serving us. Give us a greater faith and love so that we can see you in others and imitate you in love.

Friday 29 March
Good Friday
John 18:1–19:42
After Jesus had spoken these words, he went out with his disciples across the Kidron valley to a place where there was a garden, which he and his disciples entered. Now Judas, who betrayed him, also knew the place, because Jesus often met there with his disciples. So Judas brought

a detachment of soldiers together with police from the chief priests and the Pharisees, and they came there with lanterns and torches and weapons. Then Jesus, knowing all that was to happen to him, came forward and asked them, 'For whom are you looking?' They answered, 'Jesus of Nazareth.' Jesus replied, 'I am he.' Judas, who betrayed him, was standing with them. When Jesus said to them, 'I am he', they stepped back and fell to the ground. Again he asked them, 'For whom are you looking?' And they said, 'Jesus of Nazareth.' Jesus answered, 'I told you that I am he. So if you are looking for me, let these men go.' This was to fulfil the word that he had spoken, 'I did not lose a single one of those whom you gave me.' Then Simon Peter, who had a sword, drew it, struck the high priest's slave, and cut off his right ear. The slave's name was Malchus. Jesus said to Peter, 'Put your sword back into its sheath. Am I not to drink the cup that the Father has given me?'

So the soldiers, their officer, and the Jewish police arrested Jesus and bound him. First they took him to Annas, who was the father-in-law of Caiaphas, the high priest that year. Caiaphas was the one who had advised the Jews that it was better to have one person die for the people.

Simon Peter and another disciple followed Jesus. Since that disciple was known to the high priest, he went with Jesus into the courtyard of the high priest, but Peter was standing outside at the gate. So the other disciple, who was known to the high priest, went out, spoke to the woman who guarded the gate, and brought Peter in. The woman said to Peter, 'You are not also one of this man's disciples, are you?' He said, 'I am not.' Now the slaves and the police had made a charcoal fire because it was cold, and they were standing round it and warming themselves. Peter also was standing with them and warming himself.

Then the high priest questioned Jesus about his disciples and about his teaching. Jesus answered, 'I have spoken openly to the world; I have always taught in synagogues and in the temple, where all the Jews come together. I have said nothing in secret. Why do you ask me? Ask those who heard what I said to them; they know what I said.' When he had said this, one of the police standing nearby struck Jesus on the face, saying, 'Is that how you answer the high priest?' Jesus answered, 'If I have spoken wrongly, testify to the wrong. But if I have spoken rightly, why do you strike me?' Then Annas sent him bound to Caiaphas the high priest.

Now Simon Peter was standing and warming himself. They asked him, 'You are not also one of his disciples, are you?' He denied it and said, 'I am not.' One of the slaves of the high priest, a relative of the man whose ear Peter had cut off, asked, 'Did I not see you in the garden with him?' Again Peter denied it, and at that moment the cock crowed.

Then they took Jesus from Caiaphas to Pilate's headquarters. It was early in the morning. They themselves did not enter the headquarters, so as to avoid ritual defilement and to be able to eat the Passover. So Pilate went out to them and said, 'What accusation do you bring against this man?' They answered, 'If this man were not a criminal, we would not have handed him over to you.' Pilate said to them, 'Take him yourselves and judge him according to your law.' The Jews replied, 'We are not permitted to put anyone to death.' (This was to fulfil what Jesus had said when he indicated the kind of death he was to die.)

Then Pilate entered the headquarters again, summoned Jesus, and asked him, 'Are you the King of the Jews?' Jesus answered, 'Do you ask this on your own, or did others tell you about me?' Pilate replied, 'I am not a Jew, am I? Your own nation and the chief priests have handed you over to me. What have you done?' Jesus answered, 'My kingdom is not from this world. If my kingdom were from this world, my followers would be fighting to keep me from being handed over to the Jews. But as it is, my kingdom is not from here.' Pilate asked him, 'So you are a king?' Jesus answered, 'You say that I am a king. For this I was born, and for this I came into the world, to testify to the truth. Everyone who belongs to the truth listens to my voice.' Pilate asked him, 'What is truth?'

After he had said this, he went out to the Jews again and told them, 'I find no case against him. But you have a custom that I release someone for you at the Passover. Do you want me to release for you the King of the Jews?' They shouted in reply, 'Not this man, but Barabbas!' Now Barabbas was a bandit.

Then Pilate took Jesus and had him flogged. And the soldiers wove a crown of thorns and put it on his head, and they dressed him in a purple robe. They kept coming up to him, saying, 'Hail, King of the Jews!' and striking him on the face. Pilate went out again and said to them, 'Look, I am bringing him out to you to let you know that I find no case against him.' So Jesus came out, wearing the crown of thorns and the purple robe. Pilate said to them, 'Here is the man!' When the chief priests and the police saw him, they shouted, 'Crucify him! Crucify him!' Pilate said to them, 'Take him yourselves and crucify him; I find no case against him.' The Jews answered him, 'We have a law, and according to that law he ought to die because he has claimed to be the Son of God.'

Now when Pilate heard this, he was more afraid than ever. He entered his headquarters again and asked Jesus, 'Where are you from?' But Jesus gave him no answer. Pilate therefore said to him, 'Do you refuse to speak to me? Do you not know that I have power to release you, and power to crucify you?' Jesus answered him, 'You would have no power over me unless it had been given you from above; therefore the one who handed me over to you is guilty of a greater sin.' From then on Pilate tried to release him, but the Jews cried out, 'If you release this man, you are no friend of the emperor. Everyone who claims to be a king sets himself against the emperor.'

When Pilate heard these words, he brought Jesus outside and sat on the judge's bench at a place called The Stone Pavement, or in Hebrew Gabbatha. Now it was the day of Preparation for the Passover; and it was about noon. He said to the Jews, 'Here is your King!' They cried out, 'Away with him! Away with him! Crucify him!' Pilate asked them, 'Shall I crucify your King?' The chief priests answered, 'We have no king but the emperor.' Then he handed him over to them to be crucified.

So they took Jesus; and carrying the cross by himself, he went out to what is called The Place of the Skull, which in Hebrew is called Golgotha. There they crucified him, and with him two others, one on either side, with Jesus between them. Pilate also had an inscription written and put on the cross. It read, 'Jesus of Nazareth, the King of the Jews.' Many of the Jews read this inscription, because the place where Jesus was crucified was near the city; and it was written in Hebrew, in Latin, and in Greek. Then the chief priests of the Jews said to Pilate,

'Do not write, "The King of the Jews", but, "This man said, I am King of the Jews."' Pilate answered, 'What I have written I have written.' When the soldiers had crucified Jesus, they took his clothes and divided them into four parts, one for each soldier. They also took his tunic; now the tunic was seamless, woven in one piece from the top. So they said to one another, 'Let us not tear it, but cast lots for it to see who will get it.' This was to fulfil what the scripture says,

'They divided my clothes among themselves,
    and for my clothing they cast lots.'

And that is what the soldiers did.

Meanwhile, standing near the cross of Jesus were his mother, and his mother's sister, Mary the wife of Clopas, and Mary Magdalene. When Jesus saw his mother and the disciple whom he loved standing beside her, he said to his mother, 'Woman, here is your son.' Then he said to the disciple, 'Here is your mother.' And from that hour the disciple took her into his own home.

After this, when Jesus knew that all was now finished, he said (in order to fulfil the scripture), 'I am thirsty.' A jar full of sour wine was standing there. So they put a sponge full of the wine on a branch of hyssop and held it to his mouth. When Jesus had received the wine, he said, 'It is finished.' Then he bowed his head and gave up his spirit.

Since it was the day of Preparation, the Jews did not want the bodies left on the cross during the sabbath, especially because that sabbath was a day of great solemnity. So they asked Pilate to have the legs of the crucified men broken and the bodies removed. Then the soldiers came and broke the legs of the first and of the other who had been crucified with him. But when they came to Jesus and saw that he was already dead, they did not break his legs. Instead, one of the soldiers pierced his side with a spear, and at once blood and water came out. (He who saw this has testified so that you also may believe. His testimony is true, and he knows that he tells the truth.) These things occurred so that the scripture might be fulfilled, 'None of his bones shall be broken.' And again another passage of scripture says, 'They will look on the one whom they have pierced.'

After these things, Joseph of Arimathea, who was a disciple of Jesus, though a secret one because of his fear of the Jews, asked Pilate to let him take away the body of Jesus. Pilate gave him permission; so he came and removed his body. Nicodemus, who had at first come to Jesus by night, also came, bringing a mixture of myrrh and aloes, weighing about a hundred pounds. They took the body of Jesus and wrapped it with the spices in linen cloths, according to the burial custom of the Jews. Now there was a garden in the place where he was crucified, and in the garden there was a new tomb in which no one had ever been laid. And so, because it was the Jewish day of Preparation, and the tomb was nearby, they laid Jesus there.

- The passion is a love story of total self-giving. Through his prayer in the garden, Jesus came to peace in facing what lay ahead. He acknowledged who he was to those who came to arrest him – 'I am he.' Lord, help us in our search and our struggles to find you so that we may have the strength and peace to walk onwards with you.
- It could appear as if it was Pilate who was on trial. His position as governor and the threat of the crowd was enough to have him go against his own beliefs and hand Jesus over. We pray that we may hand over our lives to Jesus and have the courage to stand by the innocent who are falsely accused at this time.

Saturday 30 March
Holy Saturday
Mark 16:1–7
When the sabbath was over, Mary Magdalene, and Mary the mother of James, and Salome bought spices, so that they might go and anoint him. And very early on the first day of the week, when the sun had risen, they went to the tomb. They had been saying to one another, 'Who will roll away the stone for us from the entrance to the tomb?' When they looked up, they saw that the stone, which was very large, had already been rolled back. As they entered the tomb, they saw a young man, dressed in a white robe, sitting on the right side; and they were alarmed. But he said to them, 'Do not be alarmed; you are looking for Jesus of Nazareth, who was crucified. He has been raised; he is not

here. Look, there is the place they laid him. But go, tell his disciples and Peter that he is going ahead of you to Galilee; there you will see him, just as he told you.'

- It is the day after the funeral, with time to remember, to share stories, to take quiet time. Perhaps Peter and Judas, as flawed disciples, may speak to us in our feeble attempts to be loyal. Lord, help us to appreciate more fully who you are and what you have done for us.
- What was the day like for Mary? The prophecy of the sword of sorrow piercing her heart had become more real (Luke 2:34–36). It was painful for her see her beloved son of compassion and love being treated so cruelly. May we draw strength from the fidelity of Mary in staying with Jesus to the end.

Octave of Easter

31 March–6 April 2024

Something to think and pray about each day this week:

In the Gospels there are two bowls of water in the story of the Passion. One is Pilate's, used to wash his hands of others, pointing the accusing finger at Jesus while scrubbing himself of all responsibility. The other bowl is the one with which Jesus bathes others, soaking and drenching them in lavish love.

The two bowls are always before us in life. Jesus shows us that when you take the side of the dispossessed your spirit deepens and grows. When your self-obsession is reduced, your life expands and your horizon enlarges.

People look different from down on the floor with their feed cradled in the bowl of your lap. You look different too. But to pick up the towel is not to become a doormat. We are called, not to serve people's wants, but their needs. We serve others in the name of Christ. We share what we have but, more importantly, we share who we are, especially with people who are rejected and alienated. They are the life presence that transforms us by showing us the heart of God.

Too often homeless people are seen as a threat or at best an administrative burden and nuisance. The churches see them as objects of pity and mercy. Yet they are prophets, preachers and provocative witnesses of the Gospel. They challenge us with questions that disquiet and disturb us, as they lead us into looking at the Passion and Easter stories with new eyes and hearts.

Easter invites us to remember the Lord when we gather as a community for the Eucharist. He entrusts his future in the world to us in the Church. Let us bring the Upper Room message, action and presence to the people who are the lowest, the last, the least and the most.

John Cullen, *The Sacred Heart Messenger*, April 2022

The Presence of God
God is with me, but even more astounding, God is within me.
Let me dwell for a moment on God's life-giving presence
in my body, in my mind, in my heart,
as I sit here, right now.

Freedom
Lord, may I never take the gift of freedom for granted. You gave me
the great blessing of freedom of spirit. Fill my spirit with your peace
and joy.

Consciousness
I remind myself that I am in the presence of God, who is my strength
in times of weakness and my comforter in times of sorrow.

The Word
I take my time to read the word of God slowly, a few times, allowing
myself to dwell on anything that strikes me. *(Please turn to the Scripture on
the following pages. Inspiration points are there, should you need them. When you
are ready, return here to continue.)*

Conversation
Jesus, you always welcomed little children when you walked on this
earth. Teach me to have a childlike trust in you. Teach me to live in the
knowledge that you will never abandon me.

Conclusion
Glory be to the Father, and to the Son, and to the Holy Spirit,
As it was in the beginning, is now and ever shall be,
World without end. Amen.

Sunday 31 March
Easter Sunday of the Resurrection of the Lord
John 20:1–9

Early on the first day of the week, while it was still dark, Mary Magdalene came to the tomb and saw that the stone had been removed from the tomb. So she ran and went to Simon Peter and the other disciple, the one whom Jesus loved, and said to them, 'They have taken the Lord out of the tomb, and we do not know where they have laid him.' Then Peter and the other disciple set out and went towards the tomb. The two were running together, but the other disciple outran Peter and reached the tomb first. He bent down to look in and saw the linen wrappings lying there, but he did not go in. Then Simon Peter came, following him, and went into the tomb. He saw the linen wrappings lying there, and the cloth that had been on Jesus' head, not lying with the linen wrappings but rolled up in a place by itself. Then the other disciple, who reached the tomb first, also went in, and he saw and believed; for as yet they did not understand the scripture, that he must rise from the dead.

- There was urgency to the action of Mary Magdalene. It was like the dawn of a new creation, with light scattering darkness. Finding the stone rolled back, she ran for help. Lord, help us, as there are times when we feel that you have been removed from our lives and we do not know where to find you.

- The two disciples ran to the tomb to find it empty, with the linen wrappings lying there. Its meaning was not clear. Then the intuitive beloved disciple 'saw and believed'. We pray that we may acknowledge the empty tombs in our lives and our slowness to interpret the many signs given to us.

Monday 1 April
Matthew 28:8–15

So they left the tomb quickly with fear and great joy, and ran to tell his disciples. Suddenly Jesus met them and said, 'Greetings!' And they came to him, took hold of his feet, and worshipped him. Then Jesus said to them, 'Do not be afraid; go and tell my brothers to go to Galilee; there they will see me.'

While they were going, some of the guard went into the city and told the chief priests everything that had happened. After the priests had assembled with the elders, they devised a plan to give a large sum of money to the soldiers, telling them, 'You must say, "His disciples came by night and stole him away while we were asleep." If this comes to the governor's ears, we will satisfy him and keep you out of trouble.' So they took the money and did as they were directed. And this story is still told among the Jews to this day.

- The women left the tomb with a mixture of emotions and became apostles to the apostles, telling of their experience. Then Jesus met them and they worshipped him. Lord, enable us to move beyond our fears to share the good news that you are truly risen to a world that needs to be raised up.

- There are many who do not believe in Jesus as risen and seek excuses to justify that. Some in the Gospel did not accept it, either, and at times we are also asleep to the fact. Lord, wake us up to the truth of your resurrection and strengthen us to give witness to it.

Tuesday 2 April
John 20:11–18

But Mary stood weeping outside the tomb. As she wept, she bent over to look into the tomb; and she saw two angels in white, sitting where the body of Jesus had been lying, one at the head and the other at the feet. They said to her, 'Woman, why are you weeping?' She said to them, 'They have taken away my Lord, and I do not know where they have laid him.' When she had said this, she turned round and saw Jesus standing there, but she did not know that it was Jesus. Jesus said to her, 'Woman, why are you weeping? For whom are you looking?' Supposing him to be the gardener, she said to him, 'Sir, if you have carried him away, tell me where you have laid him, and I will take him away.' Jesus said to her, 'Mary!' She turned and said to him in Hebrew, 'Rabbouni!' (which means Teacher). Jesus said to her, 'Do not hold on to me, because I have not yet ascended to the Father. But go to my brothers and say to them, "I am ascending to my Father and your Father, to my God and your God.'" Mary Magdalene went and announced to the disciples, 'I have seen the Lord'; and she told them that he had said these things to her.

- Mary Magdalene waited at the tomb, weeping for the loss of Jesus. She searched for him, but he found her and then all was different. There are times when we do not know where to look. May we have the patience to wait and allow you, Lord, to surprise us.
- Mary Magdalene was called by name and all was changed. Jesus was no longer the gardener. This was a garden where all was made new, so it was not like Eden, or Gethsemane. Lord, there are times when we cling to the past for our own security. May we have the openness to allow the new to emerge.

Wednesday 3 April
Luke 24:13–35

Now on that same day two of them were going to a village called Emmaus, about seven miles from Jerusalem, and talking with each other about all these things that had happened. While they were talking and discussing, Jesus himself came near and went with them, but their eyes were kept from recognising him. And he said to them, 'What are you discussing with each other while you walk along?' They stood still, looking sad. Then one of them, whose name was Cleopas, answered him, 'Are you the only stranger in Jerusalem who does not know the things that have taken place there in these days?' He asked them, 'What things?' They replied, 'The things about Jesus of Nazareth, who was a prophet mighty in deed and word before God and all the people, and how our chief priests and leaders handed him over to be condemned to death and crucified him. But we had hoped that he was the one to redeem Israel. Yes, and besides all this, it is now the third day since these things took place. Moreover, some women of our group astounded us. They were at the tomb early this morning, and when they did not find his body there, they came back and told us that they had indeed seen a vision of angels who said that he was alive. Some of those who were with us went to the tomb and found it just as the women had said; but they did not see him.' Then he said to them, 'Oh, how foolish you are, and how slow of heart to believe all that the prophets have declared! Was it not necessary that the Messiah should suffer these things and then enter into his glory?' Then beginning with Moses and all the prophets, he interpreted to them the things about himself in all the scriptures.

As they came near the village to which they were going, he walked ahead as if he were going on. But they urged him strongly, saying, 'Stay with us, because it is almost evening and the day is now nearly over.' So he went in to stay with them. When he was at the table with them, he took bread, blessed and broke it, and gave it to them. Then their eyes were opened, and they recognised him; and he vanished from their sight. They said to each other, 'Were not our hearts burning within us while he was talking to us on the road, while he was opening the scriptures to us?' That same hour they got up and returned to Jerusalem; and they found the eleven and their companions gathered together. They were saying, 'The Lord has risen indeed, and he has appeared to Simon!' Then they told what had happened on the road, and how he had been made known to them in the breaking of the bread.

- On the journey of life, we often fail to recognise that the Lord is with us. Our disconsolate mood can take over and make us miserable companions to those whom we accompany. Lord, help us to recognise your presence, for it lifts our hearts in hope. May we be good companions to others, especially in difficult times.

- Jesus aroused the curiosity of the two people on the road, who were glad of his company and uplifting conversation. He threw new light on the events of the previous days, but waited to be invited in. Lord, stay with us and help us to listen to your message as you reveal yourself on the journey of life.

Thursday 4 April
Luke 24:35–48
Then they told what had happened on the road, and how he had been made known to them in the breaking of the bread.

While they were talking about this, Jesus himself stood among them and said to them, 'Peace be with you.' They were startled and terrified, and thought that they were seeing a ghost. He said to them, 'Why are you frightened, and why do doubts arise in your hearts? Look at my hands and my feet; see that it is I myself. Touch me and see; for a ghost does not have flesh and bones as you see that I have.' And when he had said this, he showed them his hands and his feet. While in their joy they were disbelieving and still wondering, he said to them, 'Have you anything here to eat?' They gave him a piece of broiled fish, and he took it and ate in their presence.

Then he said to them, 'These are my words that I spoke to you while I was still with you – that everything written about me in the law of Moses, the prophets, and the psalms must be fulfilled.' Then he opened their minds to understand the scriptures, and he said to them, 'Thus it is written, that the Messiah is to suffer and to rise from the dead on the third day, and that repentance and forgiveness of sins is to be proclaimed in his name to all nations, beginning from Jerusalem. You are witnesses of these things.'

- In a disturbed world, external and internal peace are cherished. Jesus spoke of peace to the disciples, who were distressed by his suffering and death. You call us beyond our fears. We pray for peace in the world, for others and within ourselves, as it is God's desire for us.
- The disciples were slow to believe in the resurrection. It was so unexpected and beyond their experience that they sought some proof. Jesus opened their minds to understand the scriptures to show that he fulfilled what was promised. Lord, strengthen our faith to accept the evidence and live as your witnesses.

Friday 5 April
John 21:1–14
After these things Jesus showed himself again to the disciples by the Sea of Tiberias; and he showed himself in this way. Gathered there together were Simon Peter, Thomas called the Twin, Nathanael of Cana in Galilee, the sons of Zebedee, and two others of his disciples. Simon

Peter said to them, 'I am going fishing.' They said to him, 'We will go with you.' They went out and got into the boat, but that night they caught nothing.

Just after daybreak, Jesus stood on the beach; but the disciples did not know that it was Jesus. Jesus said to them, 'Children, you have no fish, have you?' They answered him, 'No.' He said to them, 'Cast the net to the right side of the boat, and you will find some.' So they cast it, and now they were not able to haul it in because there were so many fish. That disciple whom Jesus loved said to Peter, 'It is the Lord!' When Simon Peter heard that it was the Lord, he put on some clothes, for he was naked, and jumped into the lake. But the other disciples came in the boat, dragging the net full of fish, for they were not far from the land, only about a hundred yards off.

When they had gone ashore, they saw a charcoal fire there, with fish on it, and bread. Jesus said to them, 'Bring some of the fish that you have just caught.' So Simon Peter went aboard and hauled the net ashore, full of large fish, a hundred and fifty-three of them; and though there were so many, the net was not torn. Jesus said to them, 'Come and have breakfast.' Now none of the disciples dared to ask him, 'Who are you?' because they knew it was the Lord. Jesus came and took the bread and gave it to them, and did the same with the fish. This was now the third time that Jesus appeared to the disciples after he was raised from the dead.

- The disciples were struggling to believe, so they went back to a familiar place and work. A fruitless night and then the advice of a stranger on the shore led to a bountiful catch of fish. May we be guided by the wisdom of the Lord to look in the right places so that we are fruitful in his name.
- Peter was never one for half measures, but dived in even if he was out of his depth. The intuitive beloved disciple recognised that it was the Lord who had told them what to do. Then all became clear. May we recognise the beloved disciples in our lives who introduce us to Jesus in surprising places.

Saturday 6 April
Mark 16:9–15

Now after he rose early on the first day of the week, he appeared first to Mary Magdalene, from whom he had cast out seven demons. She went out and told those who had been with him, while they were mourning and weeping. But when they heard that he was alive and had been seen by her, they would not believe it.

After this he appeared in another form to two of them, as they were walking into the country. And they went back and told the rest, but they did not believe them.

Later he appeared to the eleven themselves as they were sitting at the table; and he upbraided them for their lack of faith and stubbornness, because they had not believed those who saw him after he had risen. And he said to them, 'Go into all the world and proclaim the good news to the whole creation.'

- The end of Mark's Gospel gives a brief account of people who struggled to believe in the risen Jesus. Lord, we thank you for the witnesses you have given us to bring us to a deeper faith in the resurrection. May we have the courage to write our own ending to the Gospel, which includes our story as believers.

- The disciples were called to be companions of Jesus and share his mission. After the resurrection he commissioned them anew to proclaim the good news to all creation. Lord, you call us afresh and send us forth as your witnesses. May we rely on you to live out that call amid the many who doubt in our time.

7–13 April 2024

Something to think and pray about each day this week:

An elderly monk reached a high level of holiness. His fellow monks wanted to know how this came about, but his humility made him hesitant to speak about himself. One day he let down his guard with a close friend. 'It was through reciting the Our Father,' he explained. His friend was taken aback, 'You mean you arrived at such heights through that simple prayer?' The old monk nodded. He added, 'I was more surprised than anyone. You know, for years I had forced myself to try all sorts of unusual prayers. And after all that time, everything was so utterly straightforward. In fact, when I finally discovered how uncomplicated the path was, I felt like a real fool.'

'Why did you feel so foolish?' asked his friend. 'Because,' replied the holy monk, 'I was like someone who purchases a high-security key to open a bank vault, only to discover that the treasure is in fact lying in full view in front of me.'

Thomas G. Casey SJ, *The Mindful Our Father*

The Presence of God

Dear Lord, as I come to you today, fill my heart, my whole being, with the wonder of your presence. Help me remain receptive to you as I put aside the cares of this world. Fill my mind with your peace.

Freedom

Lord, grant me the grace to be free from the excesses of this life. Let me not get caught up with the desire for wealth. Keep my heart and mind free to love and serve you.

Consciousness

I exist in a web of relationships: links to nature, people, God. I trace out these links, giving thanks for the life that flows through them. Some links are twisted or broken; I may feel regret, anger, disappointment. I pray for the gift of acceptance and forgiveness.

The Word

God speaks to each of us individually. I listen attentively to hear what he is saying to me. Read the text a few times, then listen. *(Please turn to the Scripture on the following pages. Inspiration points are there, should you need them. When you are ready, return here to continue.)*

Conversation

Jesus, you speak to me through the words of the Gospels. May I respond to your call today. Teach me to recognise your hand at work in my daily living.

Conclusion

I thank God for these moments we have spent together and for any insights I have been given concerning the text.

Sunday 7 April
Second Sunday of Easter
John 20:19–31

When it was evening on that day, the first day of the week, and the doors of the house where the disciples had met were locked for fear of the Jews, Jesus came and stood among them and said, 'Peace be with you.' After he said this, he showed them his hands and his side. Then the disciples rejoiced when they saw the Lord. Jesus said to them again, 'Peace be with you. As the Father has sent me, so I send you.' When he had said this, he breathed on them and said to them, 'Receive the Holy Spirit. If you forgive the sins of any, they are forgiven them; if you retain the sins of any, they are retained.'

But Thomas (who was called the Twin), one of the twelve, was not with them when Jesus came. So the other disciples told him, 'We have seen the Lord.' But he said to them, 'Unless I see the mark of the nails in his hands, and put my finger in the mark of the nails and my hand in his side, I will not believe.'

A week later his disciples were again in the house, and Thomas was with them. Although the doors were shut, Jesus came and stood among them and said, 'Peace be with you.' Then he said to Thomas, 'Put your finger here and see my hands. Reach out your hand and put it in my side. Do not doubt but believe.' Thomas answered him, 'My Lord and my God!' Jesus said to him, 'Have you believed because you have seen me? Blessed are those who have not seen and yet have come to believe.'

Now Jesus did many other signs in the presence of his disciples, which are not written in this book. But these are written so that you may come to believe that Jesus is the Messiah, the Son of God, and that through believing you may have life in his name.

- Locked doors were not enough to prevent Jesus joining his disciples, who were held bound by their fears. His message of peace, combined with his showing them his hands and side helped them to accept him as real. Help us to open our minds and hearts to the wonder of new life that you offer and to the peace you alone can give.
- Thomas was always one to question. He had been caught out before so he wanted physical proof. When given the evidence he responded.

We pray that the response of Thomas, saying, 'My Lord and my God', may be true for us, too.

Monday 8 April
The Annunciation of the Lord
Luke 1:26–38

In the sixth month the angel Gabriel was sent by God to a town in Galilee called Nazareth, to a virgin engaged to a man whose name was Joseph, of the house of David. The virgin's name was Mary. And he came to her and said, 'Greetings, favoured one! The Lord is with you.' But she was much perplexed by his words and pondered what sort of greeting this might be. The angel said to her, 'Do not be afraid, Mary, for you have found favour with God. And now, you will conceive in your womb and bear a son, and you will name him Jesus. He will be great, and will be called the Son of the Most High, and the Lord God will give to him the throne of his ancestor David. He will reign over the house of Jacob for ever, and of his kingdom there will be no end.' Mary said to the angel, 'How can this be, since I am a virgin?' The angel said to her, 'The Holy Spirit will come upon you, and the power of the Most High will overshadow you; therefore the child to be born will be holy; he will be called Son of God. And now, your relative Elizabeth in her old age has also conceived a son; and this is the sixth month for her who was said to be barren. For nothing will be impossible with God.' Then Mary said, 'Here am I, the servant of the Lord; let it be with me according to your word.' Then the angel departed from her.

- There are annunciations of one kind or another in all our lives. God continues to surprise and invite us, offering signs. Being available to the Lord and others is integral to that. We ask that our hearts may be transformed, making us more open to what the Lord desires.
- It is Easter time and Mary helps us to live its message of joy and hope. Her 'yes' was to a way of life, not just one event. 'Let it be' meant that she relied on God. May we turn to the Lord for the freedom we need to respond 'yes' to our invitations.

Tuesday 9 April
John 3:7b–15

Jesus said to Nicodemus, 'Do not be astonished that I said to you, "You must be born from above." The wind blows where it chooses, and you hear the sound of it, but you do not know where it comes from or where it goes. So it is with everyone who is born of the Spirit.' Nicodemus said to him, 'How can these things be?' Jesus answered him, 'Are you a teacher of Israel, and yet you do not understand these things?

'Very truly, I tell you, we speak of what we know and testify to what we have seen; yet you do not receive our testimony. If I have told you about earthly things and you do not believe, how can you believe if I tell you about heavenly things? No one has ascended into heaven except the one who descended from heaven, the Son of Man. And just as Moses lifted up the serpent in the wilderness, so must the Son of Man be lifted up, that whoever believes in him may have eternal life.'

- The action of the Spirit is mysterious, like the wind blowing, which is better understood by its effects. Something was stirred in Nicodemus that led him to engage with Jesus. Lord, you reveal yourself in surprising ways, so we pray to know you better and to accept the gifts you offer.
- Jesus, you descended from heaven to raise us up, offering us new life. Believing in you is the way to eternal life. Deepen our faith in you so that we may be raised up with you and bring life to others in your name.

Wednesday 10 April
John 3:16–21

Jesus said to Nicodemus, 'For God so loved the world that he gave his only Son, so that everyone who believes in him may not perish but may have eternal life.

'Indeed, God did not send the Son into the world to condemn the world, but in order that the world might be saved through him. Those who believe in him are not condemned; but those who do not believe are condemned already, because they have not believed in the name of the only Son of God. And this is the judgement, that the light has come into the world, and people loved darkness rather than light because their deeds were evil. For all who do evil hate the light and do not come to the light, so that their deeds may not be exposed. But those who do what is true come to the light, so that it may be clearly seen that their deeds have been done in God.'

- Jesus is the Father's greatest gift, given to us in love that we may have eternal life. We are called to welcome him, to know him and to believe in him. May we have a deeper appreciation of who Jesus is and the gifts he has made available to us, so that we can live more fully for him.
- God's desire is for life and salvation, not condemnation. God sent Jesus, the light, into the world to scatter the darkness of unbelief. Lord, there are times when we are ambivalent about the light; please set our hearts on what is good so that we may reflect you as the true light who shows the way to life.

Thursday 11 April
John 3:31–36
Jesus said to his disciples, 'The one who comes from above is above all; the one who is of the earth belongs to the earth and speaks about earthly things. The one who comes from heaven is above all. He testifies to what he has seen and heard, yet no one accepts his testimony. Whoever has accepted his testimony has certified this, that God is true. He whom God has sent speaks the words of God, for he gives the Spirit without measure. The Father loves the Son and has placed all things in his hands. Whoever believes in the Son has eternal life; whoever disobeys the Son will not see life, but must endure God's wrath.'

- Our lives and actions reveal much about us – 'You will know them by their fruits' (Matthew 7:16). Our words can offer clarification, but they are not always consistent with our actions. We ask that we may recognise the influences in our lives so that we can choose what the Lord desires and not be trapped by earthly things.
- Jesus, sent by the Father, spoke the word of God and gave the Spirit without measure, though some do not accept his message. May we

hear your words, observe your testimony and come to believe more fully in you as the way to eternal life.

Friday 12 April
John 6:1–15

After this Jesus went to the other side of the Sea of Galilee, also called the Sea of Tiberias. A large crowd kept following him, because they saw the signs that he was doing for the sick. Jesus went up the mountain and sat down there with his disciples. Now the Passover, the festival of the Jews, was near. When he looked up and saw a large crowd coming towards him, Jesus said to Philip, 'Where are we to buy bread for these people to eat?' He said this to test him, for he himself knew what he was going to do. Philip answered him, 'Six months' wages would not buy enough bread for each of them to get a little.' One of his disciples, Andrew, Simon Peter's brother, said to him, 'There is a boy here who has five barley loaves and two fish. But what are they among so many people?' Jesus said, 'Make the people sit down.' Now there was a great deal of grass in the place; so they sat down, about five thousand in all. Then Jesus took the loaves, and when he had given thanks, he distributed them to those who were seated; so also the fish, as much as they wanted. When they were satisfied, he told his disciples, 'Gather up the fragments left over, so that nothing may be lost.' So they gathered them up, and from the fragments of the five barley loaves, left by those who had eaten, they filled twelve baskets. When the people saw the sign that he had done, they began to say, 'This is indeed the prophet who is to come into the world.'

When Jesus realised that they were about to come and take him by force to make him king, he withdrew again to the mountain by himself.

- God provided manna for the chosen people in the wilderness. Jesus gave bread to the hungry people on a mountain with Passover near. Lord, may we be more in touch with our inner hunger so that we turn to you for the food we need to continue the journey of life with others in your name.
- The disciples could see the practical difficulties of getting bread in an isolated place. Jesus saw the opportunity to invite his disciples

to enlarge their horizons. We pray for the faith to offer the little we have, knowing that you, Lord, can do more than we can ask or imagine with it (Ephesians 3:20).

Saturday 13 April
John 6:16–21

When evening came, his disciples went down to the lake, got into a boat, and started across the lake to Capernaum. It was now dark, and Jesus had not yet come to them. The lake became rough because a strong wind was blowing. When they had rowed about three or four miles, they saw Jesus walking on the lake and coming near the boat, and they were terrified. But he said to them, 'It is I; do not be afraid.' Then they wanted to take him into the boat, and immediately the boat reached the land towards which they were going.

- The disciples were rowing on stormy waters and were terrified when Jesus came to them. Lord, in the storms of life we get fearful and do not expect to find you. Give us a greater trust in your presence with us always.
- In many situations Jesus asked people not to be afraid. He provided for the disciples and will do the same for us. His presence changed the situation on the lake. We pray that on the storms of life we may rely on the Lord to be our anchor of safety.

14–20 April 2024

Something to think and pray about each day this week:

The simplest thing discloses a new aspect of God's beauty, originality, imaginativeness. To see things thus is to be enveloped in the wonderful mystery of the Beyond, and helps us to recover the contemplative capacity of our childhood when everything was full of wonder, before we named, objectified and categorised it. The loving gaze sees things in terms of their beauty prior to their usefulness or function.

A poet tells of a father and his little son watching a cart go up the street. 'That's Murphy's cart,' says the father, and turns away, but the child is captivated by the horse – its beauty and strength, its magnificence, its sheer being. The contemplative stance can revive such moments in us, and restore us to an enchanting world. Poets have this gift, and mystics too, but we can share what they see: the blind in the Gospels who are healed can include us too. As the poet William Blake puts it: 'If the doors of our perception were cleansed, everything would appear as it is, infinite'. We can cultivate this deeper perception.

Brian Grogan SJ, *Creation Walk:*
The Amazing Story of a Small Blue Planet

The Presence of God

Dear Jesus, I come to you today longing for your presence. I desire to love you as you love me. May nothing ever separate me from you.

Freedom

Lord, grant me the grace to have freedom of the spirit. Cleanse my heart and soul so that I may live joyously in your love.

Consciousness

Where am I with God? With others?
Do I have something to be grateful for? Then I give thanks.
Is there something I am sorry for? Then I ask forgiveness.

The Word

The word of God comes down to us through the Scriptures. May the Holy Spirit enlighten my mind and my heart to respond to the Gospel teachings. *(Please turn to the Scripture on the following pages. Inspiration points are there, should you need them. When you are ready, return here to continue.)*

Conversation

How has God's word moved me? Has it left me cold?
Has it consoled me or moved me to act in a new way?
I imagine Jesus standing or sitting beside me;
I turn and share my feelings with him

Conclusion

I thank God for these moments we have spent together and for any insights I have been given concerning the text.

Sunday 14 April
Third Sunday of Easter
Luke 24:35–48

Then they told what had happened on the road, and how he had been made known to them in the breaking of the bread.

While they were talking about this, Jesus himself stood among them and said to them, 'Peace be with you.' They were startled and terrified, and thought that they were seeing a ghost. He said to them, 'Why are you frightened, and why do doubts arise in your hearts? Look at my hands and my feet; see that it is I myself. Touch me and see; for a ghost does not have flesh and bones as you see that I have.' And when he had said this, he showed them his hands and his feet. While in their joy they were disbelieving and still wondering, he said to them, 'Have you anything here to eat?' They gave him a piece of broiled fish, and he took it and ate in their presence.

Then he said to them, 'These are my words that I spoke to you while I was still with you – that everything written about me in the law of Moses, the prophets, and the psalms must be fulfilled.' Then he opened their minds to understand the scriptures, and he said to them, 'Thus it is written, that the Messiah is to suffer and to rise from the dead on the third day, and that repentance and forgiveness of sins is to be proclaimed in his name to all nations, beginning from Jerusalem. You are witnesses of these things.'

- Resurrection appearances brought up a range of reactions in the disciples. With Jesus' death, their hopes had evaporated and their faith dwindled. Lord, open our hearts to the surprising ways you reveal yourself. We pray that we may grow in the sense of wonder of who you are and all you have done for us.
- The disciples sought proof of Jesus' resurrection. Showing his wounds opened their minds and being given something to eat eased some of their unbelief. Lord, transform our inner wounds and strengthen us in the sufferings of life so that we are free to share the new life you offer to us.

Monday 15 April
John 6:22–29

The next day the crowd that had stayed on the other side of the lake saw that there had been only one boat there. They also saw that Jesus had not got into the boat with his disciples, but that his disciples had gone away alone. Then some boats from Tiberias came near the place where they had eaten the bread after the Lord had given thanks. So when the crowd saw that neither Jesus nor his disciples were there, they themselves got into the boats and went to Capernaum looking for Jesus.

When they found him on the other side of the lake, they said to him, 'Rabbi, when did you come here?' Jesus answered them, 'Very truly, I tell you, you are looking for me, not because you saw signs, but because you ate your fill of the loaves. Do not work for the food that perishes, but for the food that endures for eternal life, which the Son of Man will give you. For it is on him that God the Father has set his seal.' Then they said to him, 'What must we do to perform the works of God?' Jesus answered them, 'This is the work of God, that you believe in him whom he has sent.'

- For some, searching for Jesus seemed to be motivated by curiosity as to what he would do next. Jesus wanted them to embark on something that was more internal. May our search lead to you and open us to what you want us to be and do.
- Many signs were given but they needed to be interpreted. Jesus wanted to bring the people beyond the bread that satisfied temporarily to 'the food that endures for eternal life'. May we have the freedom to read the signs and come to receive the bread that endures.

Tuesday 16 April
John 6:30–35

So they said to him, 'What sign are you going to give us then, so that we may see it and believe you? What work are you performing? Our ancestors ate the manna in the wilderness; as it is written, "He gave them bread from heaven to eat."' Then Jesus said to them, 'Very truly, I tell you, it was not Moses who gave you the bread from heaven, but it is my Father who gives you the true bread from heaven. For the bread of God is that which comes down from heaven and gives life to the world.' They said to him, 'Sir, give us this bread always.'

Jesus said to them, 'I am the bread of life. Whoever comes to me will never be hungry, and whoever believes in me will never be thirsty.'

- Another demand for a sign and proof. The signs were present but they were unable to recognise them as they were focused on externals. Lord, give us the wisdom to recognise the signs you give us so that we come to a deeper inner faith in you.

- Jesus drew on ordinary experience and events to invite people to a deeper reality. He provided food for the crowd, recalled the past but presented a new future. We pray that our hunger may lead us to receive the bread Jesus offers, knowing that it sustains us in the wilderness of this time.

Wednesday 17 April
John 6:35–40

Jesus said to them, 'I am the bread of life. Whoever comes to me will never be hungry, and whoever believes in me will never be thirsty. But I said to you that you have seen me and yet do not believe. Everything that the Father gives me will come to me, and anyone who comes to me I will never drive away; for I have come down from heaven, not to do my own will, but the will of him who sent me. And this is the will of him who sent me, that I should lose nothing of all that he has given me, but raise it up on the last day. This is indeed the will of my Father, that all who see the Son and believe in him may have eternal life; and I will raise them up on the last day.'

- It is a divided world. Many do not have drinking water whereas others have the luxury of bottled water. Lord, may we act to provide water for those in need, as we ask you to satisfy the deeper thirst in our lives.

- Jesus had a hunger for all people and desired to satisfy their deeper longings. Giving himself as the bread of life manifested his generosity to us. This is not the bread of comfort. May we who eat it be nourishment to those who hunger at all levels of life.

Thursday 18 April
John 6:44–51

Jesus said to the Jews, 'No one can come to me unless drawn by the Father who sent me; and I will raise that person up on the last day. It is written in the prophets, "And they shall all be taught by God." Everyone who has heard and learned from the Father comes to me. Not that anyone has seen the Father except the one who is from God; he has seen the Father. Very truly, I tell you, whoever believes has eternal life. I am the bread of life. Your ancestors ate the manna in the wilderness, and they died. This is the bread that comes down from heaven, so that one may eat of it and not die. I am the living bread that came down from heaven. Whoever eats of this bread will live for ever; and the bread that I will give for the life of the world is my flesh.'

- We are drawn to the Father who sent Jesus to offer us new life. The loving action of God is shared with us. We pray that the Father may draw us closer to Jesus and give us openness to the new life he offers.
- Manna gave passing sustenance in the wilderness. Jesus became 'living bread that came down from heaven', which offered eternal life. Lord, bring us beyond the practical to the deeper truth of who you are in becoming food for our journey in life.

Friday 19 April
John 6:52–59

The Jews then disputed among themselves, saying, 'How can this man give us his flesh to eat?' So Jesus said to them, 'Very truly, I tell you, unless you eat the flesh of the Son of Man and drink his blood, you have no life in you. Those who eat my flesh and drink my blood have eternal life, and I will raise them up on the last day; for my flesh is true food and my blood is true drink. Those who eat my flesh and drink my blood abide in me, and I in them. Just as the living Father sent me, and I live because of the Father, so whoever eats me will live because of me. This is the bread that came down from heaven, not like that which your ancestors ate, and they died. But the one who eats this bread will live for ever.' He said these things while he was teaching in the synagogue at Capernaum.

- The crowd was caught at the practical level with Jesus' teaching. Jesus sought to bring them from manna to living bread, which would nourish life in an enduring way. Lord, give us the faith to accept your teaching and to welcome your presence as the one who sustains us enduringly.
- The notion of sharing flesh and blood shocked Jesus' hearers. It called for a different understanding of Jesus and his message, for a vision of faith and love that went beyond the everyday. May we embrace the deeper truth of the mystery of who Jesus is, so that we may partake of his gift of life.

Saturday 20 April
John 6:60–69

When many of his disciples heard it, they said, 'This teaching is difficult; who can accept it?' But Jesus, being aware that his disciples were complaining about it, said to them, 'Does this offend you? Then what if you were to see the Son of Man ascending to where he was before? It is the spirit that gives life; the flesh is useless. The words that I have spoken to you are spirit and life. But among you there are some who do not believe.' For Jesus knew from the first who were the ones that did not believe, and who was the one that would betray him. And he said, 'For this reason I have told you that no one can come to me unless it is granted by the Father.'

Because of this many of his disciples turned back and no longer went about with him. So Jesus asked the twelve, 'Do you also wish to go away?' Simon Peter answered him, 'Lord, to whom can we go? You have the words of eternal life. We have come to believe and know that you are the Holy One of God.'

- Jesus' teaching on the bread of life was too challenging for some disciples, who walked away. There was a struggle to believe. Lord, help us when our faith is challenged that we may turn to you for what we need to believe, for you call us beyond the logical to the way of love.
- Jesus recognised the struggle of his disciples to believe in him. Peter spoke up, saying he saw no alternative to staying with Jesus. We pray that the words of Peter may help us to believe in Jesus as the Holy One of God.

21–27 April 2024

Something to think and pray about each day this week:

The stories of the humanity of Jesus are important because they help us to develop our relationship with Christ. Jesus came into the world as a dependent baby, just as we did. He needed the care of his mother and father as he grew up. We all need this nurturing in our lives. As he grew older, he learned his father's trade – that of a carpenter – and as Joseph was an expert with wood, it is likely that Jesus was also. Jesus is also recorded in the Gospel of Luke as growing in wisdom and stature – something we all wish for ourselves and for our children.

Jesus is the source of love, light and truth. These are important aspects of life. Jesus is the source of love in our lives, but we do not always recognise this. It can be very easy to become entangled in worldly affairs or in the busyness of life. We can be tempted to forget Jesus and his humanity. Jesus took time out to pray in order to discern the will of his Father and to experience a rest from the crowds of people who followed him; we too can rest, regather ourselves and discern what next step is best.

Jesus had a dual nature; he was both human and divine. He experienced temptation in the way that we do, but he did not sin. The Gospels also recount many times when Jesus ate with his friends and with the wider community. It is clear that he really liked people. Jesus truly loved God and he loved his neighbour, and that is what we are all called to do.

Deirdre M. Powell, *God in Every Day: A Whispered Prayer*

The Presence of God

As I sit here, the beating of my heart,
the ebb and flow of my breathing, the movements of my mind
are all signs of God's ongoing creation of me.
I pause for a moment and become aware
of this presence of God within me.

Freedom

I will ask God's help
to be free from my own preoccupations,
to be open to God in this time of prayer,
to come to know, love and serve God more.

Consciousness

At this moment, Lord, I turn my thoughts to you.
I will leave aside my chores and preoccupations.
I will take rest and refreshment in your presence.

The Word

Now I turn to the Scripture set out for me this day. I read slowly over
the words and see if any sentence or sentiment appeals to me. *(Please
turn to the Scripture on the following pages. Inspiration points are there, should you
need them. When you are ready, return here to continue.)*

Conversation

Begin to talk to Jesus about the Scripture you have just read. What part
of it strikes a chord in you? Perhaps the words of a friend – or some
story you have heard recently – will slowly rise to the surface of your
consciousness. If so, does the story throw light on what the Scripture
passage may be saying to you?

Conclusion

Glory be to the Father, and to the Son, and to the Holy Spirit,
As it was in the beginning, is now and ever shall be,
World without end. Amen.

Sunday 21 April
Fourth Sunday of Easter
John 10:11–18

Jesus said to them, 'I am the good shepherd. The good shepherd lays down his life for the sheep. The hired hand, who is not the shepherd and does not own the sheep, sees the wolf coming and leaves the sheep and runs away – and the wolf snatches them and scatters them. The hired hand runs away because a hired hand does not care for the sheep. I am the good shepherd. I know my own and my own know me, just as the Father knows me and I know the Father. And I lay down my life for the sheep. I have other sheep that do not belong to this fold. I must bring them also, and they will listen to my voice. So there will be one flock, one shepherd. For this reason the Father loves me, because I lay down my life in order to take it up again. No one takes it from me, but I lay it down of my own accord. I have power to lay it down, and I have power to take it up again. I have received this command from my Father.'

- The shepherd imagery is used prominently in scripture to illustrate God's love and concern. God's personal relationship is at the heart of it – 'I know my own and my own know me'. May we grow in that relationship so that we, in turn, are good shepherds for others in life.
- The good shepherd lays down his life for his sheep. Jesus lived that out in his love and concern for us. He desires unity among us all as his followers. As the lost sheep of this age, we ask the Lord to gather us and direct us to the abundant life he promises.

Monday 22 April
John 10:1–10

Jesus said to them, 'Very truly, I tell you, anyone who does not enter the sheepfold by the gate but climbs in by another way is a thief and a bandit. The one who enters by the gate is the shepherd of the sheep. The gatekeeper opens the gate for him, and the sheep hear his voice. He calls his own sheep by name and leads them out. When he has brought out all his own, he goes ahead of them, and the sheep follow him because they know his voice. They will not follow a stranger, but they will run from him because they do not know the voice of strangers.' Jesus used this figure of speech with them, but they did not understand what he was saying to them.

So again Jesus said to them, 'Very truly, I tell you, I am the gate for the sheep. All who came before me are thieves and bandits; but the sheep did not listen to them. I am the gate. Whoever enters by me will be saved, and will come in and go out and find pasture. The thief comes only to steal and kill and destroy. I came that they may have life, and have it abundantly.'

- A gate provides security. Jesus is the gate and the shepherd who enters by the gate and who desires us to do the same. He is the way in and the way out, with a personal relationship with us. Jesus, we ask you to protect us and lead us to the rich pastures that bring a fuller life.

- Jesus calls us by name and leads us. Knowing his voice helps us to trust and to follow him. He is in marked contrast to those who wish to destroy. We pray for listening ears to recognise the voice of Jesus so that we may share the fullness he desires for us.

Tuesday 23 April
John 10:22–30

At that time the festival of the Dedication took place in Jerusalem. It was winter, and Jesus was walking in the temple, in the portico of Solomon. So the Jews gathered around him and said to him, 'How long will you keep us in suspense? If you are the Messiah, tell us plainly.' Jesus answered, 'I have told you, and you do not believe. The works that I do in my Father's name testify to me; but you do not believe, because you do not belong to my sheep. My sheep hear my voice. I know them, and they follow me. I give them eternal life, and they will never perish. No one will snatch them out of my hand. What my Father has given me is greater than all else, and no one can snatch it out of the Father's hand. The Father and I are one.'

- Jesus was questioned about his identity. It should have been clear to the Jews if they understood what he did in the Father's name. We pray that amid the solemn settings of life we come to know Jesus and his message in a simple way.

- Jesus drew on the shepherd image to illustrate his relationship with the Father and with his followers. Listening, knowing and following were important aspects of this. We pray to grow in relationship with Jesus as our shepherd, knowing that he offers security and eternal life.

Wednesday 24 April
John 12:44–50

Then Jesus cried aloud: 'Whoever believes in me believes not in me but in him who sent me. And whoever sees me sees him who sent me. I have come as light into the world, so that everyone who believes in me should not remain in the darkness. I do not judge anyone who hears my words and does not keep them, for I came not to judge the world, but to save the world. The one who rejects me and does not receive my word has a judge; on the last day the word that I have spoken will serve as judge, for I have not spoken on my own, but the Father who sent me has himself given me a commandment about what to say and what to speak. And I know that his commandment is eternal life. What I speak, therefore, I speak just as the Father has told me.'

- Jesus came into the world as light. He offered direction and security as opposed to darkness, which is associated with evil. May we have faith in Jesus as the light to guide us through the darkness of this time.
- Faith in Jesus brings salvation. He came in love to offer life, not judgement. Accepting or rejecting his word will be decisive. We pray that we receive his word and are guided by it, for it is the word of light and of life.

Thursday 25 April
St Mark, Evangelist
Mark 16:15–20

And he said to them, 'Go into all the world and proclaim the good news to the whole creation. The one who believes and is baptised will be saved; but the one who does not believe will be condemned. And these signs will accompany those who believe: by using my name they will cast out demons; they will speak in new tongues; they will pick up snakes in their hands, and if they drink any deadly thing, it will not hurt them; they will lay their hands on the sick, and they will recover.'

So then the Lord Jesus, after he had spoken to them, was taken up into heaven and sat down at the right hand of God. And they went out and proclaimed the good news everywhere, while the Lord worked with them and confirmed the message by the signs that accompanied it.

- The end of the Gospel of Mark is also a beginning. Jesus was about to leave but his followers were being given the mission to 'go into all the world and proclaim the good news to all creation'. This mission is entrusted to us. May we embrace it with faith and love and go forth to share it generously.

- The eleven were assured of God's help and of how God would work through them in bringing good news and healing. Lord, may we rely on your presence and protection and recognise the signs you provide for us.

Friday 26 April
John 14:1–6

Jesus said to his disciples, 'Do not let your hearts be troubled. Believe in God, believe also in me. In my Father's house there are many dwelling-places. If it were not so, would I have told you that I go to prepare a place for you? And if I go and prepare a place for you, I will come again and will take you to myself, so that where I am, there you may be also. And you know the way to the place where I am going.' Thomas said to him, 'Lord, we do not know where you are going. How can we know the way?' Jesus said to him, 'I am the way, and the truth, and the life. No one comes to the Father except through me.'

- The Lord who abides in us has prepared dwelling places for us to abide in him and with him. He invites us to not let our hearts be troubled, assuring us of peace. May we have the trust to let the Lord lead, knowing that he will come again to take us to himself.

- Jesus' word did not seem to be enough for Thomas, who wanted assurance. Jesus told him that he, Jesus, was the way to the Father. Lord, guide us in the way, for you are the way, and living in your truth brings life to the full.

Saturday 27 April
John 14:7–14

Jesus said to his disciples, 'If you know me, you will know my Father also. From now on you do know him and have seen him.'

Philip said to him, 'Lord, show us the Father, and we will be satisfied.' Jesus said to him, 'Have I been with you all this time, Philip, and you still do not know me? Whoever has seen me has seen the Father. How can you say, "Show us the Father"? Do you not believe that I am in the Father and the Father is in me? The words that I say to you I do not speak on my own; but the Father who dwells in me does his works. Believe me that I am in the Father and the Father is in me; but if you do not, then believe me because of the works themselves. Very truly, I tell you, the one who believes in me will also do the works that I do and, in fact, will do greater works than these, because I am going to the Father. I will do whatever you ask in my name, so that the Father may be glorified in the Son. If in my name you ask me for anything, I will do it.'

- Jesus' message about going and coming perplexed the disciples. Now it was Philip's turn to question Jesus, who reveals the Father, just as the Father reveals who Jesus is. We ask Jesus to help us to know him and the Father, for we are called into their relationship of love and unity.
- Jesus and the Father were giving a similar message. The works Jesus did testified to that, though the disciples were slow to grasp it. We ask for a deeper understanding of the message so that we believe in what Jesus said and what he has promised to us in sharing his glory.

28 April–4 May 2024

Something to think and pray about each day this week:

Have you ever been to a wedding dance in which the bride and groom dance their first dance together as a married couple, alone out on the dance floor? Soon, the bride and groom each invite a parent or other relative to join the dance, and there are four people dancing. Next, other relatives may join in, until soon everyone is out on the floor. It may be surprising to consider a wedding dance as an image of forgiveness. After all, we think of forgiveness as taking place only between two people. Or we may think of forgiveness mostly in terms of *shoulds* and *oughts*. I may say to myself, *I should forgive this person because God wants me to do so.* Or, *I am required to forgive, because otherwise maybe God will not forgive me.* But forgiveness is not like this. It is much more like a dance, in which our first dance partner is God. But whenever we spend time with God and let God lead us, we are always led back to embrace other people – for example, the one whom we forgive or who forgives us. This forgiveness then gives us the freedom to go and live more generously with others in the wider human family. And then we go on to dance the dance of love with them, too.

Marina Berzins McCoy, *The Ignatian Guide to Forgiveness:*
Ten Steps to Healing

The Presence of God

'Be still, and know that I am God!' Lord, your words lead us to the calmness and greatness of your presence.

Freedom

God is not foreign to my freedom. The Spirit breathes life into my most intimate desires, gently nudging me towards all that is good. I ask for the grace to let myself be enfolded by the Spirit.

Consciousness

Where do I sense hope, encouragement and growth in my life? By looking back over the past few months, I may be able to see which activities and occasions have produced rich fruit. If I do notice such areas, I will determine to give those areas both time and space in the future.

The Word

The word of God comes down to us through the Scriptures. May the Holy Spirit enlighten my mind and my heart to respond to the Gospel teachings. *(Please turn to the Scripture on the following pages. Inspiration points are there, should you need them. When you are ready, return here to continue.)*

Conversation

What is stirring in me as I pray? Am I consoled, troubled, left cold? I imagine Jesus standing or sitting at my side, and I share my feelings with him.

Conclusion

Glory be to the Father, and to the Son, and to the Holy Spirit,
As it was in the beginning, is now and ever shall be,
World without end. Amen.

Sunday 28 April
Fifth Sunday of Easter
John 15:1–8

Jesus said, 'I am the true vine, and my Father is the vine-grower. He removes every branch in me that bears no fruit. Every branch that bears fruit he prunes to make it bear more fruit. You have already been cleansed by the word that I have spoken to you. Abide in me as I abide in you. Just as the branch cannot bear fruit by itself unless it abides in the vine, neither can you unless you abide in me. I am the vine, you are the branches. Those who abide in me and I in them bear much fruit, because apart from me you can do nothing. Whoever does not abide in me is thrown away like a branch and withers; such branches are gathered, thrown into the fire, and burned. If you abide in me, and my words abide in you, ask for whatever you wish, and it will be done for you. My Father is glorified by this, that you bear much fruit and become my disciples.'

- Jesus is the true vine who shares his life with us, his branches. We are cared for by the Father, who is the vine-grower. This describes an intimate relationship between us, Jesus and the Father. We pray to abide, to live in that relationship, accepting what facilitates bringing forth more fruit.
- Care for the vines involves pruning, but it is done for the sake of life and bearing more fruit. It reminds us that we are asked to let go of some things and attitudes in life that are not fruitful or helpful. Lord, we pray for the freedom to respond to your invitations and to be able to accept the cost.

Monday 29 April
John 14:21–26

Jesus said to his disciples, 'They who have my commandments and keep them are those who love me; and those who love me will be loved by my Father, and I will love them and reveal myself to them.' Judas (not Iscariot) said to him, 'Lord, how is it that you will reveal yourself to us, and not to the world?' Jesus answered him, 'Those who love me will keep my word, and my Father will love them, and we will come to them and make our home with them. Whoever does not love me does not keep my words; and the word that you hear is not mine, but is from the Father who sent me.

'I have said these things to you while I am still with you. But the Advocate, the Holy Spirit, whom the Father will send in my name, will teach you everything, and remind you of all that I have said to you.'

- Another disciple, Judas (not Iscariot) had a question. Did the disciples feel special because Jesus revealed himself to them and not to the world? Jesus, your message of salvation is for all. We pray for a better appreciation of who you are and of our privilege in sharing all that you offer.

- Jesus supported the disciples by his presence and the words that the Father had given them. Now that he was about to leave them he promised the Holy Spirit as an Advocate or helper. Lord, may we remember that we are not alone in our desire to live the truth you share with us.

Tuesday 30 April
John 14:27–31a

Jesus said to them, 'Peace I leave with you; my peace I give to you. I do not give to you as the world gives. Do not let your hearts be troubled, and do not let them be afraid. You heard me say to you, "I am going away, and I am coming to you." If you loved me, you would rejoice that I am going to the Father, because the Father is greater than I. And now I have told you this before it occurs, so that when it does occur, you may believe. I will no longer talk much with you, for the ruler of this world is coming. He has no power over me; but I do as the Father has commanded me, so that the world may know that I love the Father. Rise, let us be on our way.'

- The words of Jesus are pertinent in a world that lacks peace. His peace is more than the external – it is primarily an inner peace, a gift of God, which brings harmony to life. May we have that quality of peace that brings unity to our own lives and fosters better relationships with others.

- Jesus calls us to trust and not be afraid. 'Do not let your hearts be troubled.' Jesus, who is one with the Father, is greater than the forces of division. May we have trust in Jesus' message as we face the challenges ahead.

Wednesday 1 May
St Joseph the Worker
Matthew 13:54–58

He came to his home town and began to teach the people in their synagogue, so that they were astounded and said, 'Where did this man get this wisdom and these deeds of power? Is not this the carpenter's son? Is not his mother called Mary? And are not his brothers James and Joseph and Simon and Judas? And are not all his sisters with us? Where then did this man get all this?' And they took offence at him. But Jesus said to them, 'Prophets are not without honour except in their own country and in their own house.' And he did not do many deeds of power there, because of their unbelief.

- 'Is this not the carpenter's son?' Jesus' life was based in Nazareth with Mary and Joseph. It was an ordinary life where he was obedient to them (Luke 2:51). Joseph provided for the family. Lord, give us a deeper appreciation of the ordinary life, where relationships and work have an important place.
- Work is part of life and gives dignity and a sense of purpose, enabling creative gifts to be put to good use. May the example of St Joseph inspire us to see work as service, not slavery.

Thursday 2 May
John 15:9–11

Jesus said to his disciples, 'As the Father has loved me, so I have loved you; abide in my love. If you keep my commandments, you will abide in my love, just as I have kept my Father's commandments and abide in his love. I have said these things to you so that my joy may be in you, and that your joy may be complete.'

- The initiative for love rests with God, who loves us first. We tend to be slow to grasp that and can begin with our limited love. Lord, open us to the reality of your message of love and help us to accept and to respond to it.

- God's commandments teach us the way of love, how we are to relate to God and to each other. We pray for the joy Jesus promised us through living in right relationship with God and others.

Friday 3 May
Ss James and Philip, Apostles
John 14:6–14

Jesus said to Thomas, 'I am the way, and the truth, and the life. No one comes to the Father except through me. If you know me, you will know my Father also. From now on you do know him and have seen him.'

Philip said to him, 'Lord, show us the Father, and we will be satisfied.' Jesus said to him, 'Have I been with you all this time, Philip, and you still do not know me? Whoever has seen me has seen the Father. How can you say, "Show us the Father"? Do you not believe that I am in the Father and the Father is in me? The words that I say to you I do not speak on my own; but the Father who dwells in me does his works. Believe me that I am in the Father and the Father is in me; but if you do not, then believe me because of the works themselves. Very truly, I tell you, the one who believes in me will also do the works that I do and, in fact, will do greater works than these, because I am going to the Father. I will do whatever you ask in my name, so that the Father may be glorified in the Son. If in my name you ask me for anything, I will do it.'

- Today we remember two of the named apostles, though not much is known about them. The feast invites us to fill in the story and let it speak to our own lives. May we, as unnamed disciples, continue your saving mission, knowing that you continue your work through us.
- Philip desired to see the Father, but it is clear that he did not know Jesus very well. Like him, we are drawn into that relationship with Jesus. We pray to know Jesus better, so that we can live the truth, point out the way and bring others to him.

Saturday 4 May

John 15:18–21

Jesus said to his disciples, 'If the world hates you, be aware that it hated me before it hated you. If you belonged to the world, the world would love you as its own. Because you do not belong to the world, but I have chosen you out of the world – therefore the world hates you. Remember the word that I said to you, "Servants are not greater than their master." If they persecuted me, they will persecute you; if they kept my word, they will keep yours also. But they will do all these things to you on account of my name, because they do not know him who sent me.'

- The world as presented here is in opposition to Jesus. His message was different from that of those who were influential elsewhere. We pray that we may not be ruled by the popular or the convenient to the detriment of the values Jesus declared.

- Jesus reminds us that in remaining true to him we will face misunderstandings and even some persecution. His approach is to guide and support us. Lord, as your servants, we pray that we may keep your word, for it is the word of life.

5–11 May 2024

Something to think and pray about each day this week:

Pope Francis spoke on the theme of relationships at Croke Park, Dublin, in August 2018. He spoke clearly and simply about love and forgiveness in the family. He emphasised the need to say 'please, thank you, and sorry' to each other. He asked us to say the words out loud, 'PLEASE, THANK YOU, and SORRY', and to repeat them one more time. Everyone in the stadium spoke in unison, to which he replied in English, 'Thank you very much!'

He also pointed out how easy it is to be physically intimate with one another in appropriate ways. What are we afraid of? I used to hesitate to kiss my grandmother when I saw her every day. I clearly loved her through my words and other deeds, but I seemed to have saved my kisses for only special occasions. So, I followed the Pope's advice and started to do it, and it has now become second nature. Every day is a special day and an opportunity to show our love in the world.

Gavin Thomas Murphy, *Bursting Out in Praise:*
Spirituality and Mental Health

The Presence of God
'Be still, and know that I am God.' Lord, your words lead us to the calmness and greatness of your presence.

Freedom
I am free. When I look at these words in writing, they seem to create in me a feeling of awe. Yes, a wonderful feeling of freedom. Thank you, God.

Consciousness
At this moment, Lord, I turn my thoughts to you.
I will leave aside my chores and preoccupations.
I will take rest and refreshment in your presence, Lord.

The Word
The word of God comes down to us through the Scriptures. May the Holy Spirit enlighten my mind and my heart to respond to the Gospel teachings. *(Please turn to the Scripture on the following pages. Inspiration points are there, should you need them. When you are ready, return here to continue.)*

Conversation
Begin to talk with Jesus about the Scripture you have just read. What part of it strikes a chord in you? Perhaps the words of a friend – or some story you have heard recently – will slowly rise to the surface of your consciousness. If so, does the story throw light on what the Scripture passage may be trying to say to you?

Conclusion
Glory be to the Father, and to the Son, and to the Holy Spirit,
As it was in the beginning, is now and ever shall be,
World without end. Amen.

Sunday 5 May
Sixth Sunday of Easter
John 15:9–17
Jesus said to his disciples, 'As the Father has loved me, so I have loved you; abide in my love. If you keep my commandments, you will abide in my love, just as I have kept my Father's commandments and abide in his love. I have said these things to you so that my joy may be in you, and that your joy may be complete.

'This is my commandment, that you love one another as I have loved you. No one has greater love than this, to lay down one's life for one's friends. You are my friends if you do what I command you. I do not call you servants any longer, because the servant does not know what the master is doing; but I have called you friends, because I have made known to you everything that I have heard from my Father. You did not choose me but I chose you. And I appointed you to go and bear fruit, fruit that will last, so that the Father will give you whatever you ask him in my name. I am giving you these commands so that you may love one another.'

- Jesus lived and taught love by his own example of total self-giving. He laid down his life for us, his friends. May we imitate him in being people for others, reaching out to them in Jesus' name.
- It is the Lord who chose us and calls us his friends. We are to serve in the spirit of love, putting others before ourselves. Lord, may we have the humility to ask for what we need so that we bear fruit to the glory of your name.

Monday 6 May
John 15:26–16:4
Jesus said to his disciples, 'When the Advocate comes, whom I will send to you from the Father, the Spirit of truth who comes from the Father, he will testify on my behalf. You also are to testify because you have been with me from the beginning.

'I have said these things to you to keep you from stumbling. They will put you out of the synagogues. Indeed, an hour is coming when those who kill you will think that by doing so they are offering worship to God. And they will do this because they have not known the Father or me. But I have said these things to you so that when their hour comes you may remember that I told you about them.

'I did not say these things to you from the beginning, because I was with you.'

- There was opposition to Jesus and it would be the same for his disciples. Being expelled from the faith community and being killed could be seen as a form of worshipping God. We pray that we may not stumble in our following but be renewed in faith amid the misunderstandings we face.

Tuesday 7 May
John 16:5–11

Jesus said to them, 'But now I am going to him who sent me; yet none of you asks me, "Where are you going?" But because I have said these things to you, sorrow has filled your hearts. Nevertheless, I tell you the truth: it is to your advantage that I go away, for if I do not go away, the Advocate will not come to you; but if I go, I will send him to you. And when he comes, he will prove the world wrong about sin and righteousness and judgement: about sin, because they do not believe in me; about righteousness, because I am going to the Father and you will see me no longer; about judgement, because the ruler of this world has been condemned.'

- There is sadness in parting from loved ones. Jesus spoke of his going away as beneficial for the disciples, as he would send the Holy Spirit. Lord, we pray that we may remember that you are always with us in a new way and provide what we need,

Wednesday 8 May
John 16:12–15

Jesus said to his disciples, 'I still have many things to say to you, but you cannot bear them now. When the Spirit of truth comes, he will guide you into all the truth; for he will not speak on his own, but will speak whatever he hears, and he will declare to you the things that are to come. He will glorify me, because he will take what is mine and declare it to you. All that the Father has is mine. For this reason I said that he will take what is mine and declare it to you.'

- Jesus assured his disciples that they would have the help they needed for the next stage. The message would be revealed to them in due course to enable them to be ready. Lord, send us the Spirit of Truth to teach us how to know, love and serve you better.

Thursday 9 May
John 16:16–20

Jesus said to them, 'A little while, and you will no longer see me, and again a little while, and you will see me.' Then some of his disciples said to one another, 'What does he mean by saying to us, "A little while, and you will no longer see me, and again a little while, and you will see me"; and "Because I am going to the Father"?' They said, 'What does he mean by this "a little while"? We do not know what he is talking about.' Jesus knew that they wanted to ask him, so he said to them, 'Are you discussing among yourselves what I meant when I said, "A little while, and you will no longer see me, and again a little while, and you will see me"? Very truly, I tell you, you will weep and mourn, but the world will rejoice; you will have pain, but your pain will turn into joy.'

- This is a world that is in haste and short of time. There is an unwillingness to wait, even for 'a little while'. Jesus was anticipating what lay ahead in asking his disciples to trust. May we have the patience to wait, knowing that you, Lord, are faithful to your promises.
- Many desired to see Jesus, but as if from afar. Jesus wanted to meet people and be part of their lives. Lord, give us eyes of faith to truly see and the gift of understanding you so that we find true happiness

Friday 10 May
John 16:20–23

Jesus said to them, 'Very truly, I tell you, you will weep and mourn, but the world will rejoice; you will have pain, but your pain will turn into joy. When a woman is in labour, she has pain, because her hour has come. But when her child is born, she no longer remembers the anguish because of the joy of having brought a human being into the world. So you have pain now; but I will see you again, and your hearts will rejoice, and no one will take your joy from you. On that day you will ask nothing of me. Very truly, I tell you, if you ask anything of the Father in my name, he will give it to you.'

- There are times when the world is referred to as a valley of tears. On other occasions we are more conscious of being in pain because of what is happening. Jesus, may we see beyond the sufferings to the new life you have brought about by your own self-giving love.

- Jesus, you came to offer new life and brought it to birth through your suffering. Help us to accept the challenges and difficulties of life so that we may share in the joy you desire for us.

Saturday 11 May
John 16:23b–28

Jesus said to his disciples, 'On that day you will ask nothing of me. Very truly, I tell you, if you ask anything of the Father in my name, he will give it to you. Until now you have not asked for anything in my name. Ask and you will receive, so that your joy may be complete.

'I have said these things to you in figures of speech. The hour is coming when I will no longer speak to you in figures, but will tell you plainly of the Father. On that day you will ask in my name. I do not say to you that I will ask the Father on your behalf; for the Father himself loves you, because you have loved me and have believed that I came from God. I came from the Father and have come into the world; again, I am leaving the world and am going to the Father.'

- Asking for genuine gifts brings joy, as it desires to further the way of the Lord. Jesus invites us to ask in his name, as part of his family. May we have the clarity and freedom to seek good gifts that will further the Lord's kingdom.

- Jesus offers a prayerful approach in turning to him and to the Father. We are invited to come in trust, to ask and receive. Jesus' message is clear, so we ask in simple, plain language for the joy he offers.

12–18 May 2024

Something to think and pray about each day this week:

'Where will it all end up?' A question often posed today by people who value the role of the Church in their lives, their community and their society. To say that there is a lot of confusion tending towards despair about the future of the Church is commonplace.

The future lies more in creating great human beings and less about great institutions. Those who have made it to the top of the ecclesiastical structure were often people who made the institutions look great and their humanness was often not a priority. In a world that has enormous possibilities and increasingly diverse influences Christianity is desperate for more ambassadors and fewer bureaucrats.

The gospels remind us that people want to meet other people whose humanity points towards something worth striving for. 'All spoke well of him, how can this be, they asked, "isn't this Joseph's son?"' (Luke 4:22). 'And they were amazed, and asked, "what kind of man is this?"' (Matthew 8:28). 'The centurion, seeing what had happened, praised God and said, "Surely this was a righteous man?"' (Luke 23:47).

Over the last two thousand years the rituals of faith, the words of tradition, the noblest of people who allowed grace to influence their humanity have built up a great reservoir of hope and a resource of incalculable value as we foster a faith appropriate to our age.

Alan Hilliard, *Dipping into Lent*

The Presence of God

'Come to me, all you who are weary and are carrying heavy burdens, and I will give you rest.' Here I am, Lord. I come to seek your presence. I long for your healing power.

Freedom

By God's grace I was born to live in freedom. Free to enjoy the pleasures he created for me. Dear Lord, grant that I may live as you intended, with complete confidence in your loving care.

Consciousness

Knowing that God loves me unconditionally, I look honestly over the past day, its events, and my feelings. Do I have something to be grateful for? Then I give thanks. Is there something I am sorry for? Then I ask forgiveness.

The Word

God speaks to each of us individually. I listen attentively to hear what he is saying to me. Read the text a few times, then listen. *(Please turn to the Scripture on the following pages. Inspiration points are there, should you need them. When you are ready, return here to continue.)*

Conversation

I know with certainty that there were times when you carried me, Lord. There were times when it was through your strength that I got through the dark times in my life.

Conclusion

Glory be to the Father, and to the Son, and to the Holy Spirit,
As it was in the beginning, is now and ever shall be,
World without end. Amen.

Sunday 12 May
The Ascension of the Lord
Mark 16:15–20

And he said to them, 'Go into all the world and proclaim the good news to the whole creation. The one who believes and is baptised will be saved; but the one who does not believe will be condemned. And these signs will accompany those who believe: by using my name they will cast out demons; they will speak in new tongues; they will pick up snakes in their hands, and if they drink any deadly thing, it will not hurt them; they will lay their hands on the sick, and they will recover.'

So then the Lord Jesus, after he had spoken to them, was taken up into heaven and sat down at the right hand of God. And they went out and proclaimed the good news everywhere, while the Lord worked with them and confirmed the message by the signs that accompanied it.

- Jesus said farewell to the apostles and was welcomed home by the Father. Jesus has completed his part of the mission and handed it over to the disciples to carry forward. As their successors, may we bring good news and healing wherever we go.
- Jesus was taken up into heaven. His apostles were to take up his message and proclaim it. May we not be taken up with incidentals but set out to raise hearts in hope, sharing in the fruits of this day.

Monday 13 May
John 16:29–33

His disciples said, 'Yes, now you are speaking plainly, not in any figure of speech! Now we know that you know all things, and do not need to have anyone question you; by this we believe that you came from God.' Jesus answered them, 'Do you now believe? The hour is coming, indeed it has come, when you will be scattered, each one to his home, and you will leave me alone. Yet I am not alone because the Father is with me. I have said this to you, so that in me you may have peace. In the world you face persecution. But take courage; I have conquered the world!'

- Speaking plainly or proclaiming the truth does not necessarily mean ready acceptance. Jesus did so and he and his message were not understood. We pray for the gift of speaking plainly and honestly about Jesus in our time.
- Jesus promised inner peace, but it was in a world where his disciples would face persecution. He invites us to 'take courage; I have conquered the world'. May we have the conviction to proclaim and live Jesus' message in the world of now.

Tuesday 14 May
St Matthias, Apostle
John 15:9–17

Jesus said to them, 'As the Father has loved me, so I have loved you; abide in my love. If you keep my commandments, you will abide in my love, just as I have kept my Father's commandments and abide in his love. I have said these things to you so that my joy may be in you, and that your joy may be complete.

'This is my commandment, that you love one another as I have loved you. No one has greater love than this, to lay down one's life for one's friends. You are my friends if you do what I command you. I do not call you servants any longer, because the servant does not know what the master is doing; but I have called you friends, because I have made known to you everything that I have heard from my Father. You did not choose me but I chose you. And I appointed you to go and bear fruit, fruit that will last, so that the Father will give you whatever you ask him in my name. I am giving you these commands so that you may love one another.'

- Matthias was the first reserve called into the team to replace Judas. Matthias met the criteria required for being a follower from the baptism of Jesus. May we who abide in the Lord and who live as his friends bear witness to the resurrection.
- The Lord took the initiative in choosing disciples. Their lives were to be modelled on his, who laid down his life for his friends. Lord, we pray that we may know you more fully and live as your apostles in proclaiming your good news.

Wednesday 15 May
John 17:11b–19
Jesus looked up to heaven and said, 'And now I am no longer in the world, but they are in the world, and I am coming to you. Holy Father, protect them in your name that you have given me, so that they may be one, as we are one. While I was with them, I protected them in your name that you have given me. I guarded them, and not one of them was lost except the one destined to be lost, so that the scripture might be fulfilled. But now I am coming to you, and I speak these things in the world so that they may have my joy made complete in themselves. I have given them your word, and the world has hated them because they do not belong to the world, just as I do not belong to the world. I am not asking you to take them out of the world, but I ask you to protect them from the evil one. They do not belong to the world, just as I do not belong to the world. Sanctify them in the truth; your word is truth. As you have sent me into the world, so I have sent them into the world. And for their sakes I sanctify myself, so that they also may be sanctified in truth.'

- The Lord protects us as a shepherd guards his flock. We have the capacity and freedom to become lost, but that is not the Lord's desire for us. May we find security in God's protection and come to recognise that we belong to God, not to the world.
- The world is a challenging place that can trap us with what it has to offer. We are reminded that we do not belong to the world, just as Jesus did not. Lord, we pray that we may live the truth of who you are and who we are as your friends.

Thursday 16 May
John 17:20–26
Jesus said, 'I ask not only on behalf of these, but also on behalf of those who will believe in me through their word, that they may all be one. As you, Father, are in me and I am in you, may they also be in us, so that the world may believe that you have sent me. The glory that you have given me I have given them, so that they may be one, as we are one, I in them and you in me, that they may become completely one, so that the

world may know that you have sent me and have loved them even as you have loved me. Father, I desire that those also, whom you have given me, may be with me where I am, to see my glory, which you have given me because you loved me before the foundation of the world.

'Righteous Father, the world does not know you, but I know you; and these know that you have sent me. I made your name known to them, and I will make it known, so that the love with which you have loved me may be in them, and I in them.'

- Jesus was united to the Father and calls us to live in that relationship of love. He desires 'that they may all be one'. He is the source of and the reason for unity. We pray that through our union with Jesus we come to know more fully that he is the one sent by the Father.
- God's glory is shared with us in love. We are called to know Jesus and the Father who sent him. May we have the faith to follow and help others believe through our words as Jesus asked of us.

Friday 17 May
John 21:15–19

When they had finished breakfast, Jesus said to Simon Peter, 'Simon son of John, do you love me more than these?' He said to him, 'Yes, Lord; you know that I love you.' Jesus said to him, 'Feed my lambs.' A second time he said to him, 'Simon son of John, do you love me?' He said to him, 'Yes, Lord; you know that I love you.' Jesus said to him, 'Tend my sheep.' He said to him the third time, 'Simon son of John, do you love me?' Peter felt hurt because he said to him the third time, 'Do you love me?' And he said to him, 'Lord, you know everything; you know that I love you.' Jesus said to him, 'Feed my sheep. Very truly, I tell you, when you were younger, you used to fasten your own belt and to go wherever you wished. But when you grow old, you will stretch out your hands, and someone else will fasten a belt around you and take you where you do not wish to go.' (He said this to indicate the kind of death by which he would glorify God.) After this he said to him, 'Follow me.'

- Three times Peter had denied that he knew the Lord. Now he was asked three times to profess his faith in him. Peter 'felt hurt' at being asked and said, 'Lord you know everything, you know I love

you.' Lord, forgive us our denials and strengthen our faith to follow you more closely.
• Peter was being asked to let go. A time would come when others would take charge of him, just as happened to Jesus prior to his death. Lord, help us to let go of control in our ongoing call to follow you.

Saturday 18 May
John 21:20–25
Peter turned and saw the disciple whom Jesus loved following them; he was the one who had reclined next to Jesus at the supper and had said, 'Lord, who is it that is going to betray you?' When Peter saw him, he said to Jesus, 'Lord, what about him?' Jesus said to him, 'If it is my will that he remain until I come, what is that to you? Follow me!' So the rumour spread in the community that this disciple would not die. Yet Jesus did not say to him that he would not die, but, 'If it is my will that he remain until I come, what is that to you?'

This is the disciple who is testifying to these things and has written them, and we know that his testimony is true. But there are also many other things that Jesus did; if every one of them were written down, I suppose that the world itself could not contain the books that would be written.
• As we come to the end of the Easter Season we have the final part of John's Gospel. Peter seemed to be in competition with the disciple Jesus loved, asking, 'What about him?' Jesus brought attention back to Peter and his call to follow. May we seek to strengthen our own relationship with the Lord and not compare ourselves to others.
• The author acknowledged the limits of what he could write about Jesus. It was much bigger and would need far more time and space. Lord, you invite us to write the next chapter in the Gospel story and thus contribute our part in harmony and in continuity with the earlier chapters.

19–25 May 2024

Something to think and pray about each day this week:

We only start to pray when we start to love, because love is the litmus test of all prayer. Have I loved? If so, then I have also prayed. Do I love? If so, then I am really praying. Am I growing in love? If so, my prayer is deepening as well.

Jesus taught us that prayer is love by teaching us the Our Father, because every line of this prayer has something to teach us about love. The first loving aspect to this prayer is that we begin by loving God enough to place ourselves before him as 'Our Father'. We begin by contemplating his tenderness and greatness. We ask that he may be loved and that his eternal plan may be realised. In other words, we start this prayer by focusing on God and not on our selves. As a rule, when we pray, we instinctively give first priority to our own needs: we tell God what we want. We don't pause long enough to consider his desires. The Lord's Prayer teaches us to put God and his plans in first place.

Thomas G. Casey SJ, *The Mindful Our Father*

The Presence of God

'I am standing at the door, knocking,' says the Lord. What a wonderful privilege that the Lord of all creation desires to come to me. I welcome his presence.

Freedom

Everything has the potential to draw forth from me a fuller love and life. Yet my desires are often fixed, caught, on illusions of fulfilment. I ask that God, through my freedom, may orchestrate my desires in a vibrant loving melody rich in harmony.

Consciousness

To be conscious about something is to be aware of it.
Dear Lord, help me to remember that you gave me life.
Thank you for the gift of life.
Teach me to slow down, to be still and enjoy the pleasures created for me. To be aware of the beauty that surrounds me: the marvel of mountains, the calmness of lakes, the fragility of a flower petal. I need to remember that all these things come from you.

The Word

I read the word of God slowly, a few times over, and I listen to what God is saying to me. *(Please turn to the Scripture on the following pages. Inspiration points are there, should you need them. When you are ready, return here to continue.)*

Conversation

What feelings are rising in me as I pray and reflect on God's word? I imagine Jesus himself sitting or standing near me, and I open my heart to him.

Conclusion

I thank God for these moments we have spent together and for any insights I have been given concerning the text.

Sunday 19 May
Pentecost Sunday
John 20:19–23

When it was evening on that day, the first day of the week, and the doors of the house where the disciples had met were locked for fear of the Jews, Jesus came and stood among them and said, 'Peace be with you.' After he said this, he showed them his hands and his side. Then the disciples rejoiced when they saw the Lord. Jesus said to them again, 'Peace be with you. As the Father has sent me, so I send you.' When he had said this, he breathed on them and said to them, 'Receive the Holy Spirit. If you forgive the sins of any, they are forgiven them; if you retain the sins of any, they are retained.'

- Jesus, who was sent by the Father, sends the Holy Spirit, the Advocate. May we who have received the Spirit of truth as our helper give witness to the presence and action of God in our lives and in the world.
- Jesus breathed on the disciples and gave them the Holy Spirit, the breath of life. We who have received the gifts of the Spirit pray that we may be forgiving and encouraging of others in appreciation of all that we have been given.

Monday 20 May
The Blessed Virgin Mary, Mother of the Church
John 19:25–34

Meanwhile, standing near the cross of Jesus were his mother, and his mother's sister, Mary the wife of Clopas, and Mary Magdalene. When Jesus saw his mother and the disciple whom he loved standing beside her, he said to his mother, 'Woman, here is your son.' Then he said to the disciple, 'Here is your mother.' And from that hour the disciple took her into his own home.

After this, when Jesus knew that all was now finished, he said (in order to fulfil the scripture), 'I am thirsty.' A jar full of sour wine was standing there. So they put a sponge full of the wine on a branch of hyssop and held it to his mouth. When Jesus had received the wine, he said, 'It is finished.' Then he bowed his head and gave up his spirit.

Since it was the day of Preparation, the Jews did not want the bodies left on the cross during the sabbath, especially because that sabbath was a day of great solemnity. So they asked Pilate to have the legs of the crucified men broken and the bodies removed. Then the soldiers came and broke the legs of the first and of the other who had been crucified with him. But when they came to Jesus and saw that he was already dead, they did not break his legs. Instead, one of the soldiers pierced his side with a spear, and at once blood and water came out.

- Mary is the mother and disciple who was faithful to the end. Her life was lived in union with Jesus, her Son, in self-giving and in presence. May we draw strength from her to stay with Jesus through the ups and downs of life.
- Jesus on the cross, entrusted his mother, Mary, to us and us to her. Her sufferings in life were similar to his in many ways. We pray for the strength to respond as members of God's family to the many gifts and supports given to us through Mary.

Tuesday 21 May
Mark 9:30–37

They went on from there and passed through Galilee. He did not want anyone to know it; for he was teaching his disciples, saying to them, 'The Son of Man is to be betrayed into human hands, and they will kill him, and three days after being killed, he will rise again.' But they did not understand what he was saying and were afraid to ask him.

Then they came to Capernaum; and when he was in the house he asked them, 'What were you arguing about on the way?' But they were silent, for on the way they had argued with one another about who was the greatest. He sat down, called the twelve, and said to them, 'Whoever wants to be first must be last of all and servant of all.' Then he took a little child and put it among them; and taking it in his arms, he said to them, 'Whoever welcomes one such child in my name welcomes me, and whoever welcomes me welcomes not me but the one who sent me.'

- Jesus spoke of forthcoming suffering, but the disciples 'did not understand what he was saying and were afraid to ask'. Suffering was not on their agenda as they were more interested in their own importance. Lord, help us to appreciate that your greatness was in self-giving, dying that we might have life.

- Jesus' way was that of humility. He presented a little child as a model to his disciples: 'Whoever wants to be first must be last of all and servant of all.' May we welcome children with love and have a humble trust in receiving them as Jesus did.

Wednesday 22 May
Mark 9:38–40

John said to him, 'Teacher, we saw someone casting out demons in your name, and we tried to stop him, because he was not following us.' But Jesus said, 'Do not stop him; for no one who does a deed of power in my name will be able soon afterwards to speak evil of me. Whoever is not against us is for us.'

- Belonging to the right team can take on undue importance. Jesus calls us beyond external criteria to be part of the same mission. Lord, help us to recognise and appreciate the gifts of others who promote your name even though they are not 'one of us'.
- Because I am on your side does not mean that I am against those you oppose. We pray for a bigger vision, one that is more inclusive, one that is evident in humble service in the name of Jesus.

Thursday 23 May
Mark 9:41–50

Jesus said to them, 'For truly I tell you, whoever gives you a cup of water to drink because you bear the name of Christ will by no means lose the reward.

'If any of you put a stumbling-block before one of these little ones who believe in me, it would be better for you if a great millstone were hung around your neck and you were thrown into the sea. If your hand causes you to stumble, cut it off; it is better for you to enter life maimed than to have two hands and to go to hell, to the unquenchable fire. And if your foot causes you to stumble, cut it off; it is better for you to enter life lame than to have two feet and to be thrown into hell. And if your eye causes you to stumble, tear it out; it is better for you to enter the kingdom of God with one eye than to have two eyes and to be thrown into hell, where their worm never dies, and the fire is never quenched.

'For everyone will be salted with fire. Salt is good; but if salt has lost its saltiness, how can you season it? Have salt in yourselves, and be at peace with one another.'

- We are called to care for the little ones and to be supportive and helpful to others in life. Good example provides a rich source of encouragement on our journey together. May we have the freedom to see the good and show love in action affirming others who do so.
- Jesus wants us to know what is important and to be guided by it. We are called to be salt for the world, offering flavour and taste. May we have the freedom to let go of what is near and dear if it causes us to stumble from the truth.

Friday 24 May
Mark 10:1–12
He left that place and went to the region of Judea and beyond the Jordan. And crowds again gathered around him; and, as was his custom, he again taught them.

Some Pharisees came, and to test him they asked, 'Is it lawful for a man to divorce his wife?' He answered them, 'What did Moses command you?' They said, 'Moses allowed a man to write a certificate of dismissal and to divorce her.' But Jesus said to them, 'Because of your hardness of heart he wrote this commandment for you. But from the beginning of creation, "God made them male and female." "For this reason a man shall leave his father and mother and be joined to his wife, and the two shall become one flesh." So they are no longer two, but one flesh. Therefore what God has joined together, let no one separate.'

Then in the house the disciples asked him again about this matter. He said to them, 'Whoever divorces his wife and marries another commits adultery against her; and if she divorces her husband and marries another, she commits adultery.'

- Asking the right questions can be helpful in an interview. Testing the speaker is a common occurrence, especially when a stance taken challenges the prevailing culture. Lord, we pray for the courage to ask serious questions, with good intentions, to find the deeper truth.

- Jesus drew attention to fidelity, based on God's faithful love to us. He was aware that everybody did not live up to the ideal and he was compassionate in his approach. May we humbly acknowledge when we fall short and be understanding of others who do the same.

Saturday 25 May
Mark 10:13–16

People were bringing little children to him in order that he might touch them; and the disciples spoke sternly to them. But when Jesus saw this, he was indignant and said to them, 'Let the little children come to me; do not stop them; for it is to such as these that the kingdom of God belongs. Truly I tell you, whoever does not receive the kingdom of God as a little child will never enter it.' And he took them up in his arms, laid his hands on them, and blessed them.

- Jesus presented children as models of discipleship. They have a trust and honesty that can embarrass adults. May we have a childlike trust in receiving the love and care of the Lord and share it with others.
- Jesus was loving and affectionate to the children brought to him. In our culture many are hesitant to express themselves in this way. May we be respectful in how we touch the lives of children, assuring them of our love and respect.

The Eighth Week in Ordinary Time

26 May–1 June 2024

Something to think and pray about each day this week:

What does Jesus have to say about the natural world? What is the significance of the Incarnation for a theology of nature? Up to now, very little attention was given to the relationship between Jesus and the natural world, beyond the observation that he appealed to nature to talk about the coming reign of God. It is worth noting that Jesus lived much of his life in close proximity to the natural world:

- He spent forty days in the desert.
- He was with the wild animals in the desert.
- He was baptised in the River Jordan by John the Baptist.
- The transfiguration of Jesus occurred on Mount Tabor.
- He often retired to quiet places of nature to pray.
- He taught on and around the Lake of Galilee.
- He suffered in the Garden of Gethsemane.
- He appeared to Mary Magdalene in the Garden of Resurrection.

These encounters with the natural world had an influence on the life of Jesus. Many of these moments included prayerful communion with God his Father. They left a deep impression on him, so much so that when he taught about the coming reign of God, he drew on his knowledge of the natural world.

The life of Jesus was lived out of a deep Jewish creation-faith and theology. This closeness of Jesus to the natural world and the life of creation does not make him an ecologist before his time, but it does illustrate his awareness of the presence of the Spirit of God in the natural world. Miracles, such as the miracles of healing, exorcisms and nature miracles point towards a renewal of creation as part of the coming reign of God.

Dermot A. Lane, *Nature Praising God:*
Towards a Theology of the Natural World

The Presence of God
'Be still, and know that I am God!' Lord, your words lead us to the calmness and greatness of your presence.

Freedom
God is not foreign to my freedom. The Spirit breathes life into my most intimate desires, gently nudging me towards all that is good. I ask for the grace to let myself be enfolded by the Spirit.

Consciousness
Where do I sense hope, encouragement and growth in my life? By looking back over the past few months, I may be able to see which activities and occasions have produced rich fruit. If I do notice such areas, I will determine to give those areas both time and space in the future.

The Word
The word of God comes down to us through the Scriptures. May the Holy Spirit enlighten my mind and my heart to respond to the Gospel teachings. *(Please turn to the Scripture on the following pages. Inspiration points are there, should you need them. When you are ready, return here to continue.)*

Conversation
What is stirring in me as I pray? Am I consoled, troubled, left cold? I imagine Jesus standing or sitting at my side, and I share my feelings with him.

Conclusion
Glory be to the Father, and to the Son, and to the Holy Spirit,
As it was in the beginning, is now and ever shall be,
World without end. Amen.

Sunday 26 May
The Most Holy Trinity
Matthew 28:16–20

Now the eleven disciples went to Galilee, to the mountain to which Jesus had directed them. When they saw him, they worshipped him; but some doubted. And Jesus came and said to them, 'All authority in heaven and on earth has been given to me. Go therefore and make disciples of all nations, baptising them in the name of the Father and of the Son and of the Holy Spirit, and teaching them to obey everything that I have commanded you. And remember, I am with you always, to the end of the age.'

- The Trinity is a community of love. We are drawn into their life to share it. Getting inspiration from the icon of Rublev, we pray that we may avail of that open space to enter the gift our God of love desires for us.
- Much of what we celebrate in our faith lives is done in the name of the Father, the Son and the Holy Spirit. May we cherish what we have been given and anticipate what the Trinity has in store for us.

Monday 27 May
Mark 10:17–27

As he was setting out on a journey, a man ran up and knelt before him, and asked him, 'Good Teacher, what must I do to inherit eternal life?' Jesus said to him, 'Why do you call me good? No one is good but God alone. You know the commandments: "You shall not murder; You shall not commit adultery; You shall not steal; You shall not bear false witness; You shall not defraud; Honour your father and mother."' He said to him, 'Teacher, I have kept all these since my youth.' Jesus, looking at him, loved him and said, 'You lack one thing; go, sell what you own, and give the money to the poor, and you will have treasure in heaven; then come, follow me.' When he heard this, he was shocked and went away grieving, for he had many possessions.

Then Jesus looked around and said to his disciples, 'How hard it will be for those who have wealth to enter the kingdom of God!' And the disciples were perplexed at these words. But Jesus said to them again,

'Children, how hard it is to enter the kingdom of God! It is easier for a camel to go through the eye of a needle than for someone who is rich to enter the kingdom of God.' They were greatly astounded and said to one another, 'Then who can be saved?' Jesus looked at them and said, 'For mortals it is impossible, but not for God; for God all things are possible.'

- This man ran to Jesus and knelt before him. We can admire the quality of his life and his commitment, but he wanted something more. Like Martha, he lacked one thing (Luke 10:38–42). May we not drift into some form of smug satisfaction with our good deeds, but be free to let the Lord guide us to the life he promises.
- Jesus looked at the man and loved him, seeing his potential, and invited him onwards. Jesus wanted to set his heart free of the possessions that enslaved him. Lord, you remind us that all things are possible to God. May we turn to you for the freedom we need to embrace the lasting treasure you offer.

Tuesday 28 May
Mark 10:28–31
Peter began to say to him, 'Look, we have left everything and followed you.' Jesus said, 'Truly I tell you, there is no one who has left house or brothers or sisters or mother or father or children or fields, for my sake and for the sake of the good news, who will not receive a hundredfold now in this age – houses, brothers and sisters, mothers and children, and fields, with persecutions – and in the age to come eternal life. But many who are first will be last, and the last will be first.'

- It seems as if Peter was reminding Jesus of his generosity in leaving all to follow him. There was a selfish hint in Peter's remark, like 'What are we going to get for doing so?' Lord, help us to recognise where our selfish interests can be subtly present, so that we can be freer to give without counting the cost.
- Jesus referred to the rewards of discipleship. Those who left all will receive a hundredfold, but it will include some suffering. We pray to appreciate the eternal life the Lord promises, as it is much more than passing rewards.

Wednesday 29 May
Mark 10:32–45

They were on the road, going up to Jerusalem, and Jesus was walking ahead of them; they were amazed, and those who followed were afraid. He took the twelve aside again and began to tell them what was to happen to him, saying, 'See, we are going up to Jerusalem, and the Son of Man will be handed over to the chief priests and the scribes, and they will condemn him to death; then they will hand him over to the Gentiles; they will mock him, and spit upon him, and flog him, and kill him; and after three days he will rise again.'

James and John, the sons of Zebedee, came forward to him and said to him, 'Teacher, we want you to do for us whatever we ask of you.' And he said to them, 'What is it you want me to do for you?' And they said to him, 'Grant us to sit, one at your right hand and one at your left, in your glory.' But Jesus said to them, 'You do not know what you are asking. Are you able to drink the cup that I drink, or be baptised with the baptism that I am baptised with?' They replied, 'We are able.' Then Jesus said to them, 'The cup that I drink you will drink; and with the baptism with which I am baptised, you will be baptised; but to sit at my right hand or at my left is not mine to grant, but it is for those for whom it has been prepared.'

When the ten heard this, they began to be angry with James and John. So Jesus called them and said to them, 'You know that among the Gentiles those whom they recognise as their rulers lord it over them, and their great ones are tyrants over them. But it is not so among you; but whoever wishes to become great among you must be your servant, and whoever wishes to be first among you must be slave of all. For the Son of Man came not to be served but to serve, and to give his life a ransom for many.'

- Another prediction of suffering brought a familiar reaction. Jesus' ambition was to do good. The disciples were drawn to honours, importance and security. Give us the strength to find glory as you did, not in self-seeking but in self-giving.
- Competition and comparison get in the way of good relationships. They can blind us to what is most true and to who we are. May we have hearts that are free to serve in the spirit and way of Jesus.

Thursday 30 May
Mark 10:46–52

They came to Jericho. As he and his disciples and a large crowd were leaving Jericho, Bartimaeus son of Timaeus, a blind beggar, was sitting by the roadside. When he heard that it was Jesus of Nazareth, he began to shout out and say, 'Jesus, Son of David, have mercy on me!' Many sternly ordered him to be quiet, but he cried out even more loudly, 'Son of David, have mercy on me!' Jesus stood still and said, 'Call him here.' And they called the blind man, saying to him, 'Take heart; get up, he is calling you.' So throwing off his cloak, he sprang up and came to Jesus. Then Jesus said to him, 'What do you want me to do for you?' The blind man said to him, 'My teacher, let me see again.' Jesus said to him, 'Go; your faith has made you well.' Immediately he regained his sight and followed him on the way.

- The blind Bartimaeus knew what he wanted, He proclaimed his faith in Jesus as Son of David, asking for mercy and healing. His determination was evident in his shouting and continuing when others wanted him to be quiet. Lord, help me to acknowledge my blindness to your presence so that I may ask for what I need.
- Bartimaeus had energy in shouting for what he desired and when called he threw off his cloak and sprang up. May we have energy and enthusiasm in responding to Jesus' invitation and the freedom to follow him along the way.

Friday 31 May
The Visitation of the Blessed Virgin Mary
Luke 1:39–56

In those days Mary set out and went with haste to a Judean town in the hill country, where she entered the house of Zechariah and greeted Elizabeth. When Elizabeth heard Mary's greeting, the child leapt in her womb. And Elizabeth was filled with the Holy Spirit and exclaimed with a loud cry, 'Blessed are you among women, and blessed is the fruit of your womb. And why has this happened to me, that the mother of my Lord comes to me? For as soon as I heard the sound of your greeting, the child in my womb leapt for joy. And blessed is she who believed that there would be a fulfilment of what was spoken to her by the Lord.'

And Mary said,
'My soul magnifies the Lord,
  and my spirit rejoices in God my Saviour,
for he has looked with favour on the lowliness of his servant.
  Surely, from now on all generations will call me blessed;
for the Mighty One has done great things for me,
  and holy is his name.
His mercy is for those who fear him
  from generation to generation.
He has shown strength with his arm;
  he has scattered the proud in the thoughts of their hearts.
He has brought down the powerful from their thrones,
  and lifted up the lowly;
he has filled the hungry with good things,
  and sent the rich away empty.
He has helped his servant Israel,
  in remembrance of his mercy,
according to the promise he made to our ancestors,
  to Abraham and to his descendants for ever.'

And Mary remained with her for about three months and then returned to her home.

- The visitation began in haste in the unsafe hill country of Judea. It was a significant journey of compassion by a young woman newly pregnant to an older woman who was in the later stages of her pregnancy. May our visitations not be fleeting moments in haste, but genuine expressions of love and concern.
- The conversation of Mary and Elizabeth was deep and engaging, being full of faith. They acknowledged what God had done for them. May our conversations draw attention to the wonders God has done and continues to do in our lives and world.

Saturday 1 June
Mark 11:27–33

Again they came to Jerusalem. As he was walking in the temple, the chief priests, the scribes, and the elders came to him and said, 'By what authority are you doing these things? Who gave you this authority to do them?' Jesus said to them, 'I will ask you one question; answer me, and I will tell you by what authority I do these things. Did the baptism of John come from heaven, or was it of human origin? Answer me.' They argued with one another, 'If we say, "From heaven", he will say, "Why then did you not believe him?" But shall we say, "Of human origin"?' – they were afraid of the crowd, for all regarded John as truly a prophet. So they answered Jesus, 'We do not know.' And Jesus said to them, 'Neither will I tell you by what authority I am doing these things.'

- Jesus spoke and acted with authority, in contrast to the religious leaders (Mark 1:22). This authority was not of human origin, but given by the Father. Lord, you desire us to be authors in our own lives and to reveal your saving message.

- Those leaders questioned Jesus, but he turned it back on them. They had questions to answer but were afraid to do so because of how the crowd might react. May we have the courage to ask you good questions and have the freedom to accept the response.

The Ninth Week in Ordinary Time

2–8 June 2024

Something to think and pray about each day this week:

The Easter mystery continues every day in the Church. In the Eucharistic Prayer at each Mass we commemorate 'the death and resurrection of the Lord'. It can be good every now and then to look back in other seasons on some of the events, like the situation of the women who came to the tomb.

They were confused as they came there laden with the ointments – how would they get to the body of Jesus to show him this usual respect? Who would roll away the stone?

In the rising sun, it dawned on them that something very strange and unusual had happened. The stone was rolled away.

Soon they would see him. They would go ahead into Galilee; they would become the first proclaimers of the resurrection. But did they often remember their journey to the tomb?

The event reached into their ordinary lives. They probably realised that many stones in their lives had been rolled away.

The same is true for us. Think of the burdens we carry in our lives: the memories that stir pain, the grief that lasts, ill health, worries about family, bereavement and many other things. In the loving power of God, in sharing faith and difficulties with others, in the real hope that God is always near, our stones are rolled away. In love Jesus rolls away our stones.

A stone often has a crack and a little flower can grow through it. Through cracks in the stones of our lives, light and healing break through. The women at the tomb realised that morning that love was around them. It just took a while to believe. It can be the same for us.

Donal Neary SJ, *The Sacred Heart Messenger*, July 2022

The Presence of God
As I sit here, the beating of my heart,
the ebb and flow of my breathing, the movements of my mind
are all signs of God's ongoing creation of me.
I pause for a moment and become aware
of this presence of God within me.

Freedom
I will ask God's help to be free from my own preoccupations, to be open to God in this time of prayer, to come to know, love and serve God more.

Consciousness
At this moment, Lord, I turn my thoughts to you.
I will leave aside my chores and preoccupations.
I will take rest and refreshment in your presence.

The Word
Now I turn to the Scripture set out for me this day. I read slowly over the words and see if any sentence or sentiment appeals to me. *(Please turn to the Scripture on the following pages. Inspiration points are there, should you need them. When you are ready, return here to continue.)*

Conversation
Begin to talk to Jesus about the Scripture you have just read. What part of it strikes a chord in you? Perhaps the words of a friend – or some story you have heard recently – will slowly rise to the surface of your consciousness. If so, does the story throw light on what the Scripture passage may be saying to you?

Conclusion
Glory be to the Father, and to the Son, and to the Holy Spirit,
As it was in the beginning, is now and ever shall be,
World without end. Amen.

Sunday 2 June
The Most Holy Body and Blood of Christ
Mark 14:12–16.22–26

On the first day of Unleavened Bread, when the Passover lamb is sacrificed, his disciples said to him, 'Where do you want us to go and make the preparations for you to eat the Passover?' So he sent two of his disciples, saying to them, 'Go into the city, and a man carrying a jar of water will meet you; follow him, and wherever he enters, say to the owner of the house, "The Teacher asks, Where is my guest room where I may eat the Passover with my disciples?" He will show you a large room upstairs, furnished and ready. Make preparations for us there.' So the disciples set out and went to the city, and found everything as he had told them; and they prepared the Passover meal.

While they were eating, he took a loaf of bread, and after blessing it he broke it, gave it to them, and said, 'Take; this is my body.' Then he took a cup, and after giving thanks he gave it to them, and all of them drank from it. He said to them, 'This is my blood of the covenant, which is poured out for many. Truly I tell you, I will never again drink of the fruit of the vine until that day when I drink it new in the kingdom of God.'

When they had sung the hymn, they went out to the Mount of Olives.

- Jesus was initiating a new Passover and covenant. He pledged fidelity to his followers and promised to nourish them in living as his disciples. Lord, may we who share your table have the openness to be sent forth to be the bread of life to others.
- Jesus, you are the blessed one who was taken, broken and given. You invite us to share your table that we may be broken of our selfishness to be gift to others in your name. May we be good companions on the journey.

Monday 3 June
Mark 12:1–12

Then he began to speak to them in parables. 'A man planted a vineyard, put a fence around it, dug a pit for the wine press, and built a watch-tower;

then he leased it to tenants and went to another country. When the season came, he sent a slave to the tenants to collect from them his share of the produce of the vineyard. But they seized him, and beat him, and sent him away empty-handed. And again he sent another slave to them; this one they beat over the head and insulted. Then he sent another, and that one they killed. And so it was with many others; some they beat, and others they killed. He had still one other, a beloved son. Finally he sent him to them, saying, "They will respect my son." But those tenants said to one another, "This is the heir; come, let us kill him, and the inheritance will be ours." So they seized him, killed him, and threw him out of the vineyard. What then will the owner of the vineyard do? He will come and destroy the tenants and give the vineyard to others. Have you not read this scripture:

"The stone that the builders rejected
   has become the cornerstone;
this was the Lord's doing,
   and it is amazing in our eyes"?'

When they realised that he had told this parable against them, they wanted to arrest him, but they feared the crowd. So they left him and went away.

- Jesus taught in parables, giving illustrations from the life and experience of his listeners. Careful preparation of the vineyard contrasted with the selfishness of the tenants. Forgive us for the misuse of your gifts where we have sought our own comfort, not your glory.

- Jesus, the Son of the eternal Father, was not respected. His death was a means of getting him out of the way and allowing self-interest to prevail. Lord, bring us beyond short-term gain, that we may respect you as the one who offers us an eternal inheritance.

Tuesday 4 June
Mark 12:13–17
Then they sent to him some Pharisees and some Herodians to trap him in what he said. And they came and said to him, 'Teacher, we know that you are sincere, and show deference to no one; for you do not

regard people with partiality, but teach the way of God in accordance with truth. Is it lawful to pay taxes to the emperor, or not? Should we pay them, or should we not?' But knowing their hypocrisy, he said to them, 'Why are you putting me to the test? Bring me a denarius and let me see it.' And they brought one. Then he said to them, 'Whose head is this, and whose title?' They answered, 'The emperor's.' Jesus said to them, 'Give to the emperor the things that are the emperor's, and to God the things that are God's.' And they were utterly amazed at him.

- This was another attempt to trap Jesus with platitudes of sincerity and respect. As the nice person he should do what was popular. We pray for clarity and courage to face the deeper questions that lead to more honest living.
- There is much discussion of the relationship between Church and state in our time. Jesus' kingdom was of a different kind, so other criteria were needed to understand it. Lord, may we have the insight to follow you as good citizens who stand for the truth.

Wednesday 5 June
Mark 12:18–27
Some Sadducees, who say there is no resurrection, came to him and asked him a question, saying, 'Teacher, Moses wrote for us that if a man's brother dies, leaving a wife but no child, the man shall marry the widow and raise up children for his brother. There were seven brothers; the first married and, when he died, left no children; and the second married her and died, leaving no children; and the third likewise; none of the seven left children. Last of all the woman herself died. In the resurrection whose wife will she be? For the seven had married her.'

Jesus said to them, 'Is not this the reason you are wrong, that you know neither the scriptures nor the power of God? For when they rise from the dead, they neither marry nor are given in marriage, but are like angels in heaven. And as for the dead being raised, have you not read in the book of Moses, in the story about the bush, how God said to him, "I am the God of Abraham, the God of Isaac, and the God of Jacob"? He is God not of the dead, but of the living; you are quite wrong.'

- The Sadducees were familiar with the Levirate law about marrying a brother's widow (Deuteronomy 25:5–10). Jesus indicated that they were asking the wrong question in their earthbound approach. May we have your vision, Lord, and ask the further question that leads to the fullness of life.
- Jesus, as the Son of the living God, revealed the mystery of God, as occurred for Moses at the burning bush (Exodus 3). Lord, you spoke of life that is eternal. Help us to see this life as a preparation for it.

Thursday 6 June
Mark 12:28–34

One of the scribes came near and heard them disputing with one another, and seeing that he answered them well, he asked him, 'Which commandment is the first of all?' Jesus answered, 'The first is, "Hear, O Israel: the Lord our God, the Lord is one; you shall love the Lord your God with all your heart, and with all your soul, and with all your mind, and with all your strength." The second is this, "You shall love your neighbour as yourself." There is no other commandment greater than these.' Then the scribe said to him, 'You are right, Teacher; you have truly said that "he is one, and besides him there is no other"; and "to love him with all the heart, and with all the understanding, and with all the strength", and "to love one's neighbour as oneself", – this is much more important than all whole burnt-offerings and sacrifices.' When Jesus saw that he answered wisely, he said to him, 'You are not far from the kingdom of God.' After that no one dared to ask him any question.

- A scribe, who knew the law, was questioning Jesus about it. Why? Jesus responded, indicating what was important in life and in relationship with God and others. May we have the openness to hear the message afresh and put it into practice in our lives.
- The Kingdom of God is one of life that brings justice and harmony. A healthy self-love, love of God and others is at the heart of this. Lord, help us to appreciate that true worship in love is more than offering external gifts and sacrifices.

Friday 7 June
The Most Sacred Heart of Jesus
John 19:31–37

Since it was the day of Preparation, the Jews did not want the bodies left on the cross during the sabbath, especially because that sabbath was a day of great solemnity. So they asked Pilate to have the legs of the crucified men broken and the bodies removed. Then the soldiers came and broke the legs of the first and of the other who had been crucified with him. But when they came to Jesus and saw that he was already dead, they did not break his legs. Instead, one of the soldiers pierced his side with a spear, and at once blood and water came out. (He who saw this has testified so that you also may believe. His testimony is true, and he knows that he tells the truth.) These things occurred so that the scripture might be fulfilled, 'None of his bones shall be broken.' And again another passage of scripture says, 'They will look on the one whom they have pierced.'

- Death seemed like an ending but it was the beginning of something radically new. The solemn setting of the sabbath served as a preparation for what Jesus was offering. May our hearts be in tune with his, so that we are a sign of hope to others.
- The heart is a symbol of love, of self-giving, of being for others. We recall Jesus' total self-giving for us as his loved ones. May we celebrate a day where passion and love engage with each other in a life-giving way.

Saturday 8 June
The Immaculate Heart of Mary
Luke 2:41–51

Now every year his parents went to Jerusalem for the festival of the Passover. And when he was twelve years old, they went up as usual for the festival. When the festival was ended and they started to return, the boy Jesus stayed behind in Jerusalem, but his parents did not know it. Assuming that he was in the group of travellers, they went a day's journey. Then they started to look for him among their relatives and friends. When they did not find him, they returned to

Jerusalem to search for him. After three days they found him in the temple, sitting among the teachers, listening to them and asking them questions. And all who heard him were amazed at his understanding and his answers. When his parents saw him they were astonished; and his mother said to him, 'Child, why have you treated us like this? Look, your father and I have been searching for you in great anxiety.' He said to them, 'Why were you searching for me? Did you not know that I must be in my Father's house?' But they did not understand what he said to them. Then he went down with them and came to Nazareth, and was obedient to them. His mother treasured all these things in her heart.

- This feast is a parallel of yesterday, recalling Mary dedicating her life in love. Loving hearts are entwined in our salvation story as Mary made herself available for what God wanted. Her heart was pierced to see Jesus suffering. May we draw strength from her in serving her Son.

- Jesus was lost when Mary and Joseph went to Jerusalem for the Passover. They searched for him until they found him. Many people do not miss him and do not search for him. We pray that our searching for Jesus may enable us to continue the journey of life with him.

9–15 June 2024

Something to think and pray about each day this week:

A priest-colleague known for his loving, generous and kind nature would often quip that his going away on a break was a gift both to himself and to his parishioners. It was truly spiritual self-care and not a selfish act. I know his renewed spirit on his return was a blessing to all.

I have always been struck by people who say to me, 'How are you? Busy as usual, I suppose?' They seem to suggest that by being busy, my life has some meaning. In his autobiography, the writer, politician and political economist John Stuart Mill wrote movingly of his father. His dad recognise the gifted nature of his son and proceeded to cram his head with all sorts of knowledge, but he had no faith. So the father would not allow anything religious to become part of his son's education. You can almost feel the deep sense of loss when Mill wrote that his mind was stuffed with information, but his soul was starved. 'I was left at the commencement of the voyage [of life] with a well-equipped ship but no sail.'

Mill's experience was the reverse story of the early Irish monks, who set sail on small boats to spread the Gospel. In effect, they gave up their small vessel to the wind and sea, letting these elements fulfil God's will and decide their destination. In that way they converted Europe. Maybe we need to be less full of ourselves, lift up our sails and let God direct. He only asks us to 'come away' to a 'deserted place' (in life) all 'by ourselves' and finally 'rest awhile'. The prescription is still valid for our times as medicine for our souls.

Tom Cox, *The Sacred Heart Messenger*, August 2022

The Presence of God
At any time of the day or night we can call on Jesus. He is always waiting, listening for our call. What a wonderful blessing.No phone needed, no e-mails, just a whisper.

Freedom
If God were trying to tell me something, would I know?
If God were reassuring me or challenging me, would I notice?
I ask for the grace to be free of my own preoccupations
and open to what God may be saying to me.

Consciousness
Help me, Lord, become more conscious of your presence. Teach me to recognise your presence in others. Fill my heart with gratitude for the times your love has been shown to me through the care of others.

The Word
In this expectant state of mind, please turn to the text for the day with confidence. Believe that the Holy Spirit is present and may reveal whatever the passage has to say to you. Read reflectively, listening with a third ear to what may be going on in your heart. *(Please turn to the Scripture on the following pages. Inspiration points are there, should you need them. When you are ready, return here to continue.)*

Conversation
Conversation requires talking and listening.
As I talk to Jesus, may I also learn to pause and listen.
I picture the gentleness in his eyes and the love in his smile.
I can be totally honest with Jesus as I tell him my worries and cares.
I will open my heart to Jesus as I tell him my fears and doubts.
I will ask him to help me place myself fully in his care, knowing that he
    always desires good for me.

Conclusion
I thank God for these moments we have spent together and for any insights I have been given concerning the text.

Sunday 9 June
Tenth Sunday in Ordinary Time
Mark 3:20–35

And the crowd came together again, so that they could not even eat. When his family heard it, they went out to restrain him, for people were saying, 'He has gone out of his mind.' And the scribes who came down from Jerusalem said, 'He has Beelzebul, and by the ruler of the demons he casts out demons.' And he called them to him, and spoke to them in parables, 'How can Satan cast out Satan? If a kingdom is divided against itself, that kingdom cannot stand. And if a house is divided against itself, that house will not be able to stand. And if Satan has risen up against himself and is divided, he cannot stand, but his end has come. But no one can enter a strong man's house and plunder his property without first tying up the strong man; then indeed the house can be plundered.

'Truly I tell you, people will be forgiven for their sins and whatever blasphemies they utter; but whoever blasphemes against the Holy Spirit can never have forgiveness, but is guilty of an eternal sin' – for they had said, 'He has an unclean spirit.'

Then his mother and his brothers came; and standing outside, they sent to him and called him. A crowd was sitting around him; and they said to him, 'Your mother and your brothers and sisters are outside, asking for you.' And he replied, 'Who are my mother and my brothers?' And looking at those who sat around him, he said, 'Here are my mother and my brothers! Whoever does the will of God is my brother and sister and mother.'

- Jesus' family was concerned about him with his busy life. They thought he was misguided and wanted to restrain him. Lord, in our busy lives we can lose our way. Help us to find a balance and the way to you.
- There are no unforgiveable sins, but we can refuse to be open to or to ask for forgiveness. Lord, touch our stubborn hearts with your gentle spirit so that we can accept your gifts.

Monday 10 June
Matthew 5:1–12

When Jesus saw the crowds, he went up the mountain; and after he sat down, his disciples came to him. Then he began to speak, and taught them, saying:

'Blessed are the poor in spirit, for theirs is the kingdom of heaven.

'Blessed are those who mourn, for they will be comforted.

'Blessed are the meek, for they will inherit the earth.

'Blessed are those who hunger and thirst for righteousness, for they will be filled.

'Blessed are the merciful, for they will receive mercy.

'Blessed are the pure in heart, for they will see God.

'Blessed are the peacemakers, for they will be called children of God.

'Blessed are those who are persecuted for righteousness' sake, for theirs is the kingdom of heaven.

'Blessed are you when people revile you and persecute you and utter all kinds of evil against you falsely on my account. Rejoice and be glad, for your reward is great in heaven, for in the same way they persecuted the prophets who were before you.'

- In our day of mission statements we are helped by that of Jesus. Seated on a mountain, he declared what his kingdom was about. Lord, give us poverty of spirit that sets us free to embrace your way of justice, love and peace.

- Jesus' values contrast with those of multinational companies, which tend to pity those declared 'blessed'. May we turn to Jesus and be guided by him to true happiness, which comes in unexpected ways.

Tuesday 11 June
St Barnabas, Apostle
Matthew 5:13–16

Jesus said, 'You are the salt of the earth; but if salt has lost its taste, how can its saltiness be restored? It is no longer good for anything, but is thrown out and trampled under foot.

'You are the light of the world. A city built on a hill cannot be hidden. No one after lighting a lamp puts it under the bushel basket, but on the lampstand, and it gives light to all in the house. In the same way, let your light shine before others, so that they may see your good works and give glory to your Father in heaven.'

- Barnabas was a good man, filled with faith (Acts 11:24). He added flavour and taste to the message of Jesus which nourished life. We pray that we may we have a missionary spirit that enhances the lives of those we meet.
- With Paul, Barnabas brought the light of Christ to others. It served to open minds to the good news of Jesus. May our lives be inspired by him to let our light shine before others and give glory to the Father.

Wednesday 12 June
Matthew 5:17–19

Jesus said, 'Do not think that I have come to abolish the law or the prophets; I have come not to abolish but to fulfil. For truly I tell you, until heaven and earth pass away, not one letter, not one stroke of a letter, will pass from the law until all is accomplished. Therefore, whoever breaks one of the least of these commandments, and teaches others to do the same, will be called least in the kingdom of heaven; but whoever does them and teaches them will be called great in the kingdom of heaven.'

- Jesus was familiar with the commandments and the teaching of the prophets. He built on the past to open a new future. May we draw strength from this rich foundation to further the reign of God in our time.
- Jesus came to fulfil, to bring to a new place what was already present. He was the teacher who enriched his listeners with a message of hope. Lord, help us to proclaim your good news and teach your truth.

Thursday 13 June
Matthew 5:20–26

Jesus said, 'For I tell you, unless your righteousness exceeds that of the scribes and Pharisees, you will never enter the kingdom of heaven.

'You have heard that it was said to those of ancient times, "You shall not murder"; and "whoever murders shall be liable to judgement." But I say to you that if you are angry with a brother or sister, you will be liable to judgement; and if you insult a brother or sister, you will be liable to the council; and if you say, "You fool", you will be liable to the hell of fire. So when you are offering your gift at the altar, if you remember that your brother or sister has something against you, leave your gift there before the altar and go; first be reconciled to your brother or sister, and then come and offer your gift. Come to terms quickly with your accuser while you are on the way to court with him, or your accuser may hand you over to the judge, and the judge to the guard, and you will be thrown into prison. Truly I tell you, you will never get out until you have paid the last penny.'

- The scribes and Pharisees seemed preoccupied with externals in keeping the law. Jesus was focused on the interior, on converted hearts that would bring real change. We pray for a true sense of what is righteous as members of the kingdom.
- Human motivation is complex. Actions can be influenced by many factors from within. Jesus' desire is for harmony in self and with others. May we have the spirit of reconciliation with each other so that our gifts are offered in a true spirit.

Friday 14 June
Matthew 5:27–32

Jesus said, 'You have heard that it was said, "You shall not commit adultery." But I say to you that everyone who looks at a woman with lust has already committed adultery with her in his heart. If your right eye causes you to sin, tear it out and throw it away; it is better for you to lose one of your members than for your whole body to be thrown into hell. And if your right hand causes you to sin, cut it off and throw it away; it is better for you to lose one of your members than for your whole body to go into hell.

'It was also said, "Whoever divorces his wife, let him give her a certificate of divorce." But I say to you that anyone who divorces his wife, except on the ground of unchastity, causes her to commit adultery; and whoever marries a divorced woman commits adultery.'

- The old and the new are parts of life. 'You have heard that it was said … But I say to you …'. Jesus wants us to have freedom to love in action. We pray that we may be willing to sacrifice what is near and dear to us if it does not lead to the life Jesus desires.
- There were rules about adultery and divorce, as there are now. Much of what happens is symptomatic of internal struggles. Lord, give us compassion towards those who fail, knowing that we are like them in many ways.

Saturday 15 June
Matthew 5:33–37
Jesus said, 'Again, you have heard that it was said to those of ancient times, "You shall not swear falsely, but carry out the vows you have made to the Lord." But I say to you, Do not swear at all, either by heaven, for it is the throne of God, or by the earth, for it is his footstool, or by Jerusalem, for it is the city of the great King. And do not swear by your head, for you cannot make one hair white or black. Let your word be "Yes, Yes" or "No, No"; anything more than this comes from the evil one.'

- The rules of old stated clearly what harmonised with right living. Swearing falsely remains a hazard in our society. May we honour our vows and promises as part of our commitment to the Lord.
- Jesus was against needless swearing. It distracted from the truth and what was important. May our promises be a 'yes' to the glory of God, as was true of Jesus (2 Corinthians 1:20).

16–22 June 2024

Something to think and pray about each day this week:

Over the course of life, our imagery of God often changes as we grow. Perhaps, as children, we imagined God as an old man with a beard living up in heaven, high above the clouds. Later, we might imagine God as a friend or lover, as a comforting mother or, in more symbolic form, as in the image of the dove leading me, as an image of the Holy Spirit. Over my life, my image of myself may also shift, as I give up certain images of who I am in favour of others. Perhaps I imagine myself in terms of my career or as a wife or mother but later discover that my deepest identity in God is not reducible to any of those images. Likewise, when I forgive another, or experience forgiveness, my image of another may also expand beyond my earlier, narrower constructions.

Marina Berzins McCoy, *The Ignatian Guide to Forgiveness:*
Ten Steps to Healing

The Presence of God

Dear Jesus, as I call on you today, I realise that often I come asking for favours. Today I'd like just to be in your presence. Draw my heart in response to your love.

Freedom

It is so easy to get caught up with the trappings of wealth in this life. Grant, O Lord, that I may be free from greed and selfishness. Remind me that the best things in life are free: Love, laughter, caring and sharing.

Consciousness

How am I really feeling? Lighthearted? Heavy-hearted? I may be very much at peace, happy to be here. Equally, I may be frustrated, worried, or angry. I acknowledge how I really am. It is the real me whom the Lord loves.

The Word

Lord Jesus, you became human to communicate with me. You walked and worked on this earth. You endured the heat and struggled with the cold. All your time on this earth was spent in caring for humanity. You healed the sick, you raised the dead. Most important of all, you saved me from death. *(Please turn to the Scripture on the following pages. Inspiration points are there, should you need them. When you are ready, return here to continue.)*

Conversation

Do I notice myself reacting as I pray with the word of God? Do I feel challenged, comforted, angry? Imagining Jesus sitting or standing by me, I speak out my feelings, as one trusted friend to another.

Conclusion

Glory be to the Father, and to the Son, and to the Holy Spirit,
As it was in the beginning, is now and ever shall be,
World without end. Amen.

Sunday 16 June
Eleventh Sunday in Ordinary Time
Mark 4:26–34

He also said, 'The kingdom of God is as if someone would scatter seed on the ground, and would sleep and rise night and day, and the seed would sprout and grow, he does not know how. The earth produces of itself, first the stalk, then the head, then the full grain in the head. But when the grain is ripe, at once he goes in with his sickle, because the harvest has come.'

He also said, 'With what can we compare the kingdom of God, or what parable will we use for it? It is like a mustard seed, which, when sown upon the ground, is the smallest of all the seeds on earth; yet when it is sown it grows up and becomes the greatest of all shrubs, and puts forth large branches, so that the birds of the air can make nests in its shade.'

With many such parables he spoke the word to them, as they were able to hear it; he did not speak to them except in parables, but he explained everything in private to his disciples.

- There is development in life, where change can take place quietly. This can become evident over time. We pray that we may allow your word to mature in us, so that it bears fruit in your name.
- Small things and deeds in life can have much significance. What is little can lead to something greater. Lord, help us to make the small changes that bring freedom and more availability to others.

Monday 17 June
Matthew 5:38–42

Jesus said to them, 'You have heard that it was said, "An eye for an eye and a tooth for a tooth." But I say to you, Do not resist an evildoer. But if anyone strikes you on the right cheek, turn the other also; and if anyone wants to sue you and take your coat, give your cloak as well; and if anyone forces you to go one mile, go also the second mile. Give to everyone who begs from you, and do not refuse anyone who wants to borrow from you.'

- The scales of justice are to be balanced in courts of law, where the punishment is to fit the crime. Jesus' way is that of love, which follows different criteria. Lord, bring us beyond that system of justice to a spirit of compassion.
- Justice looks for equality, so if I give you something, I have less and you have more. If I give in love, both parties are enriched. May we have the generosity to go beyond what is required, in imitation of Jesus who gave all for us.

Tuesday 18 June
Matthew 5:43–48

Jesus said, 'You have heard that it was said, "You shall love your neighbour and hate your enemy." But I say to you, Love your enemies and pray for those who persecute you, so that you may be children of your Father in heaven; for he makes his sun rise on the evil and on the good, and sends rain on the righteous and on the unrighteous. For if you love those who love you, what reward do you have? Do not even the tax-collectors do the same? And if you greet only your brothers and sisters, what more are you doing than others? Do not even the Gentiles do the same? Be perfect, therefore, as your heavenly Father is perfect.'

- All of us have an inner circle of family and friends who tend to get more attention. Jesus' family was inclusive, with space for all. May we have hearts that are open to welcome and to give without expecting a return.
- It is easy to categorise people and give them a label. So, we have good and bad, just and unjust, but you love all without condition. Lord, may we imitate you in having room in our hearts for all your children.

Wednesday 19 June
Matthew 6:1–6.16–18

Jesus said to them, 'Beware of practising your piety before others in order to be seen by them; for then you have no reward from your Father in heaven.

'So whenever you give alms, do not sound a trumpet before you, as the hypocrites do in the synagogues and in the streets, so that they may be praised by others. Truly I tell you, they have received their reward. But when you give alms, do not let your left hand know what your right hand is doing, so that your alms may be done in secret; and your Father who sees in secret will reward you.

'And whenever you pray, do not be like the hypocrites; for they love to stand and pray in the synagogues and at the street corners, so that they may be seen by others. Truly I tell you, they have received their reward. But whenever you pray, go into your room and shut the door and pray to your Father who is in secret; and your Father who sees in secret will reward you.

'And whenever you fast, do not look dismal, like the hypocrites, for they disfigure their faces so as to show others that they are fasting. Truly I tell you, they have received their reward. But when you fast, put oil on your head and wash your face, so that your fasting may be seen not by others but by your Father who is in secret; and your Father who sees in secret will reward you.'

- We are called to be holy and to live according to God's directives. Doing good is different from doing well, which is overly focused on self. May we live in a way that is centred on God's glory, not our own.

- Popularity and being regarded as good are prominent in life, but they can be sought and become too important. Losing one's good name can be very challenging. Lord, may our names be written in heaven and not just on some external structure (Luke 10:20).

Thursday 20 June
Matthew 6:7–15

Jesus said to his disciples, 'When you are praying, do not heap up empty phrases as the Gentiles do; for they think that they will be heard because of their many words. Do not be like them, for your Father knows what you need before you ask him.

'Pray then in this way:
Our Father in heaven,

hallowed be your name.
Your kingdom come.
Your will be done,
on earth as it is in heaven.
Give us this day our daily bread.
And forgive us our debts,
as we also have forgiven our debtors.
And do not bring us to the time of trial,
but rescue us from the evil one.

For if you forgive others their trespasses, your heavenly Father will also forgive you; but if you do not forgive others, neither will your Father forgive your trespasses.'

- Empty phrases and hollow words do not fit with prayer, which is centred on our relationship with God. May our words be sincere, trusting God and opening us to receive what God wants to give us.
- The Our Father is a summary of all prayer, speaking of our relationship with God and each other. We pray for the freedom to honour God and we ask for forgiveness for ourselves and each other as children of the same Father.

Friday 21 June
Matthew 6:19–23

Jesus said to them, 'Do not store up for yourselves treasures on earth, where moth and rust consume and where thieves break in and steal; but store up for yourselves treasures in heaven, where neither moth nor rust consumes and where thieves do not break in and steal. For where your treasure is, there your heart will be also.

'The eye is the lamp of the body. So, if your eye is healthy, your whole body will be full of light; but if your eye is unhealthy, your whole body will be full of darkness. If then the light in you is darkness, how great is the darkness!'

- It is a world of great inequality. Many struggle for survival while the rich accumulate more. How much is enough? We pray that we may stand for justice, with genuine care for those made poor by the system.

- What is in your treasure box? All of us have something that is priceless. External possessions are vulnerable. Lord, give us your light to know what is of lasting value, with hearts that are free to attain it.

Saturday 22 June
Matthew 6:24–34

Jesus said to them, 'No one can serve two masters; for a slave will either hate the one and love the other, or be devoted to the one and despise the other. You cannot serve God and wealth.

'Therefore I tell you, do not worry about your life, what you will eat or what you will drink, or about your body, what you will wear. Is not life more than food, and the body more than clothing? Look at the birds of the air; they neither sow nor reap nor gather into barns, and yet your heavenly Father feeds them. Are you not of more value than they? And can any of you by worrying add a single hour to your span of life? And why do you worry about clothing? Consider the lilies of the field, how they grow; they neither toil nor spin, yet I tell you, even Solomon in all his glory was not clothed like one of these. But if God so clothes the grass of the field, which is alive today and tomorrow is thrown into the oven, will he not much more clothe you – you of little faith? Therefore do not worry, saying, "What will we eat?" or "What will we drink?" or "What will we wear?" For it is the Gentiles who strive for all these things; and indeed your heavenly Father knows that you need all these things. But strive first for the kingdom of God and his righteousness, and all these things will be given to you as well.

'So do not worry about tomorrow, for tomorrow will bring worries of its own. Today's trouble is enough for today.'

- There are conflicting loyalties in life that can distract from what is of lasting value. We pray that we may be free to discern what is genuinely good so that we can serve the Lord more fully.
- Everyday concerns can dominate life. The immediate can have undue influence on decisions taken. May we have a deeper trust in God, who provides what is of enduring value.

The Twelfth Week in Ordinary Time

23–29 June 2024

Something to think and pray about each day this week:

In spiritual life one of the big traps is assuming that things will happen miraculously in a spectacular fashion, and that it will all happen in one dramatic, unrepeatable moment. Many of us think of St Paul being struck blind, falling off his horse and making a dramatic shift from Pharisee to believer in one moment. The problem with this approach is that it seems to limit God's action to special people, in special places and times, and makes faith inaccessible for the majority of people whose lives don't reflect this magic and drama. It often comes as a surprise to people to learn that there was a ten-year gap between Paul's fall and his becoming an apostle; it appears that he still had to go through the slow human process of learning and making sense of his experience with the help of other believers.

This patient, 'slow work of God' (Teilhard de Chardin) is a much more helpful and humanising way to look at faith, as it allows everyone to collaborate with the work of God in their lives. The Good News is that the Spirit dwells in each one of us and we are all pilgrims on a journey to God. The Spirit is continually at work in our lives and every experience is an opportunity for growth and for a deepening of life within us.

Finding God in the messy bits and pieces of our lives is enormously challenging … The challenge remains to believe that God is with us and, while not causing life's chaos and unpredictability, works powerfully to shape and mould us through those experiences.

Brendan McManus SJ & Jim Deeds, *Discover God Daily:
Seven Life-changing Moments from the Journey of Saint Ignatius*

The Presence of God

Dear Jesus, I come to you today longing for your presence. I desire to love you as you love me. May nothing ever separate me from you.

Freedom

Lord, grant me the grace to have freedom of the Spirit. Cleanse my heart and soul so that I may live joyously in your love.

Consciousness

Where am I with God? With others?
Do I have something to be grateful for? Then I give thanks.
Is there something I am sorry for? Then I ask forgiveness.

The Word

The word of God comes down to us through the Scriptures. May the Holy Spirit enlighten my mind and my heart to respond to the Gospel teachings. *(Please turn to the Scripture on the following pages. Inspiration points are there, should you need them. When you are ready, return here to continue.)*

Conversation

How has God's word moved me? Has it left me cold?
Has it consoled me or moved me to act in a new way?
I imagine Jesus standing or sitting beside me;
I turn and share my feelings with him.

Conclusion

I thank God for these moments we have spent together and for any insights I have been given concerning the text.

Sunday 23 June
Twelfth Sunday in Ordinary Time
Mark 4:35–41

On that day, when evening had come, he said to them, 'Let us go across to the other side.' And leaving the crowd behind, they took him with them in the boat, just as he was. Other boats were with him. A great gale arose, and the waves beat into the boat, so that the boat was already being swamped. But he was in the stern, asleep on the cushion; and they woke him up and said to him, 'Teacher, do you not care that we are perishing?' He woke up and rebuked the wind, and said to the sea, 'Peace! Be still!' Then the wind ceased, and there was a dead calm. He said to them, 'Why are you afraid? Have you still no faith?' And they were filled with great awe and said to one another, 'Who then is this, that even the wind and the sea obey him?'

- In crossing the seas of life, we encounter storms that can arise in surprising ways. Lord, may we turn to you for guidance and help at those times and not rely solely on our own resources.
- Jesus' message was one of peace and calm. May we wake up from sleep and realise the Lord is present, guaranteeing safety on our journey.

Monday 24 June
The Nativity of John the Baptist
Luke 1:57–66.80

Now the time came for Elizabeth to give birth, and she bore a son. Her neighbours and relatives heard that the Lord had shown his great mercy to her, and they rejoiced with her.

On the eighth day they came to circumcise the child, and they were going to name him Zechariah after his father. But his mother said, 'No; he is to be called John.' They said to her, 'None of your relatives has this name.' Then they began motioning to his father to find out what name he wanted to give him. He asked for a writing-tablet and wrote, 'His name is John.' And all of them were amazed. Immediately his mouth was opened and his tongue freed, and he began to speak, praising God. Fear came over all their neighbours, and all these things were talked about throughout the entire hill country of Judea. All who heard them pondered them and said, 'What then will this child become?' For, indeed, the hand of the Lord was with him.

The child grew and became strong in spirit, and he was in the wilderness until the day he appeared publicly to Israel.

- John the Baptist's birth was a source of great joy for Elizabeth, Zechariah, his neighbours and relatives. May we rejoice in his birth as the dawn of a new era and pray that we may be voices to announce the presence of the eternal Word.
- Elizabeth indicated that his name was to be John, the name given by the angel. Zechariah was given a writing tablet to affirm this. We pray that our tongues may be loosened to proclaim the wonders God has done for us.

Tuesday 25 June
Matthew 7:6.12–14
Jesus said to them, 'Do not give what is holy to dogs; and do not throw your pearls before swine, or they will trample them under foot and turn and maul you.

'In everything do to others as you would have them do to you; for this is the law and the prophets.

'Enter through the narrow gate; for the gate is wide and the road is easy that leads to destruction, and there are many who take it. For the gate is narrow and the road is hard that leads to life, and there are few who find it.'

- Jesus is the pearl of great price in a world that seems more concerned with pearls of cut price. Lord, give us a fuller appreciation of your true riches so that we can set our hearts on them.
- The Lord came to bring salvation. May we have trust to receive it as a gift promised by the Lord to us.

Wednesday 26 June
Matthew 7:15–20
Jesus said, 'Beware of false prophets, who come to you in sheep's clothing but inwardly are ravenous wolves. You will know them by

their fruits. Are grapes gathered from thorns, or figs from thistles? In the same way, every good tree bears good fruit, but the bad tree bears bad fruit. A good tree cannot bear bad fruit, nor can a bad tree bear good fruit. Every tree that does not bear good fruit is cut down and thrown into the fire. Thus you will know them by their fruits.'

- There have always been more false prophets than true ones, so we need to know if they are authentic (Deuteronomy 18:22). We pray for the wisdom to know and be guided by prophets who proclaim the truth of God's ways.

Thursday 27 June
Matthew 7:21–29

Jesus said, 'Not everyone who says to me, "Lord, Lord", will enter the kingdom of heaven, but only one who does the will of my Father in heaven. On that day many will say to me, "Lord, Lord, did we not prophesy in your name, and cast out demons in your name, and do many deeds of power in your name?" Then I will declare to them, "I never knew you; go away from me, you evildoers."

'Everyone then who hears these words of mine and acts on them will be like a wise man who built his house on rock. The rain fell, the floods came, and the winds blew and beat on that house, but it did not fall, because it had been founded on rock. And everyone who hears these words of mine and does not act on them will be like a foolish man who built his house on sand. The rain fell, and the floods came, and the winds blew and beat against that house, and it fell – and great was its fall!'

Now when Jesus had finished saying these things, the crowds were astounded at his teaching, for he taught them as one having authority, and not as their scribes.

- Introductions are very revealing and may say more about the presenter than the guest. Lord, we pray that we may know you better, in a personal way, so that our introduction is genuine.
- Jesus, you are the rock, the cornerstone. May we build on you for you speak with authority.

Friday 28 June
Matthew 8:1–4

When Jesus had come down from the mountain, great crowds followed him; and there was a leper who came to him and knelt before him, saying, 'Lord, if you choose, you can make me clean.' He stretched out his hand and touched him, saying, 'I do choose. Be made clean!' Immediately his leprosy was cleansed. Then Jesus said to him, 'See that you say nothing to anyone; but go, show yourself to the priest, and offer the gift that Moses commanded, as a testimony to them.'

- Jesus' focus moved from the crowd to the leper, whose condition isolated him. Lord, heal our leprous spots, the parts of our lives that isolate us from others.

Saturday 29 June
Ss Peter and Paul, Apostles
Matthew 16:13–19

Now when Jesus came into the district of Caesarea Philippi, he asked his disciples, 'Who do people say that the Son of Man is?' And they said, 'Some say John the Baptist, but others Elijah, and still others Jeremiah or one of the prophets.' He said to them, 'But who do you say that I am?' Simon Peter answered, 'You are the Messiah, the Son of the living God.' And Jesus answered him, 'Blessed are you, Simon son of Jonah! For flesh and blood has not revealed this to you, but my Father in heaven. And I tell you, you are Peter, and on this rock I will build my church, and the gates of Hades will not prevail against it. I will give you the keys of the kingdom of heaven, and whatever you bind on earth will be bound in heaven, and whatever you loose on earth will be loosed in heaven.'

- Peter was flawed and struggled to follow. Lord, you have called us. May we, the frail disciples of this time, be more open to your working through us.
- Paul, like Peter, had a chequered story, moving from persecutor to ardent believer. Like them, we are called into relationship for service. Lord, may we who have received your revelation be apostles who continue your mission of announcing good news.

30 June–6 July 2024

Something to think and pray about each day this week:

Every so often, we catch a glimpse of the 'something more' that God has in store for us. These fleeting experiences are to be treasured: the birth of my first child, falling in love, a sense of 'being held' by God's presence. Such experiences may help us approach the Transfiguration. Like all transcendent experiences, it is fleeting, yet it etches a memory and leaves a longing. What should we do? Practise listening to him. Be not afraid. We cannot always be 'on the mountain', yet what happens on the heights can help us on the lowlands of the everyday.

Kieran J. O'Mahony OSA, *Hearers of the Word:*
Praying and Exploring the Readings for Lent and Holy Week

The Presence of God

Dear Jesus, today I call on you, but not to ask for anything. I'd like only to dwell in your presence. May my heart respond to your love.

Freedom

God my creator, you gave me life and the gift of freedom. Through your love I exist in this world. May I never take the gift of life for granted. May I always respect others' right to life.

Consciousness

I ask how I am today. Am I particularly tired, stressed or anxious? If any of these characteristics apply, can I try to let go of the concerns that disturb me?

The Word

The word of God comes down to us through the Scriptures. May the Holy Spirit enlighten my mind and my heart to respond to the Gospel teachings. *(Please turn to the Scripture on the following pages. Inspiration points are there, should you need them. When you are ready, return here to continue.)*

Conversation

I begin to talk with Jesus about the Scripture I have just read. What part of it strikes a chord in me? Perhaps the words of a friend – or some story I have heard recently – will rise to the surface in my consciousness. If so, does the story throw light on what the Scripture passage may be saying to me?

Conclusion

Glory be to the Father, and to the Son, and to the Holy Spirit,
As it was in the beginning, is now and ever shall be,
World without end. Amen.

Sunday 30 June
Thirteenth Sunday in Ordinary Time
Mark 5:21–43

When Jesus had crossed again in the boat to the other side, a great crowd gathered round him; and he was by the lake. Then one of the leaders of the synagogue named Jairus came and, when he saw him, fell at his feet and begged him repeatedly, 'My little daughter is at the point of death. Come and lay your hands on her, so that she may be made well, and live.' So he went with him.

And a large crowd followed him and pressed in on him. Now there was a woman who had been suffering from haemorrhages for twelve years. She had endured much under many physicians, and had spent all that she had; and she was no better, but rather grew worse. She had heard about Jesus, and came up behind him in the crowd and touched his cloak, for she said, 'If I but touch his clothes, I will be made well.' Immediately her haemorrhage stopped; and she felt in her body that she was healed of her disease. Immediately aware that power had gone forth from him, Jesus turned about in the crowd and said, 'Who touched my clothes?' And his disciples said to him, 'You see the crowd pressing in on you; how can you say, "Who touched me?"' He looked all round to see who had done it. But the woman, knowing what had happened to her, came in fear and trembling, fell down before him, and told him the whole truth. He said to her, 'Daughter, your faith has made you well; go in peace, and be healed of your disease.'

While he was still speaking, some people came from the leader's house to say, 'Your daughter is dead. Why trouble the teacher any further?' But overhearing what they said, Jesus said to the leader of the synagogue, 'Do not fear, only believe.' He allowed no one to follow him except Peter, James, and John, the brother of James. When they came to the house of the leader of the synagogue, he saw a commotion, people weeping and wailing loudly. When he had entered, he said to them, 'Why do you make a commotion and weep? The child is not dead but sleeping.' And they laughed at him. Then he put them all outside, and took the child's father and mother and those who were with him, and went in where the child was. He took her by the hand and said to her, 'Talitha cum', which means, 'Little girl, get up!' And immediately the girl got up and began to walk about (she was twelve years of age). At this they were overcome with amazement. He strictly ordered them that no one should know this, and told them to give her something to eat.

- Jairus, a leader in the synagogue, pleaded for the healing of his daughter, who was at the point of death. He had to wait before his request was granted. May we have the faith of Jairus to beg for what we desire and the patience to wait for a response.
- An unnamed woman was courageous in approaching Jesus from behind. She knew what she wanted and was willing to risk touching Jesus. May we have faith to act on what we want and refuse to be deterred by the crowd from doing so.

Monday 1 July
Matthew 8:18–22
Now when Jesus saw great crowds around him, he gave orders to go over to the other side. A scribe then approached and said, 'Teacher, I will follow you wherever you go.' And Jesus said to him, 'Foxes have holes, and birds of the air have nests; but the Son of Man has nowhere to lay his head.' Another of his disciples said to him, 'Lord, first let me go and bury my father.' But Jesus said to him, 'Follow me, and let the dead bury their own dead.'

- Following Jesus involves surprises. He reminds us of the rewards and costs of discipleship. May we have the love that sustains us, so that the cost is secondary.
- From the beginning, Jesus was a pilgrim in life. The infancy narratives involve much travelling, so it is not surprising to read later on that he had nowhere to lay his head. Lord, may we always remember that you are with us on our journey.

Tuesday 2 July
Matthew 8:23–27
And when he got into the boat, his disciples followed him. A gale arose on the lake, so great that the boat was being swamped by the waves;

but he was asleep. And they went and woke him up, saying, 'Lord, save us! We are perishing!' And he said to them, 'Why are you afraid, you of little faith?' Then he got up and rebuked the winds and the sea; and there was a dead calm. They were amazed, saying, 'What sort of man is this, that even the winds and the sea obey him?'

- Jesus was in the same boat as his disciples but his dispositions were different. They were concerned for themselves and their safety. May we trust Jesus to guide us through the challenges of life.
- The action of Jesus brought amazement to his disciples. He was the one to calm them in the storm. Lord, strengthen our faith so that our fears are diminished in travelling with you.

Wednesday 3 July
St Thomas, Apostle
John 20:24–29
But Thomas (who was called the Twin), one of the twelve, was not with them when Jesus came. So the other disciples told him, 'We have seen the Lord.' But he said to them, 'Unless I see the mark of the nails in his hands, and put my finger in the mark of the nails and my hand in his side, I will not believe.'

A week later his disciples were again in the house, and Thomas was with them. Although the doors were shut, Jesus came and stood among them and said, 'Peace be with you.' Then he said to Thomas, 'Put your finger here and see my hands. Reach out your hand and put it in my side. Do not doubt but believe.' Thomas answered him, 'My Lord and my God!' Jesus said to him, 'Have you believed because you have seen me? Blessed are those who have not seen and yet have come to believe.'

- Thomas was not there when Jesus came. With his enquiring mind, Thomas was searching and questioning. Lord, in our search for you, may we allow you to find us and assure us that you are always present.
- The disciples sought safety behind closed doors. In reality, their minds were closed to the message of the resurrection. May we trust the evidence Jesus provides to live the message that he is risen.

Thursday 4 July
Matthew 9:1–8
And after getting into a boat he crossed the water and came to his own town.

And just then some people were carrying a paralysed man lying on a bed. When Jesus saw their faith, he said to the paralytic, 'Take heart, son; your sins are forgiven.' Then some of the scribes said to themselves, 'This man is blaspheming.' But Jesus, perceiving their thoughts, said, 'Why do you think evil in your hearts? For which is easier, to say, "Your sins are forgiven", or to say, "Stand up and walk"? But so that you may know that the Son of Man has authority on earth to forgive sins' – he then said to the paralytic – 'Stand up, take your bed and go to your home.' And he stood up and went to his home. When the crowds saw it, they were filled with awe, and they glorified God, who had given such authority to human beings.

- Jesus went home. A paralysed man was brought to him. Jesus began with forgiveness of sins, which evoked a critical response from the scribes. Lord, there are times when we need others to carry us to you for inner healing.
- The external healing of the paralytic brought forth awe from the crowd, who glorified God, who had given such power to Jesus. We marvel at all the Lord did and pray that we may be set free from what paralyses us in glorifying God.

Friday 5 July
Matthew 9:9–13
As Jesus was walking along, he saw a man called Matthew sitting at the tax booth; and he said to him, 'Follow me.' And he got up and followed him.

And as he sat at dinner in the house, many tax-collectors and sinners came and were sitting with him and his disciples. When the Pharisees saw this, they said to his disciples, 'Why does your teacher eat with tax-collectors and sinners?' But when he heard this, he said, 'Those who are well have no need of a physician, but those who are sick. Go and learn what this means, "I desire mercy, not sacrifice." For I have come to call not the righteous but sinners.'

- Matthew was called by name from his tax booth. He was an unlikely choice as he was one of a group that was presumed to be dishonest. May we be inspired by the Lord's call and not be restricted by social criteria in following.
- Sharing table was done with family, friends and people of good reputation. Jesus went to dinner with Matthew and others, availing of the situation to teach. Lord, may we invite you to our homes to share table with us, though we are sinners.

Saturday 6 July
Matthew 9:14–17

Then the disciples of John came to him, saying, 'Why do we and the Pharisees fast often, but your disciples do not fast?' And Jesus said to them, 'The wedding-guests cannot mourn as long as the bridegroom is with them, can they? The days will come when the bridegroom is taken away from them, and then they will fast. No one sews a piece of unshrunk cloth on an old cloak, for the patch pulls away from the cloak, and a worse tear is made. Neither is new wine put into old wineskins; otherwise, the skins burst, and the wine is spilled, and the skins are destroyed; but new wine is put into fresh wineskins, and so both are preserved.'

- Jesus recognised the importance of fasting but indicated there was a time and place for it. We pray that we might have a good attitude and fast internally from what is divisive and critical.
- Jesus gave practical advice, drawing on the household image of sewing and patching. As friends of the bridegroom, may we recognise the value of the new and the old and make decisions that reflect what Jesus said.

7–13 July

Something to think and pray about each day this week:

In the Gospel parable of the sower (Luke 8:14–15), the seed of God's word is generously scattered everywhere, on rocky ground and thorny places as well as the rich soil. However, the Word of God only bears fruit, the parable concludes, when it is received by those with a 'noble and generous heart' who have 'taken the word to themselves and yield a harvest through their perseverance'.

I think of religion as the rich soil where faith takes root. It proposes a commitment to regular times for prayer and reflection and allowing thoughts and actions to be influenced by one's relationship with God. It involves familiarity with the beliefs, the symbols and the practices of religion. Its Catholic presentation emphasises the importance of belonging to the community of faith.

In the parable, the original Greek word for 'perseverance' is *hypomoné*. A word used many times in the New Testament, it is also translated as 'patience' or 'endurance'. A modern translation might be that fashionable term 'resilience'. It has been compared to a beautiful flower growing in a harsh environment. In other words, *hypomoné* is not fatalistic, just putting up with a tough situation; rather it takes charge of events, like a soldier going into battle. Pope Francis has referred to his grandmother Rosa, along with her generation, as persons who embodied the virtue. He told Fr Antonio Spadaro in an interview that 'she suffered much, also spiritually, yet she always went forward with courage.'

There is much to admire in the spiritual staying power of previous generations of Christians who cultivated their faith in an unassuming way, through their prayer and fidelity to religious practice. It gave them grace, consistency and a strength of character that many of our contemporaries would like to possess.

Gerard Condon, *The Sacred Heart Messenger*, June 2021

The Presence of God

Dear Lord, as I come to you today, fill my heart, my whole being, with the wonder of your presence. Help me remain receptive to you as I put aside the cares of this world. Fill my mind with your peace.

Freedom

Lord, grant me the grace to be free from the excesses of this life. Let me not get caught up with the desire for wealth. Keep my heart and mind free to love and serve you.

Consciousness

I exist in a web of relationships: links to nature, people, God. I trace out these links, giving thanks for the life that flows through them. Some links are twisted or broken; I may feel regret, anger, disappointment. I pray for the gift of acceptance and forgiveness.

The Word

God speaks to each of us individually. I listen attentively to hear what he is saying to me. Read the text a few times, then listen. *(Please turn to the Scripture on the following pages. Inspiration points are there, should you need them. When you are ready, return here to continue.)*

Conversation

Jesus, you speak to me through the words of the Gospels. May I respond to your call today. Teach me to recognise your hand at work in my daily living.

Conclusion

I thank God for these moments we have spent together and for any insights I have been given concerning the text.

Sunday 7 July
Fourteenth Sunday in Ordinary Time
Mark 6:1–6

He left that place and came to his home town, and his disciples followed him. On the sabbath he began to teach in the synagogue, and many who heard him were astounded. They said, 'Where did this man get all this? What is this wisdom that has been given to him? What deeds of power are being done by his hands! Is not this the carpenter, the son of Mary and brother of James and Joses and Judas and Simon, and are not his sisters here with us?' And they took offence at him. Then Jesus said to them, 'Prophets are not without honour, except in their home town, and among their own kin, and in their own house.' And he could do no deed of power there, except that he laid his hands on a few sick people and cured them. And he was amazed at their unbelief.

Then he went about among the villages teaching.

- Jesus taught in the synagogue on the sabbath in his hometown. There was surely a risk involved. His wisdom astounded some but others took offence. Give us the wisdom and courage to live our faith among our own, especially those who do not understand it.
- The carpenter's son became the preacher. His prophetic message challenged his listeners. Jesus was amazed at their lack of faith. May we be prophetic voices for Jesus among those who are hostile to the message.

Monday 8 July
Matthew 9:18–26

While he was saying these things to them, suddenly a leader of the synagogue came in and knelt before him, saying, 'My daughter has just died; but come and lay your hand on her, and she will live.' And Jesus got up and followed him, with his disciples. Then suddenly a woman who had been suffering from haemorrhages for twelve years came up behind him and touched the fringe of his cloak, for she said to herself, 'If I only touch his cloak, I will be made well.' Jesus turned, and seeing her he said, 'Take heart, daughter; your faith has made you well.' And instantly the woman was made well. When Jesus came to the leader's house and saw the flute-players and the crowd making a commotion, he said, 'Go away; for the girl is not dead but sleeping.' And they laughed at him. But when the crowd had been put outside, he went in and took her by the hand, and the girl got up. And the report of this spread throughout that district.

- Healing was a significant part of Jesus' ministry. People with various illnesses or difficulties came to him. A leader in the synagogue whose daughter had died believed Jesus could restore life. Lord, may we be open to your healing touch and to the new life you offer.
- A woman with an infirmity for twelve years took the initiative in touching Jesus' cloak to bring healing. He called her 'daughter' and praised her faith. May we have the faith to come to Jesus and to accept his healing of our brokenness.

Tuesday 9 July
Matthew 9:32–38
After they had gone away, a demoniac who was mute was brought to him. And when the demon had been cast out, the one who had been mute spoke; and the crowds were amazed and said, 'Never has anything like this been seen in Israel.' But the Pharisees said, 'By the ruler of the demons he casts out the demons.'

Then Jesus went about all the cities and villages, teaching in their synagogues, and proclaiming the good news of the kingdom, and curing every disease and every sickness. When he saw the crowds, he had compassion for them, because they were harassed and helpless, like sheep without a shepherd. Then he said to his disciples, 'The harvest is plentiful, but the labourers are few; therefore ask the Lord of the harvest to send out labourers into his harvest.'

- There were divided opinions on Jesus. At the healing of one who was mute, the crowds were amazed but the Pharisees were critical. Lord, may we have voices to declare that you are greater than the power of the demons.
- Jesus had compassion on the crowds who were harassed and helpless. In our world that is the situation of many who need leaders. May we be shepherds who reach out to them and encourage others to help in doing so.

Wednesday 10 July
Matthew 10:1–7

Then Jesus summoned his twelve disciples and gave them authority over unclean spirits, to cast them out, and to cure every disease and every sickness. These are the names of the twelve apostles: first, Simon, also known as Peter, and his brother Andrew; James son of Zebedee, and his brother John; Philip and Bartholomew; Thomas and Matthew the tax-collector; James son of Alphaeus, and Thaddaeus; Simon the Cananaean, and Judas Iscariot, the one who betrayed him.

These twelve Jesus sent out with the following instructions: 'Go nowhere among the Gentiles, and enter no town of the Samaritans, but go rather to the lost sheep of the house of Israel. As you go, proclaim the good news, "The kingdom of heaven has come near."'

- Twelve named apostles were summoned by Jesus and given authority to cure every disease and sickness. We are the unnamed disciples who are given the same mission. We pray that we may go forth with authority, knowing the Lord has called and sent us.
- The twelve were a varied group coming from different backgrounds, ways of life and talents, but they were the ones the Lord chose. As their successors, may we be guided by you, Lord, and courageously proclaim that the kingdom of heaven is near.

Thursday 11 July
Matthew 10:7–15

He said to his disciples, 'As you go, proclaim the good news, "The kingdom of heaven has come near." Cure the sick, raise the dead, cleanse the lepers, cast out demons. You received without payment; give without payment. Take no gold, or silver, or copper in your belts, no bag for your journey, or two tunics, or sandals, or a staff; for labourers deserve their food. Whatever town or village you enter, find out who in it is worthy, and stay there until you leave. As you enter the house, greet it. If the house is worthy, let your peace come upon it; but if it is not worthy, let your peace return to you. If anyone will not welcome you or listen to your words, shake off the dust from your feet as you leave that house or town. Truly I tell you, it will be more tolerable for the land of Sodom and Gomorrah on the day of judgement than for that town.'

- The disciples went to proclaim the good news that the kingdom was near. What was received without payment was to be shared in the same spirit. We pray that we may share freely what the Lord has given us in the true spirit of giftedness.
- The disciples were to travel lightly and to rely on the hospitality offered to them. They had a message of peace to offer. Lord, may we trust you to provide what we need in living out and sharing your good news.

Friday 12 July
Matthew 10:16–23
Jesus said to his disciples, 'See, I am sending you out like sheep into the midst of wolves; so be wise as serpents and innocent as doves. Beware of them, for they will hand you over to councils and flog you in their synagogues; and you will be dragged before governors and kings because of me, as a testimony to them and the Gentiles. When they hand you over, do not worry about how you are to speak or what you are to say; for what you are to say will be given to you at that time; for it is not you who speak, but the Spirit of your Father speaking through you. Brother will betray brother to death, and a father his child, and children will rise against parents and have them put to death; and you will be hated by all because of my name. But the one who endures to the end will be saved. When they persecute you in one town, flee to the next; for truly I tell you, you will not have gone through all the towns of Israel before the Son of Man comes.'

- Jesus reminded the disciples that acceptance was not guaranteed. There would be some rejection and suffering, as was his experience. We pray for the freedom and courage to go forth in Jesus' name, focused on the gift we are to share.
- In the midst of any difficulty, the call is to trust God regarding what to say, for what is needed will be given. Lord, strengthen us to accept rejection and betrayal, even by our own, knowing that your own people did not accept you (John 1:11).

Saturday 13 July
Matthew 10:24–33

Jesus said to them, 'A disciple is not above the teacher, nor a slave above the master; it is enough for the disciple to be like the teacher, and the slave like the master. If they have called the master of the house Beelzebul, how much more will they malign those of his household!

'So have no fear of them; for nothing is covered up that will not be uncovered, and nothing secret that will not become known. What I say to you in the dark, tell in the light; and what you hear whispered, proclaim from the housetops. Do not fear those who kill the body but cannot kill the soul; rather fear him who can destroy both soul and body in hell. Are not two sparrows sold for a penny? Yet not one of them will fall to the ground unperceived by your Father. And even the hairs of your head are all counted. So do not be afraid; you are of more value than many sparrows.

'Everyone therefore who acknowledges me before others, I also will acknowledge before my Father in heaven; but whoever denies me before others, I also will deny before my Father in heaven.'

- Being prophetic, like Jesus, is to risk rejection. 'A disciple is not above the teacher.' The way of Jesus could lead to misunderstanding. May we have the resilience to follow Jesus and to imitate him amid the challenges we face.
- Jesus reminds us that he is with us. We are valued by him and he provides what we need. We pray for the light that reveals the truth, knowing that God remains faithful to us.

14–20 July 2024

Something to think and pray about each day this week:

The one thing that I dislike about secularism is that it asks me to seek meaning and life in the secular world alone. I am asked to believe that 'society' itself has become the source of everything. Yet, more and more societies are falling apart as they face ever greater moral challenges. Secularism brings with it a growing interest in political and national identities as people try to chart new ways of belonging and new sources for the foundations of civil society without religion. Those who have a religious belief have to speak the language of sociology more and more just to be 'relevant'. Once your language changes you lose your power – in actual fact you give it away, particularly if it is the language of conviction.

The language of secularism is often associated with Nietzsche telling us that 'God is Dead'. However, in 1881 he wrote a note saying, 'the political madness at which I smile just as my contemporaries smile at the religious madness of earlier times, is above all secularisation, the belief in the world and the rejection of a world "beyond" and "behind".' Even the one who contributed to the evolution of secularism can see its limitations and its fanciful errors!

Whether you are deeply religious or secular there is room for wonder. I love the line from Patrick's Kavanagh's poem 'Raglan Road', where he invites you to walk along 'the enchanted way'. Maybe the nature of religious expression is changing – it might be moving away from its largely institutional identity into something more personal. Belief may have a greater element of choice rather than the heavy-handed impositions of the past. Enchantment invites people to acknowledge that science and religion are not opposing forces but are common hosts on the path towards enchantment.

Alan Hilliard, *Dipping into Life: 40 Reflections for a Fragile Faith*

The Presence of God
God is with me, but even more astounding, God is within me.
Let me dwell for a moment on God's life-giving presence
in my body, in my mind, in my heart,
as I sit here, right now.

Freedom
Lord, may I never take the gift of freedom for granted. You gave me
the great blessing of freedom of spirit. Fill my spirit with your peace
and joy.

Consciousness
I remind myself that I am in the presence of God, who is my strength
in times of weakness and my comforter in times of sorrow.

The Word
I take my time to read the word of God slowly, a few times, allowing
myself to dwell on anything that strikes me. *(Please turn to the Scripture on
the following pages. Inspiration points are there, should you need them. When you
are ready, return here to continue.)*

Conversation
Jesus, you always welcomed little children when you walked on this
earth. Teach me to have a childlike trust in you. Teach me to live in the
knowledge that you will never abandon me.

Conclusion
Glory be to the Father, and to the Son, and to the Holy Spirit,
As it was in the beginning, is now and ever shall be,
World without end. Amen.

Sunday 14 July
Fifteenth Sunday in Ordinary Time
Mark 6:7–13

He called the twelve and began to send them out two by two, and gave them authority over the unclean spirits. He ordered them to take nothing for their journey except a staff; no bread, no bag, no money in their belts; but to wear sandals and not to put on two tunics. He said to them, 'Wherever you enter a house, stay there until you leave the place. If any place will not welcome you and they refuse to hear you, as you leave, shake off the dust that is on your feet as a testimony against them.' So they went out and proclaimed that all should repent. They cast out many demons, and anointed with oil many who were sick and cured them.

- The twelve had a mission to accomplish, calling people to repentance. Lord, may we rely on you to give us what we need to continue your work on earth.
- Jesus ordered them to go forth without being weighed down by external possessions. We pray for the wisdom to reduce the amount of internal and external baggage that we carry with us.

Monday 15 July
Matthew 10:34–11:1

Jesus said to his disciples, 'Do not think that I have come to bring peace to the earth; I have not come to bring peace, but a sword.

For I have come to set a man against his father,
and a daughter against her mother,
and a daughter-in-law against her mother-in-law;
and one's foes will be members of one's own household.

Whoever loves father or mother more than me is not worthy of me; and whoever loves son or daughter more than me is not worthy of me; and whoever does not take up the cross and follow me is not worthy of me. Those who find their life will lose it, and those who lose their life for my sake will find it.

'Whoever welcomes you welcomes me, and whoever welcomes me welcomes the one who sent me. Whoever welcomes a prophet in the name of a prophet will receive a prophet's reward; and whoever welcomes a righteous person in the name of a righteous person will receive the reward of the righteous; and whoever gives even a cup of cold water to one of these little ones in the name of a disciple – truly I tell you, none of these will lose their reward.'

Now when Jesus had finished instructing his twelve disciples, he went on from there to teach and proclaim his message in their cities.

- Loving Jesus first will put all other relationships in their proper place. Welcoming the little ones we meet in Jesus' name will bring a true reward. Lord, we pray to see people through your eyes and serve them in your name.

Tuesday 16 July
Matthew 11:20–24

Then he began to reproach the cities in which most of his deeds of power had been done, because they did not repent. 'Woe to you, Chorazin! Woe to you, Bethsaida! For if the deeds of power done in you had been done in Tyre and Sidon, they would have repented long ago in sackcloth and ashes. But I tell you, on the day of judgement it will be more tolerable for Tyre and Sidon than for you. And you, Capernaum, will you be exalted to heaven?

No, you will be brought down to Hades.

For if the deeds of power done in you had been done in Sodom, it would have remained until this day. But I tell you that on the day of judgement it will be more tolerable for the land of Sodom than for you.'

- There were some who were unable to hear Jesus' message. They were like the cities of old that could not recognise the deeds of God. May we have a true spirit of repentance that opens us more fully to our need of the deeds of the Lord.
- God's gift continues to be available. It is offered freely but it needs our acceptance if it is to be fruitful. Lord, soften our hearts to receive your message and help us to be tolerant of those who find it difficult to do so.

Wednesday 17 July
Matthew 11:25–27

At that time Jesus said, 'I thank you, Father, Lord of heaven and earth, because you have hidden these things from the wise and the intelligent and have revealed them to infants; yes, Father, for such was your gracious will. All things have been handed over to me by my Father; and no one knows the Son except the Father, and no one knows the Father except the Son and anyone to whom the Son chooses to reveal him.'

- Intelligent people can be very rational and find it difficult to accept Jesus' teaching, which is of the heart. Give us a childlike spirit of trust so that we are more receptive to your words.

Thursday 18 July
Matthew 11:28–30

Jesus said, 'Come to me, all you that are weary and are carrying heavy burdens, and I will give you rest. Take my yoke upon you, and learn from me; for I am gentle and humble in heart, and you will find rest for your souls. For my yoke is easy, and my burden is light.'

- 'Come to me.' Our God continues to invite us into a relationship of love and trust. Life can become burdensome and weary. Lord, we pray to accept the rest you offer us and your promise to lighten the burdens we carry.

Friday 19 July
Matthew 12:1–8

At that time Jesus went through the cornfields on the sabbath; his disciples were hungry, and they began to pluck heads of grain and to eat. When the Pharisees saw it, they said to him, 'Look, your disciples are doing what is not lawful to do on the sabbath.' He said to them, 'Have you not read what David did when he and his companions were hungry? He entered the house of God and ate the bread of the Presence, which it was not lawful for him or his companions to eat, but only for the priests. Or have you not read in the law that on the sabbath the priests in the temple break the sabbath and yet are guiltless? I tell you, something greater than the temple is here. But if you had known what this means, "I desire mercy and not sacrifice", you would not have condemned the guiltless. For the Son of Man is lord of the sabbath.'

- Hungry disciples going through a cornfield availed of what was present. The Pharisees were preoccupied because it was the sabbath. Lord, you call us beyond external requirements to what is at the heart of life, in the spirit of the law.

Saturday 20 July
Matthew 12:14–21

But the Pharisees went out and conspired against him, how to destroy him. When Jesus became aware of this, he departed. Many crowds followed him, and he cured all of them, and he ordered them not to make him known. This was to fulfil what had been spoken through the prophet Isaiah:

'Here is my servant, whom I have chosen,
　　my beloved, with whom my soul is well pleased.
I will put my Spirit upon him,
　　and he will proclaim justice to the Gentiles.
He will not wrangle or cry aloud,
　　nor will anyone hear his voice in the streets.
He will not break a bruised reed
　　or quench a smouldering wick
until he brings justice to victory.
　　And in his name the Gentiles will hope.'

- Divided opinions of Jesus were evident again. The Pharisees went out and conspired against him, on how to destroy him, but 'many crowds followed him'. We pray for the clarity to believe and follow despite the hostility of this age.
- One of the servant songs of Isaiah describes Jesus and his mission. He was the suffering servant who offered hope to the Gentiles. As God's chosen on whom the Spirit rests, give us the resilience to follow amid the challenges we encounter.

21–27 July 2024

Something to think and pray about each day this week:

I slip on the proverbial banana skin and break my leg. Did God decide in advance that I should break my leg on that day? Did God arrange for someone to drop the banana skin on the footpath where I was walking? No, it was just an accident.

A plane crashes, five people survive, 200 die. Did God decide who should live and who should die? No, it was just an accident. Accidents and tragedies happen from time to time. It's just part of our human condition. They are neither planned not intended, not even by God.

We need to let go of the image of God as a person, who decides everything that happens. We live in a world of random, unintended events. Theologians tell us that God is 'three persons in one being', but we have no concept of what 'three persons in one being is like', for it is beyond our human imagination.

God is not a person, who controls all that happens in our world. God is love and love is God. God is present to all of us, all of the time, even in our suffering, like the parent who sits constantly by the bed of their terminally ill child, unable to prevent the child's suffering, but showering the child with all the love they have. Like the best parental love, God's love does not have favourites and is immense for all of us.

Like the sun shining through the clouds, sometimes we get a glimpse of God's love surrounding us, as when we experience the love and kindness of another human being. Human beings make visible the love of God. That is the responsibility that God has given to us. We are called to reveal the love of God by being the love of God to others.

Peter McVerry SJ, *The Sacred Heart Messenger*, October 2021

The Presence of God

God is with me, but more,
God is within me, giving me existence.
Let me dwell for a moment on God's life-giving presence
in my body, my mind, my heart,
and in the whole of my life.

Freedom

Lord, you created me to live in freedom. May your Holy Spirit guide
me to follow you freely. Instil in my heart a desire to know and love you
more each day.

Consciousness

In God's loving presence I unwind the past day,
starting from now and looking back, moment by moment.
I gather in all the goodness and light, in gratitude.
I attend to the shadows and what they say to me,
seeking healing, courage, forgiveness.

The Word

God speaks to each of us individually. I listen attentively to hear what
he is saying to me. Read the text a few times, then listen. *(Please turn to
the Scripture on the following pages. Inspiration points are there, should you need
them. When you are ready, return here to continue.)*

Conversation

Jesus, you always welcomed little children when you walked on this
earth. Teach me to have a childlike trust in you. Teach me to live in the
knowledge that you will never abandon me.

Conclusion

I thank God for these moments we have spent together and for any
insights I have been given concerning the text.

Sunday 21 July

Sixteenth Sunday in Ordinary Time
Mark 6:30–34

The apostles gathered around Jesus, and told him all that they had done and taught. He said to them, 'Come away to a deserted place all by yourselves and rest a while.' For many were coming and going, and they had no leisure even to eat. And they went away in the boat to a deserted place by themselves. Now many saw them going and recognised them, and they hurried there on foot from all the towns and arrived ahead of them. As he went ashore, he saw a great crowd; and he had compassion for them, because they were like sheep without a shepherd; and he began to teach them many things.

- It is a busy world, where many are stressed and need some rest and relaxation. Jesus invited the apostles to come on a short retreat. Lord, with the pace of life and many demands, may we have the wisdom to take quiet time to regain perspective.
- The planned retreat was interrupted by the crowd who hastened to find Jesus. He responded with compassion, seeing their situation. May we have a compassionate response when things do not work out for us as we planned.

Monday 22 July

John 20:1–2.11–18

Early on the first day of the week, while it was still dark, Mary Magdalene came to the tomb and saw that the stone had been removed from the tomb. So she ran and went to Simon Peter and the other disciple, the one whom Jesus loved, and said to them, 'They have taken the Lord out of the tomb, and we do not know where they have laid him.'

But Mary stood weeping outside the tomb. As she wept, she bent over to look into the tomb; and she saw two angels in white, sitting where the body of Jesus had been lying, one at the head and the other at the feet. They said to her, 'Woman, why are you weeping?' She said to them, 'They have taken away my Lord, and I do not know where they have laid him.' When she had said this, she turned round and saw Jesus standing there, but she did not know that it was Jesus. Jesus said to her, 'Woman, why are you weeping? For whom are you looking?' Supposing him to be the gardener, she said to him, 'Sir, if you have carried him away, tell me where you have laid him, and I will take him away.' Jesus said to her, 'Mary!' She turned and said to him in Hebrew, 'Rabbouni!' (which means Teacher). Jesus said to her, 'Do not hold on to me, because I have not yet ascended to the Father. But go to my brothers and say to them, "I am ascending to my Father and your Father, to my God and your God."' Mary Magdalene went and announced to the disciples, 'I have seen the Lord'; and she told them that he had said these things to her.

- Mary Magdalene tells us much about discipleship. She came to the tomb at first light, ran to tell the apostles what she found, returned and waited. We pray that we may share her enthusiasm in our searching for Jesus.
- Mary's waiting took an unexpected turn when she was called by name. She recognised the stranger as more than a gardener. Lord, bring us beyond our expectations to a fuller recognition of you as our risen Lord.

Tuesday 23 July
Matthew 12:46–50

While he was still speaking to the crowds, his mother and his brothers were standing outside, wanting to speak to him. Someone told him, 'Look, your mother and your brothers are standing outside, wanting to speak to you.' But to the one who had told him this, Jesus replied, 'Who is my mother, and who are my brothers?' And pointing to his disciples, he said, 'Here are my mother and my brothers! For whoever does the will of my Father in heaven is my brother and sister and mother.'

- We are members of families. Some cultures have a good sense of the extended family, with a clear sense of belonging. This invites us to reflect on where we are at home. Lord, your family was inclusive. May we feel at home with you as you do with us.
- God's will is the way to the fullness of life. This was of great significance in the life of Jesus, as it was for Mary. May we learn from their example and pray that God's will may be done on earth as it is in heaven.

Wednesday 24 July
Matthew 13:1–9

That same day Jesus went out of the house and sat beside the lake. Such great crowds gathered around him that he got into a boat and sat there, while the whole crowd stood on the beach. And he told them many things in parables, saying: 'Listen! A sower went out to sow. And as he sowed, some seeds fell on the path, and the birds came and ate them up. Other seeds fell on rocky ground, where they did not have much soil, and they sprang up quickly, since they had no depth of soil. But when the sun rose, they were scorched; and since they had no root, they withered away. Other seeds fell among thorns, and the thorns grew up and choked them. Other seeds fell on good soil and brought forth grain, some a hundredfold, some sixty, some thirty. Let anyone with ears listen!'

- Jesus spoke from the boat, while the crowd stood on the beach. Now many are at sea in their lives and cannot listen to Jesus who stands on a firm foundation. We pray for the wisdom to acknowledge our situation and the freedom to listen afresh to Jesus.
- Jesus' teaching gave rise to different responses. It is important to note that some seed did grow and there was a fruitful outcome. Lord, may your word enlighten and inspire us to bear fruit in your name.

Thursday 25 July
St James, Apostle
Matthew 20:20–28

Then the mother of the sons of Zebedee came to him with her sons, and kneeling before him, she asked a favour of him. And he said to her, 'What do you want?' She said to him, 'Declare that these two sons of mine will sit, one at your right hand and one at your left, in your kingdom.' But Jesus answered, 'You do not know what you are asking. Are you able to drink the cup that I am about to drink?' They said to him, 'We are able.' He said to them, 'You will indeed drink my cup, but to sit at my right hand and at my left, this is not mine to grant, but it is for those for whom it has been prepared by my Father.'

When the ten heard it, they were angry with the two brothers. But Jesus called them to him and said, 'You know that the rulers of the Gentiles lord it over them, and their great ones are tyrants over them. It will not be so among you; but whoever wishes to be great among you must be your servant, and whoever wishes to be first among you must be your slave; just as the Son of Man came not to be served but to serve, and to give his life a ransom for many.'

- James and John were ambitious, even if their mother presented their request. Having left their boat and occupation, they desired to secure their future. May we be honest with our ambitions so that they can be transformed into ambitions to do good in a Christ-like way (Philippians 2:3).
- For Jesus, true greatness was shown in service, as was evident from his life and teaching. May we be available to others, for it is in giving that we truly receive.

Friday 26 July
Matthew 13:18–23

'Hear then the parable of the sower. When anyone hears the word of the kingdom and does not understand it, the evil one comes and snatches away what is sown in the heart; this is what was sown on the path. As for what was sown on rocky ground, this is the one who hears the word and immediately receives it with joy; yet such a person has no root, but endures only for a while, and when trouble or persecution arises on account of the word, that person immediately falls away. As for what was sown among thorns, this is the one who hears the word, but the cares of the world and the lure of wealth choke the word, and it yields nothing. But as for what was sown on good soil, this is the one who hears the word and understands it, who indeed bears fruit and yields, in one case a hundredfold, in another sixty, and in another thirty.'

- Hearing and responding is an ongoing challenge in a world of conflicting voices. There are many temptations and distractions from living the message. May we have ears that listen and hearts that are engaged with the word so that we can respond with fidelity.

- This is one of the few parables Jesus explained. It speaks to the gift bearing fruit and the obstacles that can prevent it. We pray for help to live the message as our commitment to Jesus, the living word.

Saturday 27 July
Matthew 13:24–30

He put before them another parable: 'The kingdom of heaven may be compared to someone who sowed good seed in his field; but while everybody was asleep, an enemy came and sowed weeds among the wheat, and then went away. So when the plants came up and bore grain, then the weeds appeared as well. And the slaves of the householder came and said to him, "Master, did you not sow good seed in your field? Where, then, did these weeds come from?" He answered, "An enemy has done this." The slaves said to him, "Then do you want us to go and gather them?" But he replied, "No; for in gathering the weeds you would uproot the wheat along with them. Let both of them grow together until the harvest; and at harvest time I will tell the reapers, Collect the weeds first and bind them in bundles to be burned, but gather the wheat into my barn."'

- Something can begin well and then lose momentum and direction. Temptations can distract from the original good intention. Lord, help us to recognise the weeds that can infiltrate our lives and take away from the harvest you desire.
- Life involves wheat and weeds, good and bad, genuine intentions and distractions. Progress is not automatic or to be taken for granted. May we have an awareness of the different attractions so that with discerning hearts we are guided to the truth.

28 July–3 August 2024

Something to think and pray about each day this week:

One of my favourite gardens is an orchard in the suburbs of Dublin. There is a small summer house to relax in and enjoy the delights of the garden: the trees with their bending arms, the neatly cut grass and the sweet singing of the birds. The orchard is secluded. It is a haven of peace and sometimes feels like a piece of heaven. The orchard has an 'Olde Worlde' feeling about it. I can imagine running into a character from a Jane Austen novel there.

In the Bible there are several times when God or Jesus is referred to as being present in a garden. In the Old Testament, God was present in the Garden of Eden, where he walked with Adam and Eve. In the New Testament, Jesus suffered in the Garden of Gethsemane before his passion and death. After the resurrection, he was also mistaken for the gardener by Mary of Magdalene.

The garden is a great place to find God in an everyday way. It is strange to think of God as being interested in sowing flowers and vegetables, digging for worms, or just being close to the earth that is often the source of new life. Yet, God is a gardener! Sometimes he is the great 'sower' and at other times he is the great 'mower'. God tends to his garden, and we can find him in ours.

Deirdre M. Powell, *God in Every Day: A Whispered Prayer*

The Presence of God

I pause for a moment and think of the love and the grace that God showers on me. I am created in the image and likeness of God; I am God's dwelling place.

Freedom

I am free. When I look at these words in writing, they seem to create in me a feeling of awe. Yes, a wonderful feeling of freedom. Thank you, God.

Consciousness

In the presence of my loving Creator, I look honestly at my feelings over the past day: the highs, the lows, and the level ground. Can I see where the Lord has been present?

The Word

I read the word of God slowly, a few times over, and I listen to what God is saying to me. *(Please turn to the Scripture on the following pages. Inspiration points are there, should you need them. When you are ready, return here to continue.)*

Conversation

Remembering that I am still in God's presence,
I imagine Jesus standing or sitting beside me,
and I say whatever is on my mind, whatever is in my heart,
speaking as one friend to another.

Conclusion

Glory be to the Father, and to the Son, and to the Holy Spirit,
As it was in the beginning, is now and ever shall be,
World without end. Amen.

Sunday 28 July
Seventeenth Sunday in Ordinary Time
John 6:1–15

After this Jesus went to the other side of the Sea of Galilee, also called the Sea of Tiberias. A large crowd kept following him, because they saw the signs that he was doing for the sick. Jesus went up the mountain and sat down there with his disciples. Now the Passover, the festival of the Jews, was near. When he looked up and saw a large crowd coming towards him, Jesus said to Philip, 'Where are we to buy bread for these people to eat?' He said this to test him, for he himself knew what he was going to do. Philip answered him, 'Six months' wages would not buy enough bread for each of them to get a little.' One of his disciples, Andrew, Simon Peter's brother, said to him, 'There is a boy here who has five barley loaves and two fish. But what are they among so many people?' Jesus said, 'Make the people sit down.' Now there was a great deal of grass in the place; so they sat down, about five thousand in all. Then Jesus took the loaves, and when he had given thanks, he distributed them to those who were seated; so also the fish, as much as they wanted. When they were satisfied, he told his disciples, 'Gather up the fragments left over, so that nothing may be lost.' So they gathered them up, and from the fragments of the five barley loaves, left by those who had eaten, they filled twelve baskets. When the people saw the sign that he had done, they began to say, 'This is indeed the prophet who is to come into the world.'

When Jesus realised that they were about to come and take him by force to make him king, he withdrew again to the mountain by himself.

- The location, the setting and the occasion give us a framework to understand what Jesus was doing. A mountain, the Passover and the signs Jesus performed drew people to him. Lord, you call us to yourself and nourish us in surprising ways. Give us the ability to recognise the signs and to respond to you.

- Jesus was the prophet who taught and provided for the crowd. He used the little they had to give food, but his own food was to do the will of the Father who sent him (John 3:34). May we hunger for the food Jesus gives and remain focused on what he can do.

Monday 29 July
Ss Martha, Mary and Lazarus
John 11:19–27

And many of the Jews had come to Martha and Mary to console them about their brother. When Martha heard that Jesus was coming, she went and met him, while Mary stayed at home. Martha said to Jesus, 'Lord, if you had been here, my brother would not have died. But even now I know that God will give you whatever you ask of him.' Jesus said to her, 'Your brother will rise again.' Martha said to him, 'I know that he will rise again in the resurrection on the last day.' Jesus said to her, 'I am the resurrection and the life. Those who believe in me, even though they die, will live, and everyone who lives and believes in me will never die. Do you believe this?' She said to him, 'Yes, Lord, I believe that you are the Messiah, the Son of God, the one coming into the world.'

- Martha, Mary and Lazarus were friends of Jesus whom he could visit on his journeys (Luke 10:38–42). He welcomed their hospitality but called them onwards in faith. May we, as friends of the Lord, be open to his ongoing invitation to share table and grow in discipleship.
- Martha was seen as the active one who desired to serve Jesus. She was a woman of deep faith. We pray that her profession of faith may be ours as we say, 'Yes, Lord, I believe that you are the Messiah, the Son of God.'

Tuesday 30 July
Matthew 13:36–43

Then he left the crowds and went into the house. And his disciples approached him, saying, 'Explain to us the parable of the weeds of the field.' He answered, 'The one who sows the good seed is the Son of Man; the field is the world, and the good seed are the children of the kingdom; the weeds are the children of the evil one, and the enemy who sowed them is the devil; the harvest is the end of the age, and the reapers are angels. Just as the weeds are collected and burned up with fire, so will it be at the end of the age. The Son of Man will send his angels, and they will collect out of his kingdom all causes of sin and all evildoers, and they will throw them into the furnace of fire, where there will be weeping and gnashing of teeth. Then the righteous will shine like the sun in the kingdom of their Father. Let anyone with ears listen!'

- This is another parable that Jesus explained. Good and evil elements can co-exist in life. There are always weeds present but they do not have to dominate. Lord, help us to focus on the genuine gift, that we may bring forth a harvest in your name.

- There is an invitation to be patient with change and growth. All the weeds in life cannot be pulled up quickly and put into bundles to be burned. May we have the faith to know that there is a harvest time when the righteous shine in the kingdom of the Father.

Wednesday 31 July
St Ignatius of Loyola
Matthew 13:44–46
He said to his disciples, 'The kingdom of heaven is like treasure hidden in a field, which someone found and hid; then in his joy he goes and sells all that he has and buys that field.

'Again, the kingdom of heaven is like a merchant in search of fine pearls; on finding one pearl of great value, he went and sold all that he had and bought it.'

- Jesus gives a clear focus in two short parables of the treasure in the field and the pearl of great value. They invite us to reflect on his words: 'where your treasure is, there will your heart be also' (Matthew 6:21). May we search diligently in life for what is authentic and of value.

- There are three short words – 'go', 'sell' and 'buy' – but they are very challenging if we are to live them out. We pray for the wisdom to discern and the freedom to put the decision into action.

Thursday 1 August
Matthew 13:47–53
Jesus said to his disciples, 'Again, the kingdom of heaven is like a net that was thrown into the sea and caught fish of every kind; when it was

full, they drew it ashore, sat down, and put the good into baskets but threw out the bad. So it will be at the end of the age. The angels will come out and separate the evil from the righteous and throw them into the furnace of fire, where there will be weeping and gnashing of teeth.

'Have you understood all this?' They answered, 'Yes.' And he said to them, 'Therefore every scribe who has been trained for the kingdom of heaven is like the master of a household who brings out of his treasure what is new and what is old.' When Jesus had finished these parables, he left that place.

- In making choices in life, we are helped by knowing what is of lasting value. The decisions made tell much about the quality of life. Lord, help us to see what the nets gather and offer to us so that we can choose what is of quality and enriches life.
- The new in life can be given undue attention, as if all the old is bad. We need to see what is good in both. We pray for discerning hearts that can help us to choose what is better.

Friday 2 August
Matthew 13:54–58

He came to his home town and began to teach the people in their synagogue, so that they were astounded and said, 'Where did this man get this wisdom and these deeds of power? Is not this the carpenter's son? Is not his mother called Mary? And are not his brothers James and Joseph and Simon and Judas? And are not all his sisters with us? Where then did this man get all this?' And they took offence at him. But Jesus said to them, 'Prophets are not without honour except in their own country and in their own house.' And he did not do many deeds of power there, because of their unbelief.

- Expectations of self and others can be very influential in life and in relationships. They can reveal openness or prejudice, hopes or fears. Jesus did not meet expectations at the local level. We pray that we may clarify our expectations so that they are a source of hope and promise.
- Putting people into categories can offer some security. Where people come from, what they do and their family situation can be

used for good or ill. We pray that we may have the freedom to assess people on their merits and not on some preconceived category that is convenient.

Saturday 3 August
Matthew 14:1–12

At that time Herod the ruler heard reports about Jesus; and he said to his servants, 'This is John the Baptist; he has been raised from the dead, and for this reason these powers are at work in him.' For Herod had arrested John, bound him, and put him in prison on account of Herodias, his brother Philip's wife, because John had been telling him, 'It is not lawful for you to have her.' Though Herod wanted to put him to death, he feared the crowd, because they regarded him as a prophet. But when Herod's birthday came, the daughter of Herodias danced before the company, and she pleased Herod so much that he promised on oath to grant her whatever she might ask. Prompted by her mother, she said, 'Give me the head of John the Baptist here on a platter.' The king was grieved, yet out of regard for his oaths and for the guests, he commanded it to be given; he sent and had John beheaded in the prison. The head was brought on a platter and given to the girl, who brought it to her mother. His disciples came and took the body and buried it; then they went and told Jesus.

- This is a familiar story. John the Baptist was a prophet who evoked a variety of responses. He was put in prison for declaring that the union of Herod and Herodias unlawful. Jesus, you too suffered for declaring the truth, so please help us to live by your way with conviction.
- It is the role of the prophet to declare God's message and call people back from their errant ways. John the Baptist, like Jesus and the prophets of old, suffered for doing so. May we have the faith and wisdom to be prophetic voices amid the noisy parties of our time.

The Eighteenth Week in Ordinary Time

4–10 August 2024

Something to think and pray about each day this week:

As we walk the long time-line of Creation we find that the truths of Sacred Scripture are interwoven with those of contemporary science to enrich our understanding of our Common Home. God is author both of the book of Scriptures and the book of Nature. If you find God in small things you will be more able to find God on the macro-level. A feather, a leaf, a drop of water, a single breath – any tiny and passing thing can open a window onto the divine. The eighteenth-century botanist Linnaeus noted that 'Nature is most to be marvelled at in the smallest of creatures'. Pope Francis's landmark encyclical on the environment, *Laudato Si'*, 2015, says that Nature is 'a continuing revelation of the divine' (LS, 85). When you accept this fact the everyday world around you is transfigured and life becomes a song of gratitude.

But *Laudato Si'* carries a challenge too: 'If we approach nature without openness to awe and wonder, if we no longer speak the language of fraternity in our relationship with the world, our attitude will be that of ruthless exploiters. … But if we feel intimately united with all that exists, then care will well up spontaneously in us' (LS, 11).

Brian Grogan SJ, *Creation Walk:*
The Amazing Story of a Small Blue Planet

The Presence of God

I pause for a moment and think of the love and the grace that God showers on me. I am created in the image and likeness of God; I am God's dwelling place.

Freedom

Lord, you granted me the great gift of freedom. In these times, O Lord, grant that I may be free from any form of racism or intolerance. Remind me that we are all equal in your loving eyes.

Consciousness

Knowing that God loves me unconditionally, I can afford to be honest about how I am.
How has the day been, and how do I feel now? I share my feelings openly with the Lord.

The Word

I take my time to read the word of God slowly, a few times, allowing myself to dwell on anything that strikes me. *(Please turn to the Scripture on the following pages. Inspiration points are there, should you need them. When you are ready, return here to continue.)*

Conversation

Sometimes I wonder what I might say if I were to meet you in person, Lord. I think I might say, 'Thank you', because you are always there for me.

Conclusion

I thank God for these moments we have spent together and for any insights I have been given concerning the text.

Sunday 4 August
Eighteenth Sunday in Ordinary Time
John 6:24–35

So when the crowd saw that neither Jesus nor his disciples were there, they themselves got into the boats and went to Capernaum looking for Jesus.

When they found him on the other side of the lake, they said to him, 'Rabbi, when did you come here?' Jesus answered them, 'Very truly, I tell you, you are looking for me, not because you saw signs, but because you ate your fill of the loaves. Do not work for the food that perishes, but for the food that endures for eternal life, which the Son of Man will give you. For it is on him that God the Father has set his seal.' Then they said to him, 'What must we do to perform the works of God?' Jesus answered them, 'This is the work of God, that you believe in him whom he has sent.' So they said to him, 'What sign are you going to give us then, so that we may see it and believe you? What work are you performing? Our ancestors ate the manna in the wilderness; as it is written, "He gave them bread from heaven to eat."' Then Jesus said to them, 'Very truly, I tell you, it was not Moses who gave you the bread from heaven, but it is my Father who gives you the true bread from heaven. For the bread of God is that which comes down from heaven and gives life to the world.' They said to him, 'Sir, give us this bread always.'

Jesus said to them, 'I am the bread of life. Whoever comes to me will never be hungry, and whoever believes in me will never be thirsty.'

- Capernaum and the lake were significant places in the ministry of Jesus. He taught and drew people to himself in that area and offered many signs. Lord, may we have the ability to interpret the signs and live by the deeper truth of who you are.

Monday 5 August
Matthew 14:13–21

Now when Jesus heard this, he withdrew from there in a boat to a deserted place by himself. But when the crowds heard it, they followed him on foot from the towns. When he went ashore, he saw a great crowd; and he had compassion for them and cured their sick. When it was evening, the disciples came to him and said, 'This is a deserted place, and the hour is now late; send the crowds away so that they may go into the villages and buy food for themselves.' Jesus said to them, 'They need not go away; you give them something to eat.' They replied, 'We have nothing here but five loaves and two fish.' And he said, 'Bring them here to me.' Then he ordered the crowds to sit down on the grass. Taking the five loaves and the two fish, he looked up to heaven, and blessed and broke the loaves, and gave them to the disciples, and the disciples gave them to the crowds. And all ate and were filled; and they took up what was left over of the broken pieces, twelve baskets full. And those who ate were about five thousand men, besides women and children.

- The crowds were attracted to Jesus, who found it difficult to find a deserted place for himself. Crossing the lake in a boat was not sufficient as a great crowd met him on arrival. Lord, we find it difficult to get away in our busy lives. We ask for compassion for ourselves and for others.

- Jesus engaged his disciples in finding what food was available, in distributing it and collecting what was left over. May we help the Lord in finding food for the hungry and sharing it with them.

Tuesday 6 August
The Transfiguration of the Lord
Mark 9:2–10

Six days later, Jesus took with him Peter and James and John, and led them up a high mountain apart, by themselves. And he was transfigured before them, and his clothes became dazzling white, such as no one on earth could bleach them. And there appeared to them Elijah with Moses, who were talking with Jesus. Then Peter said to Jesus, 'Rabbi, it is good for us to be here; let us make three dwellings, one for you, one for Moses, and one for Elijah.' He did not know what to say, for they were terrified. Then a cloud overshadowed them, and from the cloud there came a voice, 'This is my Son, the Beloved; listen to him!' Suddenly when they looked around, they saw no one with them any more, but only Jesus.

As they were coming down the mountain, he ordered them to tell no one about what they had seen, until after the Son of Man had risen from the dead. So they kept the matter to themselves, questioning what this rising from the dead could mean.

- Mountains were seen as places to meet God. Jesus took the inner circle of Peter, James and John up a high mountain. There, something of Jesus' glory was revealed to them. May we take time to get away from the crowd to go to a meeting place with the Lord.

Wednesday 7 August
Matthew 15:21–28

Jesus left that place and went away to the district of Tyre and Sidon. Just then a Canaanite woman from that region came out and started shouting, 'Have mercy on me, Lord, Son of David; my daughter is tormented by a demon.' But he did not answer her at all. And his disciples came and urged him, saying, 'Send her away, for she keeps shouting after us.' He answered, 'I was sent only to the lost sheep of the house of Israel.' But she came and knelt before him, saying, 'Lord, help me.' He answered, 'It is not fair to take the children's food and throw it to the dogs.' She said, 'Yes, Lord, yet even the dogs eat the crumbs that fall from their masters' table.' Then Jesus answered her, 'Woman, great is your faith! Let it be done for you as you wish.' And her daughter was healed instantly.

- The woman from an outside territory approached Jesus. She was an inconvenience to the disciples as she kept shouting for what she wanted. Lord, give us ears to listen to the calls of the outsiders who ask for our attention and help.
- We are the lost sheep that Jesus desires to gather and give a sense of belonging to. May we recognise our situation but have faith, like the Canaanite woman, to come to Jesus for what we need.

Thursday 8 August
Matthew 16:13–23

Now when Jesus came into the district of Caesarea Philippi, he asked his disciples, 'Who do people say that the Son of Man is?' And they said, 'Some say John the Baptist, but others Elijah, and still others Jeremiah or one of the prophets.' He said to them, 'But who do you say that I am?' Simon Peter answered, 'You are the Messiah, the Son of the living God.' And Jesus answered him, 'Blessed are you, Simon son of Jonah! For flesh and blood has not revealed this to you, but my Father in heaven. And I tell you, you are Peter, and on this rock I will build my church, and the gates of Hades will not prevail against it. I will give you the keys of the kingdom of heaven, and whatever you bind on earth will be bound in heaven, and whatever you loose on earth will be loosed in heaven.' Then he sternly ordered the disciples not to tell anyone that he was the Messiah.

From that time on, Jesus began to show his disciples that he must go to Jerusalem and undergo great suffering at the hands of the elders and chief priests and scribes, and be killed, and on the third day be raised. And Peter took him aside and began to rebuke him, saying, 'God forbid it, Lord! This must never happen to you.' But he turned and said to Peter, 'Get behind me, Satan! You are a stumbling-block to me; for you are setting your mind not on divine things but on human things.'

- 'Do you know who I am?' can be asked for different reasons. Jesus was asking his disciples for their sakes, not his own. We pray that we may come to know more fully who Jesus is as our Lord and Messiah.
- Peter's wonderful expression of faith was followed soon afterwards by his concern for the direction Jesus was taking. Glory was more attractive for him than the cross. Lord, help us to grow in our relationship with you so that we are not stumbling blocks to each other in following you.

Friday 9 August
Matthew 16:24–28

Then Jesus told his disciples, 'If any want to become my followers, let them deny themselves and take up their cross and follow me. For those who want to save their life will lose it, and those who lose their life for my sake will find it. For what will it profit them if they gain the whole world but forfeit their life? Or what will they give in return for their life?

'For the Son of Man is to come with his angels in the glory of his Father, and then he will repay everyone for what has been done. Truly I tell you, there are some standing here who will not taste death before they see the Son of Man coming in his kingdom.'

- In our time there is much reference to finding self and having a healthy sense of self and being fulfilled in life. Jesus turns some of that on its head in how it is to be accomplished. May we be able to let go of what is selfish so that we can find our true selves in him.

Saturday 10 August
St Lawrence, Deacon and Martyr
John 12:24–26

Jesus said to them, 'Very truly, I tell you, unless a grain of wheat falls into the earth and dies, it remains just a single grain; but if it dies, it bears much fruit. Those who love their life lose it, and those who hate their life in this world will keep it for eternal life. Whoever serves me must follow me, and where I am, there will my servant be also. Whoever serves me, the Father will honour.'

- Life has many paradoxes. The example of the grain of wheat dying, as Jesus did, to bring forth new life provides a rich message. May we have the ability to let go, so that we have more freedom to receive the true gift.
- Being possessive and accumulating much has its hazards. We know that here are no pockets in shrouds or roof racks on hearses. Lord, help us to know what is the genuine treasure so that we do not settle for short-term convenience.

11–17 August 2024

Something to think and pray about each day this week:

In Celtic spirituality there are 'thin places'. Such numinous environments are places where there is a sense of a thin veil between the material and spiritual. The fact remains that the 'world is something we apprehend but cannot comprehend'. We comprehend some of our apprehensions, but not all. Thin places can facilitate an intuitive experience that senses a divine, otherworldly, transcendent presence, which raises questions about our experience of human limitation and why there is something rather than nothing. For many, such an experience can take place in rugged landscapes or beautiful seascapes or when a baby is born. Many people share their experience of such a common phenomenon. Is it subjective? Or is there more to it? Can spirituality bring this experience to a level of understanding?

The idea of a global 'thin place' is echoed in Pope Francis's *Laudato Si'*: 'The entire material universe speaks of God's love and boundless affection for us. Soil, water, mountains: everything is a caress of God' (LS, 84). Spirituality is learning how to detect the caress of that ultimate reality and how to respond to that caress in a way that enriches our experience of life and contributes to the care of our common home and those with whom we share it.

Jim Maher SJ, *Reimagining Religion: A Jesuit Vision*

The Presence of God
I pause for a moment
and reflect on God's life-giving presence
in every part of my body,
in everything around me,
in the whole of my life.

Freedom
Many countries are at this moment suffering the agonies of war. I bow my head in thanksgiving for my freedom. I pray for all prisoners and captives.

Consciousness
Knowing that God loves me unconditionally, I look honestly over the past day, its events, and my feelings. Do I have something to be grateful for? Then I give thanks. Is there something I am sorry for? Then I ask forgiveness.

The Word
Now I turn to the Scripture set out for me this day. I read slowly over the words and see if any sentence or sentiment appeals to me. *(Please turn to the Scripture on the following pages. Inspiration points are there, should you need them. When you are ready, return here to continue.)*

Conversation
I know with certainty that there were times when you carried me, Lord. There were times when it was through your strength that I got through the dark times in my life.

Conclusion
Glory be to the Father, and to the Son, and to the Holy Spirit,
As it was in the beginning, is now and ever shall be,
World without end. Amen.

Sunday 11 August
Nineteenth Sunday in Ordinary Time
John 6:41–51

Then the Jews began to complain about him because he said, 'I am the bread that came down from heaven.' They were saying, 'Is not this Jesus, the son of Joseph, whose father and mother we know? How can he now say, "I have come down from heaven"?' Jesus answered them, 'Do not complain among yourselves. No one can come to me unless drawn by the Father who sent me; and I will raise that person up on the last day. It is written in the prophets, "And they shall all be taught by God." Everyone who has heard and learned from the Father comes to me. Not that anyone has seen the Father except the one who is from God; he has seen the Father. Very truly, I tell you, whoever believes has eternal life. I am the bread of life. Your ancestors ate the manna in the wilderness, and they died. This is the bread that comes down from heaven, so that one may eat of it and not die. I am the living bread that came down from heaven. Whoever eats of this bread will live for ever; and the bread that I will give for the life of the world is my flesh.'

- There is a challenge to break out of the prevailing system and do something differently. This can be too much for some. Lord, may we not be confined by the comfortable or mediocre but have the courage to live our gifts more fully for you.
- Many people are held bound by the mundane. Jesus revealed a new way beyond the ordinary and everyday where the action of God was more evident. We pray for openness to the deeper gifts and the surprising ways in which God is present in our lives and world.

Monday 12 August
Matthew 17:22–27

As they were gathering in Galilee, Jesus said to them, 'The Son of Man is going to be betrayed into human hands, and they will kill him, and on the third day he will be raised.' And they were greatly distressed.

When they reached Capernaum, the collectors of the temple tax came to Peter and said, 'Does your teacher not pay the temple tax?' He said,

'Yes, he does.' And when he came home, Jesus spoke of it first, asking, 'What do you think, Simon? From whom do kings of the earth take toll or tribute? From their children or from others?' When Peter said, 'From others', Jesus said to him, 'Then the children are free. However, so that we do not give offence to them, go to the lake and cast a hook; take the first fish that comes up; and when you open its mouth, you will find a coin; take that and give it to them for you and me.'

- The disciples' image of Jesus as Messiah did not envisage betrayal, suffering, death and resurrection, though they did not seem to hear of 'being raised'. Lord, we can find suffering distressful, so we ask your help to appreciate your offering of new life beyond death.
- In many situations of conflict about people and the sabbath Jesus held on to his compassionate approach. This matter of the temple tax did not merit the same attention. We pray for perspective in dealing with the conflicts we encounter in life.

Tuesday 13 August
Matthew 18:1–5.10.12–14
At that time the disciples came to Jesus and asked, 'Who is the greatest in the kingdom of heaven?' He called a child, whom he put among them, and said, 'Truly I tell you, unless you change and become like children, you will never enter the kingdom of heaven. Whoever becomes humble like this child is the greatest in the kingdom of heaven. Whoever welcomes one such child in my name welcomes me.

'Take care that you do not despise one of these little ones; for, I tell you, in heaven their angels continually see the face of my Father in heaven. What do you think? If a shepherd has a hundred sheep, and one of them has gone astray, does he not leave the ninety-nine on the mountains and go in search of the one that went astray? And if he finds it, truly I tell you, he rejoices over it more than over the ninety-nine that never went astray. So it is not the will of your Father in heaven that one of these little ones should be lost.'

- It is a world where self-importance plays a prominent role. Being the greatest has a popular place in many fields of life and endeavour.

In the Lord's kingdom it is the little ones who are cherished. Lord, give us humble hearts like your own that help us to welcome with childlike trust.

- Jesus had great love for the little ones and for the lost, as is evident from his teaching and his ministry. May we have his love and concern so that we can share his joy in finding and serving as he desires.

Wednesday 14 August
Matthew 18:15–20

Jesus said to them, 'If another member of the church sins against you, go and point out the fault when the two of you are alone. If the member listens to you, you have regained that one. But if you are not listened to, take one or two others along with you, so that every word may be confirmed by the evidence of two or three witnesses. If the member refuses to listen to them, tell it to the church; and if the offender refuses to listen even to the church, let such a one be to you as a Gentile and a tax-collector. Truly I tell you, whatever you bind on earth will be bound in heaven, and whatever you loose on earth will be loosed in heaven. Again, truly I tell you, if two of you agree on earth about anything you ask, it will be done for you by my Father in heaven. For where two or three are gathered in my name, I am there among them.'

- We are given some common-sense advice on reconciliation, but it needs courage to be able to point out some fault to another. Lord, may we be sensitive to the failings of others, knowing that we have our own frailty, too.
- The presence of the Lord among us helps us to retain perspective. When we are gathered in the Lord's name, he is present. In our gatherings may we remember that the Lord is with us, as this will strengthen the bond between us and bring true peace.

Thursday 15 August
The Assumption of the Blessed Virgin Mary
Luke 1:39–56

In those days Mary set out and went with haste to a Judean town in the hill country, where she entered the house of Zechariah and greeted

Elizabeth. When Elizabeth heard Mary's greeting, the child leapt in her womb. And Elizabeth was filled with the Holy Spirit and exclaimed with a loud cry, 'Blessed are you among women, and blessed is the fruit of your womb. And why has this happened to me, that the mother of my Lord comes to me? For as soon as I heard the sound of your greeting, the child in my womb leapt for joy. And blessed is she who believed that there would be a fulfilment of what was spoken to her by the Lord.'

And Mary said,
'My soul magnifies the Lord,
   and my spirit rejoices in God my Saviour,
for he has looked with favour on the lowliness of his servant.
   Surely, from now on all generations will call me blessed;
for the Mighty One has done great things for me,
   and holy is his name.
His mercy is for those who fear him
   from generation to generation.
He has shown strength with his arm;
   he has scattered the proud in the thoughts of their hearts.
He has brought down the powerful from their thrones,
   and lifted up the lowly;
he has filled the hungry with good things,
   and sent the rich away empty.
He has helped his servant Israel,
   in remembrance of his mercy,
according to the promise he made to our ancestors,
   to Abraham and to his descendants for ever.'

And Mary remained with her for about three months and then returned to her home.

- At the end of his earthly life, Jesus ascended into heaven. At the end of Mary's life, she was honoured by God for her faithful service to Jesus. In life, she was blessed by God and responded with great generosity. May we imitate her faith in our lives of service and remain open to God's generosity to us.
- Mary was united to Jesus throughout his life on earth. Having completed her earthly life she was re-united with him in glory. Lord,

may we be affirmed by your promises from generation to generation in your fidelity to us.

Friday 16 August
Matthew 19:3–12

Some Pharisees came to him, and to test him they asked, 'Is it lawful for a man to divorce his wife for any cause?' He answered, 'Have you not read that the one who made them at the beginning "made them male and female", and said, "For this reason a man shall leave his father and mother and be joined to his wife, and the two shall become one flesh"? So they are no longer two, but one flesh. Therefore what God has joined together, let no one separate.' They said to him, 'Why then did Moses command us to give a certificate of dismissal and to divorce her?' He said to them, 'It was because you were so hard-hearted that Moses allowed you to divorce your wives, but at the beginning it was not so. And I say to you, whoever divorces his wife, except for unchastity, and marries another commits adultery.'

His disciples said to him, 'If such is the case of a man with his wife, it is better not to marry.' But he said to them, 'Not everyone can accept this teaching, but only those to whom it is given. For there are eunuchs who have been so from birth, and there are eunuchs who have been made eunuchs by others, and there are eunuchs who have made themselves eunuchs for the sake of the kingdom of heaven. Let anyone accept this who can.'

- God is a God of union and desires us to share in that. God is committed to us and does not break that bond. Lord, we pray for greater faith to live in response to that, knowing that we can be hard-hearted and fail in our fidelity to you.
- Jesus understood the human situation, with its limitations. Not everyone could accept or respond to his teaching, yet he continued to call people onwards. May we have generosity to aspire to the gift he offers and compassion towards those who fail.

Saturday 17 August

Matthew 19:13–15

Then little children were being brought to him in order that he might lay his hands on them and pray. The disciples spoke sternly to those who brought them; but Jesus said, 'Let the little children come to me, and do not stop them; for it is to such as these that the kingdom of heaven belongs.' And he laid his hands on them and went on his way.

- Jesus was at home with children and felt free to lay hands on them. He had love and respect for them and presented them as models of discipleship. Lord, give us the childlike qualities of love and trust so that we may draw closer to you.
- Children have a significant place in the scriptures. There were 'promised children', who were part of the salvation story. Jesus spoke of them as having the qualities of belonging to his kingdom. As children of promise may we continue God's salvation story at this time.

18–24 August 2024

Something to think and pray about each day this week:

What brings you joy? A beautiful book. A chat with a friend, A YouTube clip shared. A child you know. An older person you know. Dancing. Food. A piece of music. Relaxing. Sleep. Dressing up. Doing your hair. A quiet house. A noisy house. A cup of tea. The joy of success. Exam results. Knowing you helped someone. Laughing. Sport. The adrenalin of exercise. The birds singing. Warmth. A familiar smell. The joy of joy.

May God be gracious to us and bless us
    and make his face to shine upon us,
Selah
that your way may be known upon earth,
    your saving power among all nations.
Let the peoples praise you, O God;
    let all the peoples praise you.

Let the nations be glad and sing for joy,
    for you judge the peoples with equity
    and guide the nations upon earth.
    Selah
Let the peoples praise you, O God;
    let all the peoples praise you.

Psalm 67:1–5

Gráinne Delaney, *Occasional Prayers for the School Year*

The Presence of God

I remind myself that I am in the presence of God, who is my strength in times of weakness and my comforter in times of sorrow.

Freedom

St Ignatius thought that a thick and shapeless tree trunk would never believe that it could become a statue, admired as a miracle of sculpture, and would never submit itself to the chisel of the sculptor, who sees by her genius what she can make of it. I ask for the grace to let myself be shaped by my loving Creator.

Consciousness

Dear Lord, help me to remember that you gave me life. Teach me to slow down, to be still and enjoy the pleasures created for me. To be aware of the beauty that surrounds me: the marvel of mountains, the calmness of lakes, the fragility of a flower petal. I need to remember that all these things come from you.

The Word

In this expectant state of mind, please turn to the text for the day with confidence. Believe that the Holy Spirit is present and may reveal whatever the passage has to say to you. Read reflectively, listening with a third ear to what may be going on in your heart. *(Please turn to the Scripture on the following pages. Inspiration points are there, should you need them. When you are ready, return here to continue.)*

Conversation

What feelings are rising in me as I pray and reflect on God's word? I imagine Jesus himself sitting or standing near me, and I open my heart to him.

Conclusion

I thank God for these moments we have spent together and for any insights I have been given concerning the text.

Sunday 18 August
Twentieth Sunday in Ordinary Time
John 6:51–58

Jesus said to them, 'I am the living bread that came down from heaven. Whoever eats of this bread will live for ever; and the bread that I will give for the life of the world is my flesh.'

The Jews then disputed among themselves, saying, 'How can this man give us his flesh to eat?' So Jesus said to them, 'Very truly, I tell you, unless you eat the flesh of the Son of Man and drink his blood, you have no life in you. Those who eat my flesh and drink my blood have eternal life, and I will raise them up on the last day; for my flesh is true food and my blood is true drink. Those who eat my flesh and drink my blood abide in me, and I in them. Just as the living Father sent me, and I live because of the Father, so whoever eats me will live because of me. This is the bread that came down from heaven, not like that which your ancestors ate, and they died. But the one who eats this bread will live for ever.'

- It is a world where the poor look for bread and the rich wonder what kind of bread they will have. What Jesus provides may not suit all tastes but it is genuine and satisfies the deeper hunger. Lord, may we value what you offer and allow it to nourish us for life that is eternal.
- The Jews did not understand what Jesus was saying and disputed among themselves what this bread could mean. May we have the faith and clarity that brings us beyond the logical and practical to what the Lord is offering to us.

Monday 19 August
Matthew 19:16–22

Then someone came to him and said, 'Teacher, what good deed must I do to have eternal life?' And he said to him, 'Why do you ask me about what is good? There is only one who is good. If you wish to enter into life, keep the commandments.' He said to him, 'Which ones?' And Jesus said, 'You shall not murder; You shall not commit adultery; You shall not steal; You shall not bear false witness; Honour your father and mother; also, You shall love your neighbour as yourself.' The young man said to him, 'I have kept all these; what do I still lack?' Jesus said to him, 'If you wish to be perfect, go, sell your possessions, and give the money to the poor, and you will have treasure in heaven; then come, follow me.' When the young man heard this word, he went away grieving, for he had many possessions.

- 'What good deed must I do to have eternal life?' Having life of quality is about more than deeds, as it is rooted in relationship, in a heart that is free. Lord, may we focus on you and ask for openness to the treasure you desire for us, as your followers.

Tuesday 20 August
Matthew 19:23–30
Then Jesus said to his disciples, 'Truly I tell you, it will be hard for a rich person to enter the kingdom of heaven. Again I tell you, it is easier for a camel to go through the eye of a needle than for someone who is rich to enter the kingdom of God.' When the disciples heard this, they were greatly astounded and said, 'Then who can be saved?' But Jesus looked at them and said, 'For mortals it is impossible, but for God all things are possible.'

Then Peter said in reply, 'Look, we have left everything and followed you. What then will we have?' Jesus said to them, 'Truly I tell you, at the renewal of all things, when the Son of Man is seated on the throne of his glory, you who have followed me will also sit on twelve thrones, judging the twelve tribes of Israel. And everyone who has left houses or brothers or sisters or father or mother or children or fields, for my name's sake, will receive a hundredfold, and will inherit eternal life. But many who are first will be last, and the last will be first.'

- Possessions can be all-consuming, taking over life. Securing, protecting or enlarging them can dominate. Lord, may we be open to the true riches that you offer so that we know what is of lasting value.
- Jesus pointed out those riches to Peter. They were not to be found in external treasures but in relationship to God. May the honours you offer be the treasure that holds our hearts.

Wednesday 21 August
Matthew 20:1–16

Jesus told them this parable, 'For the kingdom of heaven is like a landowner who went out early in the morning to hire labourers for his vineyard. After agreeing with the labourers for the usual daily wage, he sent them into his vineyard. When he went out about nine o'clock, he saw others standing idle in the market-place; and he said to them, "You also go into the vineyard, and I will pay you whatever is right." So they went. When he went out again about noon and about three o'clock, he did the same. And about five o'clock he went out and found others standing around; and he said to them, "Why are you standing here idle all day?" They said to him, "Because no one has hired us." He said to them, "You also go into the vineyard." When evening came, the owner of the vineyard said to his manager, "Call the labourers and give them their pay, beginning with the last and then going to the first." When those hired about five o'clock came, each of them received the usual daily wage. Now when the first came, they thought they would receive more; but each of them also received the usual daily wage. And when they received it, they grumbled against the landowner, saying, "These last worked only one hour, and you have made them equal to us who have borne the burden of the day and the scorching heat." But he replied to one of them, "Friend, I am doing you no wrong; did you not agree with me for the usual daily wage? Take what belongs to you and go; I choose to give to this last the same as I give to you. Am I not allowed to do what I choose with what belongs to me? Or are you envious because I am generous?" So the last will be first, and the first will be last.'

- Labour unions continue to ask for a living wage for all workers. They want what is fair and that the promises made to their members are honoured. Lord, you are committed to your promises. May we be guided by your criteria and the generosity that you manifest.
- God's generosity is shown in many different ways. It is one of extravagant love taught in parables and shown in action. May we have a similar disposition that enables us to go beyond what is required or seems equitable.

Thursday 22 August
Matthew 22:1–14
Once more Jesus spoke to them in parables, saying: 'The kingdom of heaven may be compared to a king who gave a wedding banquet for his son. He sent his slaves to call those who had been invited to the wedding banquet, but they would not come. Again he sent other slaves, saying, "Tell those who have been invited: Look, I have prepared my dinner, my oxen and my fat calves have been slaughtered, and everything is ready; come to the wedding banquet." But they made light of it and went away, one to his farm, another to his business, while the rest seized his slaves, maltreated them, and killed them. The king was enraged. He sent his troops, destroyed those murderers, and burned their city. Then he said to his slaves, "The wedding is ready, but those invited were not worthy. Go therefore into the main streets, and invite everyone you find to the wedding banquet." Those slaves went out into the streets and gathered all whom they found, both good and bad; so the wedding hall was filled with guests.

'But when the king came in to see the guests, he noticed a man there who was not wearing a wedding robe, and he said to him, "Friend, how did you get in here without a wedding robe?" And he was speechless. Then the king said to the attendants, "Bind him hand and foot, and throw him into the outer darkness, where there will be weeping and gnashing of teeth." For many are called, but few are chosen.'

- As friends of the bridegroom, the Lord invites us to the wedding banquet. We can accept or reject the invitation. Lord, with our many commitments we can make excuses for not attending. May we have the honesty to accept your invitation.

Friday 23 August
Matthew 22:34–40
When the Pharisees heard that he had silenced the Sadducees, they gathered together, and one of them, a lawyer, asked him a question to test him. 'Teacher, which commandment in the law is the greatest?' He said to him, '"You shall love the Lord your God with all your heart, and with all your soul, and with all your mind." This is the greatest

and first commandment. And a second is like it: "You shall love your neighbour as yourself." On these two commandments hang all the law and the prophets.'

- Questioning Jesus was a common tactic. Lord, your way is that of love and you invite us, as you invited them, to let this be the rule of life.
- Loving God and neighbour is at the heart of the law and the prophets, as it is in the teaching and way of Jesus. May we increase in that love that puts God and others first as well as growing in a healthy self-love.

Saturday 24 August
St Bartholomew, Apostle
John 1:45–51

Philip found Nathanael and said to him, 'We have found him about whom Moses in the law and also the prophets wrote, Jesus son of Joseph from Nazareth.' Nathanael said to him, 'Can anything good come out of Nazareth?' Philip said to him, 'Come and see.' When Jesus saw Nathanael coming towards him, he said of him, 'Here is truly an Israelite in whom there is no deceit!' Nathanael asked him, 'Where did you come to know me?' Jesus answered, 'I saw you under the fig tree before Philip called you.' Nathanael replied, 'Rabbi, you are the Son of God! You are the King of Israel!' Jesus answered, 'Do you believe because I told you that I saw you under the fig tree? You will see greater things than these.' And he said to him, 'Very truly, I tell you, you will see heaven opened and the angels of God ascending and descending upon the Son of Man.'

- Bartholomew expressed his newfound faith in Jesus as Son of God and King of Israel. Jesus promised something greater when he would be revealed more fully. Lord, we pray for openness to the ways in which you are revealed so that we may follow you more closely.

The Twenty-first Week in Ordinary Time

25–31 August 2024

Something to think and pray about each day this week:

John the Baptist must have been a very dynamic and inspiring preacher. He probably seemed a bit quirky, roaming around in the wilderness, calling people to change their ways. The crowds speculated 'in their hearts' if John was the one they had been waiting for, but he used all of this attention and popularity for one purpose only: to point people to Jesus. There are many people in our own lives who have pointed us towards Jesus, perhaps by an invitation to an event or sharing with us a new insight at just the right time: teachers, grandparents, religious, inspirational speakers, friends … In them we see something special that makes us *wonder* so that our hearts are moved to *seek* a little further. They are the John the Baptists in our lives, signposts along the way.

Tríona Doherty and Jane Mellett, *The Deep End*

The Presence of God

I remind myself that, as I sit here now, God is gazing on me with love and holding me in being. I pause for a moment and think of this.

Freedom

'There are very few people who realise what God would make of them if they abandoned themselves into his hands, and let themselves be formed by his grace' (St Ignatius). I ask for the grace to trust myself totally to God's love.

Consciousness

Where do I sense hope, encouragement and growth in my life? By looking back over the past few months, I may be able to see which activities and occasions have produced rich fruit. If I do notice such areas, I will determine to give those areas both time and space in the future.

The Word

Lord Jesus, you became human to communicate with me.
You walked and worked on this earth.
You endured the heat and struggled with the cold.
All your time on this earth was spent in caring for humanity.
You healed the sick, you raised the dead.
Most important of all, you saved me from death.
(Please turn to the Scripture on the following pages. Inspiration points are there, should you need them. When you are ready, return here to continue.)

Conversation

What is stirring in me as I pray? Am I consoled, troubled, left cold? I imagine Jesus standing or sitting at my side, and I share my feelings with him.

Conclusion

Glory be to the Father, and to the Son, and to the Holy Spirit,
As it was in the beginning, is now and ever shall be,
World without end. Amen.

Sunday 25 August
Twenty-first Sunday in Ordinary Time
John 6:60–69
When many of his disciples heard it, they said, 'This teaching is difficult; who can accept it?' But Jesus, being aware that his disciples were complaining about it, said to them, 'Does this offend you? Then what if you were to see the Son of Man ascending to where he was before? It is the spirit that gives life; the flesh is useless. The words that I have spoken to you are spirit and life. But among you there are some who do not believe.' For Jesus knew from the first who were the ones that did not believe, and who was the one that would betray him. And he said, 'For this reason I have told you that no one can come to me unless it is granted by the Father.'

Because of this many of his disciples turned back and no longer went about with him. So Jesus asked the twelve, 'Do you also wish to go away?' Simon Peter answered him, 'Lord, to whom can we go? You have the words of eternal life. We have come to believe and know that you are the Holy One of God.'

- The disciples were challenged by the teaching of Jesus and the departure of others who could not accept his message on the bread of life. May we have the insight and courage to be open to the guidance of the spirit that gives life.
- Jesus asked his disciples directly if they too wished to go away. Peter professed faith, but he did not understand the full implications of what he said. Lord, may we have the freedom to follow you even if we do not understand very well where you are leading us.

Monday 26 August
Matthew 23:13–22
Then Jesus said to the crowds and to his disciples, 'But woe to you, scribes and Pharisees, hypocrites! For you lock people out of the kingdom of heaven. For you do not go in yourselves, and when others are going in, you stop them. Woe to you, scribes and Pharisees, hypocrites! For you cross sea and land to make a single convert, and you make the new convert twice as much a child of hell as yourselves.

'Woe to you, blind guides, who say, "Whoever swears by the sanctuary is bound by nothing, but whoever swears by the gold of the sanctuary is bound by the oath." You blind fools! For which is greater, the gold or the sanctuary that has made the gold sacred? And you say, "Whoever swears by the altar is bound by nothing, but whoever swears by the gift that is on the altar is bound by the oath." How blind you are! For which is greater, the gift or the altar that makes the gift sacred? So whoever swears by the altar, swears by it and by everything on it; and whoever swears by the sanctuary, swears by it and by the one who dwells in it; and whoever swears by heaven, swears by the throne of God and by the one who is seated upon it.'

- The religious leaders, the scribes and Pharisees, were accused of being hypocrites. They were like masked actors playing roles but the real persons were not being seen. Amid the pressures of life and popularity, may we discard our masks, so that we can hear and live the truth.

- Jesus came to open the way to the kingdom of heaven, being authentic in word and action. He called people beyond external conformity to a change of heart. Lord, heal our blindness and pretence so that we may guide others in a way that is genuine and life-giving.

Tuesday 27 August
Matthew 23:23–26

Jesus said, 'Woe to you, scribes and Pharisees, hypocrites! For you tithe mint, dill and cummin, and have neglected the weightier matters of the law: justice and mercy and faith. It is these you ought to have practised without neglecting the others. You blind guides! You strain out a gnat but swallow a camel!

'Woe to you, scribes and Pharisees, hypocrites! For you clean the outside of the cup and of the plate, but inside they are full of greed and self-indulgence. You blind Pharisee! First clean the inside of the cup, so that the outside also may become clean.'

- Many of the actions of the religious leaders were good from an external point of view, but their inner dispositions were sadly lacking. May we recognise what is important and carry it out with a good disposition.

- Jesus frequently drew attention to the inner attitude, to doing something for the right motives. The external actions said something but did not manifest the full meaning of what was being done. We pray for purity of heart, which will enable us to see God more clearly and continue to serve in that spirit.

Wednesday 28 August
Matthew 23:27–32

Jesus said, 'Woe to you, scribes and Pharisees, hypocrites! For you are like whitewashed tombs, which on the outside look beautiful, but inside they are full of the bones of the dead and of all kinds of filth. So you also on the outside look righteous to others, but inside you are full of hypocrisy and lawlessness.

'Woe to you, scribes and Pharisees, hypocrites! For you build the tombs of the prophets and decorate the graves of the righteous, and you say, "If we had lived in the days of our ancestors, we would not have taken part with them in shedding the blood of the prophets." Thus you testify against yourselves that you are descendants of those who murdered the prophets. Fill up, then, the measure of your ancestors.'

- We live in a world where looking good and being popular have much appeal. The external pressure to conform can be very influential. May our true beauty that is within be more significant in how we live and present ourselves.

- There are many monuments to people who were prophetic and who suffered for it, but their message is often ignored. We pray that their lives and example may lead to a change of heart where we can live for justice and truth in our modern world.

Thursday 29 August
The Passion of St John the Baptist
Mark 6:17–29

For Herod himself had sent men who arrested John, bound him, and put him in prison on account of Herodias, his brother Philip's wife, because Herod had married her. For John had been telling Herod, 'It is not lawful for you to have your brother's wife.' And Herodias had a grudge against him, and wanted to kill him. But she could not, for Herod feared John, knowing that he was a righteous and holy man, and he protected him. When he heard him, he was greatly perplexed; and yet he liked to listen to him. But an opportunity came when Herod on his birthday gave a banquet for his courtiers and officers and for the leaders of Galilee. When his daughter Herodias came in and danced, she pleased Herod and his guests; and the king said to the girl, 'Ask me for whatever you wish, and I will give it.' And he solemnly swore to her, 'Whatever you ask me, I will give you, even half of my kingdom.' She went out and said to her mother, 'What should I ask for?' She replied, 'The head of John the baptiser.' Immediately she rushed back to the king and requested, 'I want you to give me at once the head of John the Baptist on a platter.' The king was deeply grieved; yet out of regard for his oaths and for the guests, he did not want to refuse her. Immediately the king sent a soldier of the guard with orders to bring John's head. He went and beheaded him in the prison, brought his head on a platter, and gave it to the girl. Then the girl gave it to her mother. When his disciples heard about it, they came and took his body, and laid it in a tomb.

- At euphoric times, we can make foolish or rash promises that we come to regret later. Herod grieved for what he had done. May we have the courage not to compound our error with another disastrous decision, but face up to our responsibility in the situation.

Friday 30 August
Matthew 25:1–13

Jesus said, 'Then the kingdom of heaven will be like this. Ten bridesmaids took their lamps and went to meet the bridegroom. Five of them were foolish, and five were wise. When the foolish took their lamps, they took no oil with them; but the wise took flasks of oil with their lamps. As the bridegroom was delayed, all of them became drowsy and slept. But at midnight there was a shout, "Look! Here is the bridegroom! Come out to meet him." Then all those bridesmaids got up and trimmed their lamps. The foolish said to the wise, "Give us some of your oil, for our lamps are going out." But the wise replied, "No! there will not be enough for you and for us; you had better go to the dealers and buy some for yourselves." And while they went to buy it, the bridegroom came, and those who were ready went with him into the wedding banquet; and the door was shut. Later the other bridesmaids came also, saying, "Lord, lord, open to us." But he replied, "Truly I tell you, I do not know you." Keep awake therefore, for you know neither the day nor the hour.'

- Important occasions and events are given careful preparation. Great attention is given to planning a wedding. May we have the wisdom and foresight to acknowledge what is needed in life and take action in the light of that.
- In the parable, all the bridesmaids fell asleep, but some had taken what was required, so the occasion was more important to them. Lord, you are the bridegroom who invites us to the celebration. May our relationship with you guide us to take appropriate action to be alert, awake and prepared.

Saturday 31 August
Matthew 25:14–30
Jesus said to them, 'For it is as if a man, going on a journey, summoned his slaves and entrusted his property to them; to one he gave five talents, to another two, to another one, to each according to his ability. Then he went away. The one who had received the five talents went off at once and traded with them, and made five more talents. In the same way, the one who had the two talents made two more talents. But the one who had received the one talent went off and dug a hole in the ground and hid his master's money. After a long time the master of those slaves came and settled accounts with them. Then the one who had received the five talents came forward, bringing five more talents, saying, "Master, you handed over to me five talents; see, I have made five more talents." His master said to him, "Well done, good and trustworthy slave; you have been trustworthy in a few things, I will put you in charge of many things; enter into the joy of your master." And

the one with the two talents also came forward, saying, "Master, you handed over to me two talents; see, I have made two more talents." His master said to him, "Well done, good and trustworthy slave; you have been trustworthy in a few things, I will put you in charge of many things; enter into the joy of your master." Then the one who had received the one talent also came forward, saying, "Master, I knew that you were a harsh man, reaping where you did not sow, and gathering where you did not scatter seed; so I was afraid, and I went and hid your talent in the ground. Here you have what is yours." But his master replied, "You wicked and lazy slave! You knew, did you, that I reap where I did not sow, and gather where I did not scatter? Then you ought to have invested my money with the bankers, and on my return I would have received what was my own with interest. So take the talent from him, and give it to the one with the ten talents. For to all those who have, more will be given, and they will have an abundance; but from those who have nothing, even what they have will be taken away. As for this worthless slave, throw him into the outer darkness, where there will be weeping and gnashing of teeth.'"

- Our creator God has entrusted many talents to us. These gifts are meant to be used in a fruitful way. May we have gratitude for the gifts we have received and use them to bring glory to God (Matthew 5:12).
- There is the contrast between taking the initiative and being too passive, between trusting and being too cautious in applying what we have been given. Lord, may we have gratitude for the gifts and be responsible in developing them and not letting them lie dormant.

The Twenty-second Week in Ordinary Time

1–7 September 2024

Something to think and pray about each day this week:

Many of us seek joy outside of ourselves, in food and drink, or in riches and reputation. Mary found an inner joy that came from encountering God, a joy that was immeasurably greater than any material joy: 'You have put into my heart a greater joy than they have from abundance of corn and new wine' (Psalm 4:8). By giving Mary a place in our hearts, we can find true joy in God as well.

Joy is something deeper than an artificial smile or a forced grin, and in fact a cheery expression that is permanently fixed on the face suggests superficiality. Mary's joy was not something superficial because it was above all an internal joy, as all true joy is. Mary lived in joy because she was in tune with God. If we can't experience God as joy, we're in tune with something much less than God. The only God who is believable is the God who wakens us into wonder, the wonder of joy.

Thomas Casey SJ, *Smile of Joy: Mary of Nazareth*

The Presence of God

Lord, help me to be fully alive to your holy presence. Enfold me in your love. Let my heart become one with yours. My soul longs for your presence, Lord. When I turn my thoughts to you, I find peace and contentment.

Freedom

Your death on the cross has set me free. I can live joyously and freely without fear of death. Your mercy knows no bounds.

Consciousness

At this moment, Lord, I turn my thoughts to you.
I will leave aside my chores and preoccupations.
I will take rest and refreshment in your presence.

The Word

The word of God comes down to us through the Scriptures.
May the Holy Spirit enlighten my mind and my heart
to respond to the Gospel teachings:
to love my neighbour as myself,
to care for my sisters and brothers in Christ.
(Please turn to the Scripture on the following pages. Inspiration points are there, should you need them. When you are ready, return here to continue.)

Conversation

Begin to talk to Jesus about the Scripture you have just read. What part of it strikes a chord in you? Perhaps the words of a friend – or some story you have heard recently – will slowly rise to the surface of your consciousness. If so, does the story throw light on what the Scripture passage may be saying to you?

Conclusion

I thank God for these moments we have spent together and for any insights I have been given concerning the text.

Sunday 1 September
Twenty-second Sunday in Ordinary Time
Mark 7:1–8.14–15.21–23

Now when the Pharisees and some of the scribes who had come from Jerusalem gathered around him, they noticed that some of his disciples were eating with defiled hands, that is, without washing them. (For the Pharisees, and all the Jews, do not eat unless they thoroughly wash their hands, thus observing the tradition of the elders; and they do not eat anything from the market unless they wash it; and there are also many other traditions that they observe, the washing of cups, pots, and bronze kettles.) So the Pharisees and the scribes asked him, 'Why do your disciples not live according to the tradition of the elders, but eat with defiled hands?' He said to them, 'Isaiah prophesied rightly about you hypocrites, as it is written,

"This people honours me with their lips,
    but their hearts are far from me;
in vain do they worship me,
    teaching human precepts as doctrines."

You abandon the commandment of God and hold to human tradition.'

Then he called the crowd again and said to them, 'Listen to me, all of you, and understand: there is nothing outside a person that by going in can defile, but the things that come out are what defile.' For it is from within, from the human heart, that evil intentions come: fornication, theft, murder, adultery, avarice, wickedness, deceit, licentiousness, envy, slander, pride, folly. All these evil things come from within, and they defile a person.'

- Ritual handwashing was prominent in the lives of the Pharisees. Jesus was pointing beyond the practical and the hygienic to the need for inner cleanliness. We pray for hearts that are clean so that we may truly honour God.
- External actions have an internal source. Evil intentions can find expression in life. May we have the honesty to look behind our actions to come to a deeper freedom to live in the truth.

Monday 2 September
Luke 4:16–30

When he came to Nazareth, where he had been brought up, he went to the synagogue on the sabbath day, as was his custom. He stood up to read, and the scroll of the prophet Isaiah was given to him. He unrolled the scroll and found the place where it was written:
    'The Spirit of the Lord is upon me,
        because he has anointed me
        to bring good news to the poor.
    He has sent me to proclaim release to the captives
        and recovery of sight to the blind,
        to let the oppressed go free,
    to proclaim the year of the Lord's favour.'
And he rolled up the scroll, gave it back to the attendant, and sat down. The eyes of all in the synagogue were fixed on him. Then he began to say to them, 'Today this scripture has been fulfilled in your hearing.' All spoke well of him and were amazed at the gracious words that came from his mouth. They said, 'Is not this Joseph's son?' He said to them, 'Doubtless you will quote to me this proverb, "Doctor, cure yourself!" And you will say, "Do here also in your home town the things that we have heard you did at Capernaum."' And he said, 'Truly I tell you, no prophet is accepted in the prophet's home town. But the truth is, there were many widows in Israel in the time of Elijah, when the heaven was shut up for three years and six months, and there was a severe famine over all the land; yet Elijah was sent to none of them except to a widow at Zarephath in Sidon. There were also many lepers in Israel in the time of the prophet Elisha, and none of them was cleansed except Naaman the Syrian.' When they heard this, all in the synagogue were filled with rage. They got up, drove him out of the town, and led him to the brow of the hill on which their town was built, so that they might hurl him off the cliff. But he passed through the midst of them and went on his way.

- Jesus went to the synagogue on the sabbath as was his custom. He chose a text from Isaiah to announce his mission of bringing good news and freedom to the oppressed. May this message be fulfilled today when many lack good news and need healing of their blindness.

- Jesus gave the example of outsiders responding to the prophets Elijah and Elisha, whereas the people of Nazareth found it difficult to accept his prophetic message. We pray for openness to hear you, Lord, and that we may not seek to drive you out of our lives.

Tuesday 3 September
Luke 4:31–37

He went down to Capernaum, a city in Galilee, and was teaching them on the sabbath. They were astounded at his teaching, because he spoke with authority. In the synagogue there was a man who had the spirit of an unclean demon, and he cried out with a loud voice, 'Let us alone! What have you to do with us, Jesus of Nazareth? Have you come to destroy us? I know who you are, the Holy One of God.' But Jesus rebuked him, saying, 'Be silent, and come out of him!' When the demon had thrown him down before them, he came out of him without having done him any harm. They were all amazed and kept saying to one another, 'What kind of utterance is this? For with authority and power he commands the unclean spirits, and out they come!' And a report about him began to reach every place in the region.

- Jesus got a good reception in Capernaum where he taught on the sabbath. They were astounded at his teaching because he spoke and acted with authority. May we accept the evidence and speak with authority in your name.
- A demon recognised Jesus as the Holy One of God. Many people struggle to come to that level of recognition. May we have the faith to recognise the authority and power of Jesus as greater than any opposing forces.

Wednesday 4 September
Luke 4:38–44

After leaving the synagogue he entered Simon's house. Now Simon's mother-in-law was suffering from a high fever, and they asked him about her. Then he stood over her and rebuked the fever, and it left her. Immediately she got up and began to serve them.

As the sun was setting, all those who had any who were sick with various kinds of diseases brought them to him; and he laid his hands on each of them and cured them. Demons also came out of many, shouting, 'You are the Son of God!' But he rebuked them and would not allow them to speak, because they knew that he was the Messiah.

At daybreak he departed and went into a deserted place. And the crowds were looking for him; and when they reached him, they wanted to prevent him from leaving them. But he said to them, 'I must proclaim the good news of the kingdom of God to the other cities also; for I was sent for this purpose.' So he continued proclaiming the message in the synagogues of Judea.

- Jesus had spoken of healing and he lived it out, rebuking the fever of Simon's mother-in-law. He also cured many who were sick with various kinds of diseases. Lord, we come to you with our sickness and ask you to lay your healing hands on us.
- Jesus found some quiet time in the early morning. It was interrupted when the crowds found him and wanted to detain him. May we have the freedom to take quiet time but also to move on as messengers of the good news of Jesus.

Thursday 5 September
Luke 5:1–11

Once while Jesus was standing beside the lake of Gennesaret, and the crowd was pressing in on him to hear the word of God, he saw two boats there at the shore of the lake; the fishermen had gone out of them and were washing their nets. He got into one of the boats, the one belonging to Simon, and asked him to put out a little way from the shore. Then he sat down and taught the crowds from the boat. When he had finished speaking, he said to Simon, 'Put out into the deep water and let down your nets for a catch.' Simon answered, 'Master, we have worked all night long but have caught nothing. Yet if you say so, I will let down the nets.' When they had done this, they caught so many fish that their nets were beginning to break. So they signalled to their partners in the other boat to come and help them. And they came and filled both boats, so that they began to sink. But when Simon Peter saw it, he fell down at Jesus' knees, saying, 'Go away from me, Lord, for I am a sinful man!' For he and all who were with him were amazed at the catch of fish that they had taken; and so also were James and John, sons of Zebedee, who were partners with Simon. Then Jesus said to Simon, 'Do not be afraid; from now on you will be catching people.' When they had brought their boats to shore, they left everything and followed him.

- This a story with different levels. It began on the shore and ended up in the deep, where the disciples went to fish. Lord, you call us and invite us to go into the deep where the better catch is to be found.

- Peter knew the lake and the time to fish, but he put that wisdom aside on hearing Jesus telling him to put into the deep water and lower the nets. May we be open to the surprising invitations of the Lord, so that we may catch people in his name.

Friday 6 September
Luke 5:33–39
Then they said to him, 'John's disciples, like the disciples of the Pharisees, frequently fast and pray, but your disciples eat and drink.' Jesus said to them, 'You cannot make wedding-guests fast while the bridegroom is with them, can you? The days will come when the bridegroom will be taken away from them, and then they will fast in those days.' He also told them a parable: 'No one tears a piece from a new garment and sews it on an old garment; otherwise the new will be torn, and the piece from the new will not match the old. And no one puts new wine into old wineskins; otherwise the new wine will burst the skins and will be spilled, and the skins will be destroyed. But new wine must be put into fresh wineskins. And no one after drinking old wine desires new wine, but says, "The old is good."'

- Fasting can be primarily an external act done for different reasons, such as impressing others (Matthew 6:16). It is meant to help us to recognise the limits of life and to honour God. Lord, help us to recognise our motives and to know the times and occasions when it is more appropriate to fast.

- Jesus said there would be a time and place for fasting and for celebrating. As the bridegroom, he was advocating the best of the old and the new. We pray for discerning hearts that enable us to make wise choices and to act accordingly

Saturday 7 September
Luke 6:1–5

One sabbath while Jesus was going through the cornfields, his disciples plucked some heads of grain, rubbed them in their hands, and ate them. But some of the Pharisees said, 'Why are you doing what is not lawful on the sabbath?' Jesus answered, 'Have you not read what David did when he and his companions were hungry? He entered the house of God and took and ate the bread of the Presence, which it is not lawful for any but the priests to eat, and gave some to his companions?' Then he said to them, 'The Son of Man is lord of the sabbath.'

- Jesus drew on the everyday, using seeds, wheat, sowing and harvest to illustrate his message. When the disciples ate some corn while walking through cornfields on the sabbath it raised questions. Lord, help us to retain perspective in life and not be imprisoned by the letter of the law.

- David was a significant figure in the history of Israel and the salvation story. Jesus was a descendant of David, so quoting his example added weight to Jesus' stance. May we be guided by Jesus as Lord in our living as sabbath people.

The Twenty-third Week in Ordinary Time

8–14 September 2024

Something to think and pray about each day this week:

Few things in life are certain, but one of the certainties of life is this: we will make mistakes. We will make a lot of mistakes. Early in life we often feel guilty and ashamed of our mistakes, perhaps thinking that we are the only ones who make them. As we grow older, however, we see that making mistakes – messing things up and failure – is part of life for everyone. While mistakes are not to be sought out, they are not the end of the story.

Mistakes are to be learned from and grown out of. They are opportunities for us to sheepishly, maybe, and humbly, definitively, turn back to God in search of the forgiveness or strength that will inevitably await us and help us to move on along a better path. One of the best lines in the New Testament dealing with failure comes in the story of the Prodigal Son, or the Forgiving Father, as it is increasingly known. When the wayward son, who has really messed up, comes back to his father seeking forgiveness for his mistakes we read the following about the father's reaction to the son: 'He fell on his neck and kissed him.'

How wonderful to have a God who falls on our neck and kisses us when we mess up and ask for his forgiveness! And what better way to be his presence in the world than to do the same for others in our lives?

Brendan McManus SJ & Jim Deeds,
Deeper into the Mess: Praying Through Tough Times

The Presence of God

The more we call on God the more we can feel God's presence. Day by day we are drawn closer to the loving heart of God.

Freedom

I am free. When I look at these words in writing, they seem to create in me a feeling of awe. Yes, a wonderful feeling of freedom. Thank you, God.

Consciousness

Help me, Lord, become more conscious of your presence. Teach me to recognise your presence in others. Fill my heart with gratitude for the times your love has been shown to me through the care of others.

The Word

The word of God comes down to us through the Scriptures. May the Holy Spirit enlighten my mind and my heart to respond to the Gospel teachings. *(Please turn to the Scripture on the following pages. Inspiration points are there, should you need them. When you are ready, return here to continue.)*

Conversation

Conversation requires talking and listening.
As I talk to Jesus, may I also learn to pause and listen.
I picture the gentleness in his eyes and the love in his smile.
I can be totally honest with Jesus as I tell him my worries and cares.
I will open my heart to Jesus as I tell him my fears and doubts.
I will ask him to help me place myself fully in his care, knowing that he always desires good for me.

Conclusion

Glory be to the Father, and to the Son, and to the Holy Spirit,
As it was in the beginning, is now and ever shall be,
World without end. Amen.

Sunday 8 September
Twenty-third Sunday in Ordinary Time
Mark 7:31–37

Then he returned from the region of Tyre, and went by way of Sidon towards the Sea of Galilee, in the region of the Decapolis. They brought to him a deaf man who had an impediment in his speech; and they begged him to lay his hand on him. He took him aside in private, away from the crowd, and put his fingers into his ears, and he spat and touched his tongue. Then looking up to heaven, he sighed and said to him, 'Ephphatha', that is, 'Be opened.' And immediately his ears were opened, his tongue was released, and he spoke plainly. Then Jesus ordered them to tell no one; but the more he ordered them, the more zealously they proclaimed it. They were astounded beyond measure, saying, 'He has done everything well; he even makes the deaf to hear and the mute to speak.'

- Jesus took the deaf man aside, away from the crowd, to heal him. Jesus did not want to draw attention but the word was proclaimed zealously. We pray for the freedom to speak and not to be rendered silent by the crowd.
- Putting fingers into the deaf man's ears and spitting to touch his tongue could have been offensive. Jesus' desire to open up life to this man was decisive in what he did. May our tongues be released to proclaim Jesus who has done everything well.

Monday 9 September
Luke 6:6–11

On another sabbath he entered the synagogue and taught, and there was a man there whose right hand was withered. The scribes and the Pharisees watched him to see whether he would cure on the sabbath, so that they might find an accusation against him. Even though he knew what they were thinking, he said to the man who had the withered hand, 'Come and stand here.' He got up and stood there. Then Jesus said to them, 'I ask you, is it lawful to do good or to do harm on the sabbath, to save life or to destroy it?' After looking around at all of them, he said to him, 'Stretch out your hand.' He did so, and his hand was restored. But they were filled with fury and discussed with one another what they might do to Jesus.

- The situation, the occasion, the presence of the religious leaders and a man with an infirmity provided an occasion for Jesus to make a significant intervention. We ask for clarity of focus in the complex situations we encounter.

- Jesus put a question to the scribes and Pharisees about the legality of doing good or evil on the sabbath. They were unwilling to respond but were furious at what Jesus did. May we have the courage to do good in challenging situations to offer life and hope.

Tuesday 10 September
Luke 6:12–19

Now during those days he went out to the mountain to pray; and he spent the night in prayer to God. And when day came, he called his disciples and chose twelve of them, whom he also named apostles: Simon, whom he named Peter, and his brother Andrew, and James, and John, and Philip, and Bartholomew, and Matthew, and Thomas, and James son of Alphaeus, and Simon, who was called the Zealot, and Judas son of James, and Judas Iscariot, who became a traitor.

He came down with them and stood on a level place, with a great crowd of his disciples and a great multitude of people from all Judea, Jerusalem, and the coast of Tyre and Sidon. They had come to hear him and to be healed of their diseases; and those who were troubled with unclean spirits were cured. And all in the crowd were trying to touch him, for power came out from him and healed all of them.

- Prayer was very important in the life of Jesus. Before choosing the twelve he spent the night in prayer to God on a mountain. This was a significant event early in his mission. Lord, may we have the same spirit of prayer in responding to your call to us.

- A great crowd came from all around to hear Jesus and be healed of their diseases. He asks us to come down from the mountain with him to a level place. May we have the freedom to follow and serve the Lord as he desires in the ordinary.

Wednesday 11 September
Luke 6:20–26

Then he looked up at his disciples and said:
'Blessed are you who are poor,
   for yours is the kingdom of God.
'Blessed are you who are hungry now,
   for you will be filled.
'Blessed are you who weep now,
   for you will laugh.
'Blessed are you when people hate you, and when they exclude you, revile you, and defame you on account of the Son of Man. Rejoice on that day and leap for joy, for surely your reward is great in heaven; for that is what their ancestors did to the prophets.
'But woe to you who are rich,
   for you have received your consolation.
'Woe to you who are full now,
   for you will be hungry.
'Woe to you who are laughing now,
   for you will mourn and weep.
'Woe to you when all speak well of you, for that is what their ancestors did to the false prophets.'

- The poor who recognise their situation have a great capacity to receive. All of us are poor in one way or another. May our poverty open us to the gifts of God, the source of all blessing, so that we have grateful hearts to respond.
- Fame is unreliable as it rests on an insecure foundation. It can crumble or disappear very quickly. In the woes of life may we rely on you, Lord, for what matters is that all is your gift to us.

Thursday 12 September
Luke 6:27–38

'But I say to you that listen, Love your enemies, do good to those who hate you, bless those who curse you, pray for those who abuse you. If anyone strikes you on the cheek, offer the other also; and from anyone who takes away your coat do not withhold even your shirt. Give to everyone who begs from you; and if anyone takes away your goods, do not ask for them again. Do to others as you would have them do to you.

'If you love those who love you, what credit is that to you? For even sinners love those who love them. If you do good to those who do good to you, what credit is that to you? For even sinners do the same. If you lend to those from whom you hope to receive, what credit is that to you? Even sinners lend to sinners, to receive as much again. But love your enemies, do good, and lend, expecting nothing in return. Your reward will be great, and you will be children of the Most High; for he is kind to the ungrateful and the wicked. Be merciful, just as your Father is merciful.

'Do not judge, and you will not be judged; do not condemn, and you will not be condemned. Forgive, and you will be forgiven; give, and it will be given to you. A good measure, pressed down, shaken together, running over, will be put into your lap; for the measure you give will be the measure you get back.'

- Jesus, your love and forgiveness were not measured, but available freely to all. You were not confined by the legal requirements of justice, but gave all in love. We ask for the grace of imitating you in generosity, giving beyond what is expected.

Friday 13 September
Luke 6:39–42

Jesus also told them a parable: 'Can a blind person guide a blind person? Will not both fall into a pit? A disciple is not above the teacher, but everyone who is fully qualified will be like the teacher. Why do you see the speck in your neighbour's eye, but do not notice the log in your own eye? Or how can you say to your neighbour, "Friend, let me take out the speck in your eye", when you yourself do not see the log in your own eye? You hypocrite, first take the log out of your own eye, and then you will see clearly to take the speck out of your neighbour's eye.'

Jesus said to his disciples, 'But I say to you that listen, Love your enemies, do good to those who hate you, bless those who curse you, pray for those who abuse you. If anyone strikes you on the cheek, offer the other also; and from anyone who takes away your coat do not withhold even your shirt. Give to everyone who begs from you; and if anyone takes away your goods, do not ask for them again. Do to others as you would have them do to you.'

- Visual impairment puts limits on life. Moving around in safety is not guaranteed. In many ways, our sight is restricted too. Lord, give us eyes that see as you do, so that we are good guides to others in negotiating the hazards of life.
- We can be blind to our own faults and keenly observant of those of others. They are not given the benefit of the doubt. May we notice our own benign interpretations so that we are honest about them, and not be overly focused on the failings of other people.

Saturday 14 September
The Exaltation of the Holy Cross
John 3:13–17
Jesus said to Nicodemus, 'No one has ascended into heaven except the one who descended from heaven, the Son of Man. And just as Moses lifted up the serpent in the wilderness, so must the Son of Man be lifted up, that whoever believes in him may have eternal life.

'For God so loved the world that he gave his only Son, so that everyone who believes in him may not perish but may have eternal life.

'Indeed, God did not send the Son into the world to condemn the world, but in order that the world might be saved through him.'

- The cross can be seen as a symbol of death, but for us it is one of life. Jesus being raised up was his glorification, offering us salvation. May we draw strength from his being raised up to find meaning in the sufferings of life.
- Jesus' self-giving on the cross is the ultimate expression of love; he laid down his life for us, his friends (John 15:13). Lord, inspire us with a spirit of self-giving so that we can bring hope and life to others.

The Twenty-fourth Week in Ordinary Time

15–21 September 2024

Something to think and pray about each day this week:

In *Laudato Si'*, Pope Francis calls each of us to become 'painfully aware' of what is happening to our world. We know now that the past 200 years of 'development' have caused widespread destruction of our planet, altering the very fabric of our ecosystems. We want to maintain that pattern as if infinite economic growth could continue indefinitely, but this is simply not possible on a planet with finite resources. Levels of consumption by humans are out of control.

The Season of Creation is a time to reconnect with the beauty of God's creation so that we can set out on more sustainable paths. This involves breaking away from systems on which we are dependent and embracing a gentler way of walking on this earth. It requires a drastic change of heart so that we can set out on new paths as a global community.

Tríona Doherty and Jane Mellett, *The Deep End*

The Presence of God

'Be still, and know that I am God!' Lord, your words lead us to the calmness and greatness of your presence.

Freedom

'In these days, God taught me as a schoolteacher teaches a pupil' (Saint Ignatius). I remind myself that there are things God has to teach me yet, and I ask for the grace to hear them and let them change me.

Consciousness

How am I really feeling? Lighthearted? Heavyhearted? I may be very much at peace, happy to be here. Equally, I may be frustrated, worried, or angry. I acknowledge how I really am. It is the real me whom the Lord loves.

The Word

God speaks to each of us individually. I listen attentively to hear what he is saying to me. Read the text a few times, then listen. *(Please turn to the Scripture on the following pages. Inspiration points are there, should you need them. When you are ready, return here to continue.)*

Conversation

Do I notice myself reacting as I pray with the word of God? Do I feel challenged, comforted, angry? Imagining Jesus sitting or standing by me, I speak out my feelings, as one trusted friend to another.

Conclusion

I thank God for these moments we have spent together and for any insights I have been given concerning the text.

Sunday 15 September
Twenty-fourth Sunday in Ordinary Time
Mark 8:27–35

Jesus went on with his disciples to the villages of Caesarea Philippi; and on the way he asked his disciples, 'Who do people say that I am?' And they answered him, 'John the Baptist; and others, Elijah; and still others, one of the prophets.' He asked them, 'But who do you say that I am?' Peter answered him, 'You are the Messiah.' And he sternly ordered them not to tell anyone about him.

Then he began to teach them that the Son of Man must undergo great suffering, and be rejected by the elders, the chief priests, and the scribes, and be killed, and after three days rise again. He said all this quite openly. And Peter took him aside and began to rebuke him. But turning and looking at his disciples, he rebuked Peter and said, 'Get behind me, Satan! For you are setting your mind not on divine things but on human things.'

He called the crowd with his disciples, and said to them, 'If any want to become my followers, let them deny themselves and take up their cross and follow me. For those who want to save their life will lose it, and those who lose their life for my sake, and for the sake of the gospel, will save it.'

- Jesus called his disciples by name into a personal relationship with him. Knowing, loving and serving him was central to the mission he shared with them. May we be prophetic in announcing Jesus as the Messiah amid the many discordant voices of this age.

Monday 16 September
Luke 7:1–10

After Jesus had finished all his sayings in the hearing of the people, he entered Capernaum. A centurion there had a slave whom he valued highly, and who was ill and close to death. When he heard about Jesus, he sent some Jewish elders to him, asking him to come and heal his slave. When they came to Jesus, they appealed to him earnestly, saying, 'He is worthy of having you do this for him, for he loves our people, and it is he who built our synagogue for us.' And Jesus went with them, but when he was not far from the house, the centurion sent friends to say to him, 'Lord, do not trouble yourself, for I am not worthy to have you come under my roof; therefore I did not presume to come to you. But only speak the word, and let my servant be healed. For I also am a man set under authority, with soldiers under me; and I say to one, "Go", and he goes, and to another, "Come", and he comes, and to my slave, "Do this", and the slave does it.' When Jesus heard this he was amazed at him, and turning to the crowd that followed him, he said, 'I tell you, not even in Israel have I found such faith.' When those who had been sent returned to the house, they found the slave in good health.

- A centurion, an outsider, believed Jesus could help his highly valued slave. This was a man with authority and generosity, who built the synagogue and sent Jewish elders to Jesus for help. Lord, may we have the faith to ask others to intercede for us, to pray on our behalf.
- The spoken word can be powerful and very influential. Human testimony is of great significance on many occasions. May we believe in the power of the spoken word to bring healing and hope.

Tuesday 17 September
Luke 7:11–17

Soon afterwards he went to a town called Nain, and his disciples and a large crowd went with him. As he approached the gate of the town, a man who had died was being carried out. He was his mother's only son, and she was a widow; and with her was a large crowd from the town. When the Lord saw her, he had compassion for her and said to her, 'Do not weep.' Then he came forward and touched the bier, and the bearers stood still. And he said, 'Young man, I say to you, rise!' The dead man sat up and began to speak, and Jesus gave him to his mother. Fear seized all of them; and they glorified God, saying, 'A great prophet has risen among us!' and 'God has looked favourably on his people!' This word about him spread throughout Judea and all the surrounding country.

- Aware of this widow, whose only son had died, Jesus intervened. Her security was gone. Widows were vulnerable and needed protection. We pray that we may be people of compassion to the vulnerable and the poor.

- Jesus had compassion for the widow and entered deeply into her grief and loss. Was he the only son of a widowed mother at this stage? Jesus raised the widow's son and 'gave him to his mother'. May we enter more fully into the lives of those who grieve and suffer, to offer comfort and hope.

Wednesday 18 September
Luke 7:31–35

Jesus said to the crowds, 'To what then will I compare the people of this generation, and what are they like? They are like children sitting in the market-place and calling to one another,

"We played the flute for you, and you did not dance;
we wailed, and you did not weep."

'For John the Baptist has come eating no bread and drinking no wine, and you say, "He has a demon"; the Son of Man has come eating and drinking, and you say, "Look, a glutton and a drunkard, a friend of tax-collectors and sinners!" Nevertheless, wisdom is vindicated by all her children.'

- We can be stubborn and blind in many ways. Events and messages can be interpreted to fit with our own prejudices and what is convenient for us. We pray for the insight to see each situation on its merits and to live in the truth.
- There was a contrast between the ascetic life of John and that of Jesus, who went to parties with tax collectors and sinners. Both were reaching out to people in prophetic ways and in different circumstances. May we have the wisdom to assess each situation and to act as Jesus would.

Thursday 19 September
Luke 7:36–50

One of the Pharisees asked Jesus to eat with him, and he went into the Pharisee's house and took his place at the table. And a woman in the city, who was a sinner, having learned that he was eating in the Pharisee's house, brought an alabaster jar of ointment. She stood behind him at his feet, weeping, and began to bathe his feet with her tears and to dry them with her hair. Then she continued kissing his feet and anointing them with the ointment. Now when the Pharisee who had invited him saw it, he said to himself, 'If this man were a prophet, he would have known who and what kind of woman this is who is touching him – that she is a sinner.' Jesus spoke up and said to him, 'Simon, I have something to say to you.' 'Teacher,' he replied, 'speak.' 'A certain creditor had two debtors; one owed five hundred denarii, and the other fifty. When they could not pay, he cancelled the debts for both of them. Now which of them will love him more?' Simon answered, 'I suppose the one for whom he cancelled the greater debt.' And Jesus said to him, 'You have judged rightly.' Then turning towards the woman, he said to Simon, 'Do you see this woman? I entered your house; you gave me no water for my feet, but she has bathed my feet with her tears and dried them with her hair. You gave me no kiss, but from the time I came in she has not stopped kissing my feet. You did not anoint my head with oil, but she has anointed my feet with ointment. Therefore, I tell you, her sins, which were many, have been forgiven; hence she has shown great love. But the one to whom little is forgiven, loves little.' Then he said to her, 'Your sins are forgiven.' But those who were at the table with him began to say among themselves, 'Who is this who even forgives sins?' And he said to the woman, 'Your faith has saved you; go in peace.'

- An unnamed sinner broke in on a party in the house of Simon, a Pharisee. An unwelcome guest provided an opportunity for Simon to test Jesus on how he would deal with the situation. Simon had his labels ready for the woman and Jesus. We ask for the freedom and generosity to welcome the unlikely guests in life.
- Simon failed miserably as host in all aspects of welcoming Jesus. This woman met all the desired requirements. May we have the openness of the woman to show love and to receive forgiving love, so that like her we can embark on a new future.

Friday 20 September
Luke 8:1–3

Soon afterwards he went on through cities and villages, proclaiming and bringing the good news of the kingdom of God. The twelve were with him, as well as some women who had been cured of evil spirits and infirmities: Mary, called Magdalene, from whom seven demons had gone out, and Joanna, the wife of Herod's steward Chuza, and Susanna, and many others, who provided for them out of their resources.

- Much attention is given to the twelve who travelled around with Jesus, but there were also female disciples, who got little attention. Like them, may we provide for Jesus and his company out of our resources so that they can continue the mission.
- Mary Magdalene, Chuza and Susanna were named (Luke 23:49; 55), but there were many others. Lord, may we emulate these women who followed Jesus faithfully on his journey from Galilee to Jerusalem.

Saturday 21 September
St Matthew, Apostle and Evangelist
Matthew 9:9–13

As Jesus was walking along, he saw a man called Matthew sitting at the tax booth; and he said to him, 'Follow me.' And he got up and followed him.

And as he sat at dinner in the house, many tax-collectors and sinners came and were sitting with him and his disciples. When the Pharisees saw this, they said to his disciples, 'Why does your teacher eat with tax-collectors and sinners?' But when he heard this, he said, 'Those who are well have no need of a physician, but those who are sick. Go and learn what this means, "I desire mercy, not sacrifice." For I have come to call not the righteous but sinners.'

- Matthew was called from his tax office, to give up his way of life and to follow Jesus. His way of life was presumed to be dishonest. We pray that we may give up our dishonest ways, even in small things, to follow the Lord more closely.

22–28 September 2024

Something to think and pray about each day this week:

As the years go by, more and more of them, you can't help being a bit more aware of the destiny that's waiting for all of us. But what has long cheered me is the memory of a great line spoken by a great man when he reached a significant milestone.

We can become too preoccupied by the attempt to preserve ourselves from death or from natural decline. On his eightieth birthday the composer Stravinsky was asked in an interview what it felt like to be eighty. The great man looked puzzled. 'I don't know what you mean', he said, 'It's just another day for music.'

Another day for music. And even for the vast majority of us who will never compose anything the music of each day can be sensed in many forms – a child's laughter, a robin on a winter branch, a good joke. The music is all around us if we take time to be aware of it, and don't waste our time worrying about the destiny we inherited at birth.

Denis Tuohy, *Streets and Secret Places: Reflections of a News Reporter*

The Presence of God

To be present is to arrive as one is and open up to the other.
At this instant, as I arrive here, God is present waiting for me.
God always arrives before me, desiring to connect with me
even more than my most intimate friend.
I take a moment and greet my loving God.

Freedom

Leave me here freely all alone. / In cell where never sunlight shone. /
Should no one ever speak to me. / This golden silence makes me free!

— Part of a poem by Bl. Titus Brandsma, written while he was a
prisoner at Dachau concentration camp

Consciousness

Where am I with God? With others?
Do I have something to be grateful for? Then I give thanks.
Is there something I am sorry for? Then I ask forgiveness.

The Word

I take my time to read the word of God slowly, a few times, allowing
myself to dwell on anything that strikes me. *(Please turn to the Scripture on
the following pages. Inspiration points are there, should you need them. When you
are ready, return here to continue.)*

Conversation

How has God's word moved me? Has it left me cold?
Has it consoled me or moved me to act in a new way?
I imagine Jesus standing or sitting beside me;
I turn and share my feelings with him.

Conclusion

Glory be to the Father, and to the Son, and to the Holy Spirit,
As it was in the beginning, is now and ever shall be,
World without end. Amen.

Sunday 22 September
Twenty-fifth Sunday in Ordinary Time
Mark 9:30–37

They went on from there and passed through Galilee. He did not want anyone to know it; for he was teaching his disciples, saying to them, 'The Son of Man is to be betrayed into human hands, and they will kill him, and three days after being killed, he will rise again.' But they did not understand what he was saying and were afraid to ask him.

Then they came to Capernaum; and when he was in the house he asked them, 'What were you arguing about on the way?' But they were silent, for on the way they had argued with one another about who was the greatest. He sat down, called the twelve, and said to them, 'Whoever wants to be first must be last of all and servant of all.' Then he took a little child and put it among them; and taking it in his arms, he said to them, 'Whoever welcomes one such child in my name welcomes me, and whoever welcomes me welcomes not me but the one who sent me.'

- Jesus reminded his disciples of the direction of his prophetic life. Each time he mentioned suffering and death they did not hear his message or could not accept it. May we hear the truth of your good news, where glory is attained through suffering (Luke 24:26).
- The disciples seemed more concerned about themselves and their own glory. They were discussing who was the greatest among them. Lord, give us childlike hearts that can truly welcome you and help us to be welcoming of others, as your children.

Monday 23 September
Luke 8:16–18

He said in a parable, 'No one after lighting a lamp hides it under a jar, or puts it under a bed, but puts it on a lampstand, so that those who enter may see the light. For nothing is hidden that will not be disclosed, nor is anything secret that will not become known and come to light. Then pay attention to how you listen; for to those who have, more will be given; and from those who do not have, even what they seem to have will be taken away.'

- The theme of light is frequently used in scripture, from the creation story to Jesus as the light of the world. Light is not to be hidden but should show the way to safety. We pray that we may be a light to others who are caught in darkness.
- We need a gentle hold on life as it is God's gift to us. Holding on to anything in a possessive way is doomed to fail. It is in giving that we receive. Lord, give us the openness to live your message, for it is not to be kept secret but to show the way to others.

Tuesday 24 September
Luke 8:19–21

Then his mother and his brothers came to him, but they could not reach him because of the crowd. And he was told, 'Your mother and your brothers are standing outside, wanting to see you.' But he said to them, 'My mother and my brothers are those who hear the word of God and do it.'

- Everybody wants to belong, to feel included, for we are social beings. May we notice what excludes us from the Lord's company and take appropriate action to open the way to it.
- Hearing the word was significant for Mary, who said at the annunciation, 'Let it be with me according to your word' (Luke 1:38). We pray to hear the word anew and allow it to guide us to the fullness of life.

Wednesday 25 September
Luke 9:1–6

Then Jesus called the twelve together and gave them power and authority over all demons and to cure diseases, and he sent them out to proclaim the kingdom of God and to heal. He said to them, 'Take nothing for your journey, no staff, nor bag, nor bread, nor money – not even an extra tunic. Whatever house you enter, stay there, and leave from there. Wherever they do not welcome you, as you are leaving that town shake the dust off your feet as a testimony against them.' They departed and went through the villages, bringing the good news and curing diseases everywhere.

- Jesus is the good news of salvation. He shares his mission with us, as he did with the twelve. We are given authority to proclaim the kingdom and to heal. Lord, in our broken world, many need healing. May we trust you to work in us in ministering to them.
- We spend much time planning and coming up with projects for the way ahead. We can do so without giving sufficient space to Jesus, who sends us. May we have a deeper trust to rely more on him for what we need.

Thursday 26 September
Luke 9:7–9
Now Herod the ruler heard about all that had taken place, and he was perplexed, because it was said by some that John had been raised from the dead, by some that Elijah had appeared, and by others that one of the ancient prophets had arisen. Herod said, 'John I beheaded; but who is this about whom I hear such things?' And he tried to see him.

- Herod had a guilty conscience for having John beheaded. It was as if John was coming back to haunt him for his cowardice. May we have honesty in accepting our past and entrust it to Jesus to free us for the future.
- Jesus was a curiosity for Herod, who had heard reports and wanted to see him. Jesus was clearly placed among the prophets. Lord, we desire to meet you, not just see you as a wonder-worker.

Friday 27 September
Luke 9:18–22
Once when Jesus was praying alone, with only the disciples near him, he asked them, 'Who do the crowds say that I am?' They answered, 'John the Baptist; but others, Elijah; and still others, that one of the ancient prophets has arisen.' He said to them, 'But who do you say that I am?' Peter answered, 'The Messiah of God.'

He sternly ordered and commanded them not to tell anyone, saying, 'The Son of Man must undergo great suffering, and be rejected by the elders, chief priests, and scribes, and be killed, and on the third day be raised.'

- Coming from a time of prayer, Jesus asked his disciples how he was seen. Prayer was a special meeting place with the Father, who confirmed his identity as the beloved Son (Luke 3:22; 9:35). May our prayer deepen our identity as beloved sons and daughters of our heavenly Father.
- We are called to know and accept Jesus as Messiah and to have prophetic voices to announce it. May we have the faith and courage to do so, despite the rejection and suffering it may bring.

Saturday 28 September
Luke 9:43b–45

And all were astounded at the greatness of God.

While everyone was amazed at all that he was doing, he said to his disciples, 'Let these words sink into your ears: The Son of Man is going to be betrayed into human hands.' But they did not understand this saying; its meaning was concealed from them, so that they could not perceive it. And they were afraid to ask him about this saying.

- In the midst of all the acclaim about his ministry, Jesus brought his disciples back to reality by telling them where it was leading. We are told that everyone was amazed, but in truth some were not. Lord, we acknowledge our own betrayals of you and ask you to strengthen us to follow you better.
- The disciples were slow to grasp the full picture of Jesus and his mission. Being more concerned about themselves they were afraid to ask. May we be astonished at the greatness of God as revealed through the life of Jesus.

The Twenty-sixth Week in Ordinary Time

29 September–5 October 2024

Something to think and pray about each day this week:

During the month of October, we are invited to examine how we can be missionary disciples, sending out a message of faith, hope and love. In other words, what does it mean for our lives to have the 'flavour of the Gospel'? The Gospels offer a blueprint for all those who consider themselves followers of Christ. Do we have a 'taste' for God, an ability to savour God's presence in the world and God's goodness in all those we meet? To love as Jesus loved, to have a 'flavour of the Gospel', means to see everyone through the eyes of our loving God and to treat them as Jesus did with immediate and generous welcome. We will notice in particular that Jesus is always on the side of those who are marginalised, those whom society wants to condemn.

Jesus urges us to open our eyes and hearts to those who are excluded in our communities. This exclusion exists, even if it does not affect us personally. When we live with the 'flavour of the Gospel', we welcome all, and we model the radical hospitality and compassion of Jesus. Tuned in to the divine presence all around us, our lives will reflect the Spirit of God, who is loving, compassionate, and always on the side of those who are excluded. We have an active role to play in the mission of Jesus, who came to 'bring good news to the poor ... to proclaim release to captives and recovery of sight to the blind, to let the oppressed go free' (Luke 4:18).

Jane Mellett and Triona Doherty,
The Sacred Heart Messenger, October 2021

The Presence of God

What is present to me is what has a hold on my becoming. I reflect on the presence of God always there in love, amidst the many things that have a hold on me. I pause and pray that I may let God affect my becoming in this precise moment.

Freedom

By God's grace I was born to live in freedom. Free to enjoy the pleasures he created for me. Dear Lord, grant that I may live as you intended, with complete confidence in your loving care.

Consciousness

To be conscious about something is to be aware of it.

Dear Lord, help me to remember that you gave me life. Thank you for the gift of life. Teach me to slow down, to be still and enjoy the pleasures created for me. To be aware of the beauty that surrounds me: the marvel of mountains, the calmness of lakes, the fragility of a flower petal. I need to remember that all these things come from you.

The Word

God speaks to each of us individually. I listen attentively to hear what he is saying to me. Read the text a few times, then listen. *(Please turn to the Scripture on the following pages. Inspiration points are there, should you need them. When you are ready, return here to continue.)*

Conversation

I begin to talk with Jesus about the Scripture I have just read. What part of it strikes a chord in me? Perhaps the words of a friend – or some story I have heard recently – will rise to the surface in my consciousness. If so, does the story throw light on what the Scripture passage may be saying to me?

Conclusion

Glory be to the Father, and to the Son, and to the Holy Spirit,
As it was in the beginning, is now and ever shall be,
World without end. Amen.

Sunday 29 September
Twenty-sixth Sunday in Ordinary Time
Mark 9:38–43.45.47–48

John said to him, 'Teacher, we saw someone casting out demons in your name, and we tried to stop him, because he was not following us.' But Jesus said, 'Do not stop him; for no one who does a deed of power in my name will be able soon afterwards to speak evil of me. Whoever is not against us is for us. For truly I tell you, whoever gives you a cup of water to drink because you bear the name of Christ will by no means lose the reward.

'If any of you put a stumbling-block before one of these little ones who believe in me, it would be better for you if a great millstone were hung around your neck and you were thrown into the sea. If your hand causes you to stumble, cut it off; it is better for you to enter life maimed than to have two hands and to go to hell, to the unquenchable fire. And if your foot causes you to stumble, cut it off; it is better for you to enter life lame than to have two feet and to be thrown into hell. And if your eye causes you to stumble, tear it out; it is better for you to enter the kingdom of God with one eye than to have two eyes and to be thrown into hell, where the worm never dies, and the fire is never quenched.'

- Divisions can be formed on many grounds – who is in or out, who belongs and by what criteria. Jesus' way is that of union, of working together with him and for him. Lord, may we concentrate on the deeper values and not get caught in surface matters that break harmony.
- Jesus, you desire unity with you and with one another, just as you want integrity for us in our own lives. Give us the wisdom to choose what is beneficial and the freedom to let go of what is not.

Monday 30 September
Luke 9:46–50

An argument arose among them as to which one of them was the greatest. But Jesus, aware of their inner thoughts, took a little child and put it by his side, and said to them, 'Whoever welcomes this child in my name welcomes me, and whoever welcomes me welcomes the one who sent me; for the least among all of you is the greatest.'

John answered, 'Master, we saw someone casting out demons in your name, and we tried to stop him, because he does not follow with us.' But Jesus said to him, 'Do not stop him; for whoever is not against you is for you.'

- Children have much to teach us about trust and honesty and can embarrass us in our shortcomings. May we know what is truly great and have the humility to be guided by it as the little ones the Lord loves.
- Artificial divisions are evident in life. Distinctions are made that are not helpful. Lord, it is you who calls us together. May we find our unity in you and not be separated by little things of no enduring value.

Tuesday 1 October
Luke 9:51–56

When the days drew near for him to be taken up, he set his face to go to Jerusalem. And he sent messengers ahead of him. On their way they entered a village of the Samaritans to make ready for him; but they did not receive him, because his face was set towards Jerusalem. When his disciples James and John saw it, they said, 'Lord, do you want us to command fire to come down from heaven and consume them?' But he turned and rebuked them. Then they went on to another village.

- At the age of twelve Jesus made a journey to Jerusalem, where he declared he had to be in his Father's house (Luke 2:49). Now we have a decisive moment when 'he set his face to go to Jerusalem', as it was where all things of note should happen. We pray that we may make the journey with him as it was where he would complete his mission.
- 'When the days drew near for him to be taken up … '. The journey to Jerusalem had a clear goal. Lord, may we have clarity on the direction you were taking so that we are not distracted by sideshows on the way.

Wednesday 2 October
The Guardian Angels
Matthew 18:1–5.10

At that time the disciples came to Jesus and asked, 'Who is the greatest in the kingdom of heaven?' He called a child, whom he put among them, and said, 'Truly I tell you, unless you change and become like children, you will never enter the kingdom of heaven. Whoever becomes humble like this child is the greatest in the kingdom of heaven. Whoever welcomes one such child in my name welcomes me.

'Take care that you do not despise one of these little ones; for, I tell you, in heaven their angels continually see the face of my Father in heaven.'

- Our creator God, recognising our gifts and frailties, did not leave us to our own devices. God's loving care is provided in different ways. May we value the angels God has given us to guide and guard us on the journey of life.
- We are not self-sufficient, even if we like to think so. God looks after us, little ones who need direction and security. May we have the honesty to accept what God has in store for us and the humility of beloved children to be led to it.

Thursday 3 October
Luke 10:1–12

After this the Lord appointed seventy others and sent them on ahead of him in pairs to every town and place where he himself intended to go. He said to them, 'The harvest is plentiful, but the labourers are few; therefore ask the Lord of the harvest to send out labourers into his harvest. Go on your way. See, I am sending you out like lambs into the midst of wolves. Carry no purse, no bag, no sandals; and greet no one on the road. Whatever house you enter, first say, "Peace to this house!" And if anyone is there who shares in peace, your peace will rest on that person; but if not, it will return to you. Remain in the same house, eating and drinking whatever they provide, for the labourer deserves to be paid. Do not move about from house to house. Whenever you enter a town and its people welcome you, eat what is set before you; cure the sick who are there, and say to them, "The kingdom of God has come near to you." But whenever you enter a town and they do not welcome you, go out into its streets and say, "Even the dust of your town that clings to our feet, we wipe off in protest against you. Yet know this: the kingdom of God has come near." I tell you, on that day it will be more tolerable for Sodom than for that town.'

- Jesus appointed and sent out seventy in pairs to prepare the way for him. It was his desire that they help to gather the harvest. Lord, may we who are sent out in your name trust you to provide what we need for the mission.
- Jesus' message is one of peace and of proclaiming that the kingdom of God is near. There are people who welcome the message and the messengers, just as there are others who do not do so. May we have the strength to continue the Lord's work and not be put off by those unwilling to hear the good news.

Friday 4 October
Luke 10:13–16
'Woe to you, Chorazin! Woe to you, Bethsaida! For if the deeds of power done in you had been done in Tyre and Sidon, they would have repented long ago, sitting in sackcloth and ashes. But at the judgement it will be more tolerable for Tyre and Sidon than for you. And you, Capernaum, will you be exalted to heaven?

No, you will be brought down to Hades.

'Whoever listens to you listens to me, and whoever rejects you rejects me, and whoever rejects me rejects the one who sent me.'

- Tyre and Sidon rejected God's message but they did not witness the person and ministry of Jesus. Chorazin and Bethsaida were more familiar with Jesus but they were unwilling to respond. We pray for the faith to receive the message, learning from those who rejected it, as the way of life.
- God's word is proclaimed as good news. The invitation is to listen and take it to heart. It is the acceptance or rejection of Jesus, not just his word. May we have ears to hear and hearts to live his message as our good news of salvation.

Saturday 5 October
Luke 10:17–24

The seventy returned with joy, saying, 'Lord, in your name even the demons submit to us!' He said to them, 'I watched Satan fall from heaven like a flash of lightning. See, I have given you authority to tread on snakes and scorpions, and over all the power of the enemy; and nothing will hurt you. Nevertheless, do not rejoice at this, that the spirits submit to you, but rejoice that your names are written in heaven.'

At that same hour Jesus rejoiced in the Holy Spirit and said, 'I thank you, Father, Lord of heaven and earth, because you have hidden these things from the wise and the intelligent and have revealed them to infants; yes, Father, for such was your gracious will. All things have been handed over to me by my Father; and no one knows who the Son is except the Father, or who the Father is except the Son and anyone to whom the Son chooses to reveal him.'

Then turning to the disciples, Jesus said to them privately, 'Blessed are the eyes that see what you see! For I tell you that many prophets and kings desired to see what you see, but did not see it, and to hear what you hear, but did not hear it.'

- The seventy who had been sent out rejoiced in what they had accomplished. They had evidence of the power and authority of God working through them. Lord, you remind us that our deeper joy is more than the deeds we perform, for we are special to you, with our names written in heaven.
- We are blessed to know the Lord and live in relationship with him. We have been given eyes to see and ears to hear so that as children of God we can live in a spirit of gratitude for what we have been given. May we grow in faith and openness to God's ongoing revelation to us.

6–12 October 2024

Something to think and pray about each day this week:

I knew a man who fought cancer to the end. He took to every type of possible healing. We had all been told it wouldn't work. I know another who just opened himself to it all and wouldn't even take chemo. These are different approaches to suffering. One fought it and the other accepted. I admired the both of them.

Many people go into hospital wondering about their illness, and worry that death might be close. That's part of life. As for Jesus: it's a fearful time, confusing, and sometimes draws us into more faith. We can transform our pain into suffering, and find some great graces in it. There is the challenge to find new life in it. Pain becomes suffering. Jesus doesn't want the chalice of the garden, but he allows it become fully part of him so that his inner strength is big! It doesn't mean a simplistic approach, rather it means an acceptance of darkness in life.

Jesus found in his passion that God the Father is near. This can be our way and we can find that through helping each other. We can help people at times of suffering – listening, being present. We find this in our hearts, not in books – we find that we can grow through suffering and we realise on a bad day that peace invades the soul, or that there is a bright light in the darkness.

Donal Neary SJ, *Gospel Reflections for Sundays of Year B*

The Presence of God
'Be still, and know that I am God!' Lord, your words lead us to the calmness and greatness of your presence.

Freedom
Everything has the potential to draw forth from me a fuller love and life. Yet my desires are often fixed, caught, on illusions of fulfilment. I ask that God, through my freedom, may orchestrate my desires in a vibrant loving melody rich in harmony.

Consciousness
I exist in a web of relationships: links to nature, people, God. I trace out these links, giving thanks for the life that flows through them. Some links are twisted or broken; I may feel regret, anger, disappointment. I pray for the gift of acceptance and forgiveness.

The Word
I read the word of God slowly, a few times over, and I listen to what God is saying to me. *(Please turn to the Scripture on the following pages. Inspiration points are there, should you need them. When you are ready, return here to continue.)*

Conversation
Jesus, you speak to me through the words of the Gospels. May I respond to your call today. Teach me to recognise your hand at work in my daily living.

Conclusion
I thank God for these moments we have spent together and for any insights I have been given concerning the text.

Sunday 6 October
Twenty-seventh Sunday in Ordinary Time
Mark 10:2–16

Some Pharisees came, and to test him they asked, 'Is it lawful for a man to divorce his wife?' He answered them, 'What did Moses command you?' They said, 'Moses allowed a man to write a certificate of dismissal and to divorce her.' But Jesus said to them, 'Because of your hardness of heart he wrote this commandment for you. But from the beginning of creation, "God made them male and female." "For this reason a man shall leave his father and mother and be joined to his wife, and the two shall become one flesh." So they are no longer two, but one flesh. Therefore what God has joined together, let no one separate.'

Then in the house the disciples asked him again about this matter. He said to them, 'Whoever divorces his wife and marries another commits adultery against her; and if she divorces her husband and marries another, she commits adultery.'

People were bringing little children to him in order that he might touch them; and the disciples spoke sternly to them. But when Jesus saw this, he was indignant and said to them, 'Let the little children come to me; do not stop them; for it is to such as these that the kingdom of God belongs. Truly I tell you, whoever does not receive the kingdom of God as a little child will never enter it.' And he took them up in his arms, laid his hands on them, and blessed them.

- The Pharisees set out to test Jesus on the issue of divorce, referring to the stance of Moses. Jesus stated God's desire but he was aware that all did not meet the ideal. May we have the faith to teach the truth and be compassionate to those who do not meet the ideal.
- From marriage there is the move to children. Jesus was happy to meet and engage with children, despite the indignation of the disciples. We pray for the freedom of children to approach Jesus and to be better members of his kingdom.

Monday 7 October
Luke 10:25–37

Just then a lawyer stood up to test Jesus. 'Teacher,' he said, 'what must I do to inherit eternal life?' He said to him, 'What is written in the law? What do you read there?' He answered, 'You shall love the Lord your God with all your heart, and with all your soul, and with all your strength, and with all your mind; and your neighbour as yourself.' And he said to him, 'You have given the right answer; do this, and you will live.'

But wanting to justify himself, he asked Jesus, 'And who is my neighbour?' Jesus replied, 'A man was going down from Jerusalem to Jericho, and fell into the hands of robbers, who stripped him, beat him, and went away, leaving him half dead. Now by chance a priest was going down that road; and when he saw him, he passed by on the other side. So likewise a Levite, when he came to the place and saw him, passed by on the other side. But a Samaritan while travelling came near him; and when he saw him, he was moved with pity. He went to him and bandaged his wounds, having poured oil and wine on them. Then he put him on his own animal, brought him to an inn, and took care of him. The next day he took out two denarii, gave them to the innkeeper, and said, "Take care of him; and when I come back, I will repay you whatever more you spend." Which of these three, do you think, was a neighbour to the man who fell into the hands of the robbers?' He said, 'The one who showed him mercy.' Jesus said to him, 'Go and do likewise.'

- A lawyer stood up to test Jesus, who put a question back to him. The criterion for inheriting eternal life was love of God, neighbour and self. Jesus affirmed the response. Lord, your law is one of love. May we have hearts to embrace it and allow it to guide us in life.
- The story of the good Samaritan is one of compassion, of love in action, of going beyond the expected. Others walked by the stricken man but the Samaritan took decisive action. We pray for a similarly compassionate and caring response.

Tuesday 8 October
Luke 10:38–42

Now as they went on their way, he entered a certain village, where a woman named Martha welcomed him into her home. She had a sister named Mary, who sat at the Lord's feet and listened to what he was saying. But Martha was distracted by her many tasks; so she came to him and asked, 'Lord, do you not care that my sister has left me to do all the work by myself? Tell her then to help me.' But the Lord answered her, 'Martha, Martha, you are worried and distracted by many things; there is need of only one thing. Mary has chosen the better part, which will not be taken away from her.'

- While on a journey Jesus called in to visit his friends. Martha welcomed him to her home but was overly concerned with feeding Jesus. Lord, we ask that we may have the hospitality to welcome you into our homes and not be distracted by what we have to do.
- Mary sat and listened. Her focus was Jesus, not the kitchen. She wanted to be nourished, to be fed by Jesus and his word. We pray that we may be free to choose the better part that will sustain us on our journey.

Wednesday 9 October
Luke 11:1–4

He was praying in a certain place, and after he had finished, one of his disciples said to him, 'Lord, teach us to pray, as John taught his disciples.' He said to them, 'When you pray, say:
Father, hallowed be your name.
  Your kingdom come.
  Give us each day our daily bread.
  And forgive us our sins,
  for we ourselves forgive everyone indebted to us.
  And do not bring us to the time of trial.'

- Jesus is the teacher of prayer, which had a prominent place in his life. In making the request, the disciple recognised that there was something different about Jesus' prayer. Lord, we ask you to teach us to pray and to be more in tune with you and the Father.

- Jesus proclaimed that the kingdom of God was near. He asked us to pray that it may become a reality in our lives and world where there are many competing kingdoms. Help us to accept our need and let it turn us to God to provide.

Thursday 10 October
Luke 11:5–13
And he said to them, 'Suppose one of you has a friend, and you go to him at midnight and say to him, "Friend, lend me three loaves of bread; for a friend of mine has arrived, and I have nothing to set before him." And he answers from within, "Do not bother me; the door has already been locked, and my children are with me in bed; I cannot get up and give you anything." I tell you, even though he will not get up and give him anything because he is his friend, at least because of his persistence he will get up and give him whatever he needs.

'So I say to you, Ask, and it will be given to you; search, and you will find; knock, and the door will be opened for you. For everyone who asks receives, and everyone who searches finds, and for everyone who knocks, the door will be opened. Is there anyone among you who, if your child asks for a fish, will give a snake instead of a fish? Or if the child asks for an egg, will give a scorpion? If you then, who are evil, know how to give good gifts to your children, how much more will the heavenly Father give the Holy Spirit to those who ask him!'

- A friend arriving at an inconvenient time asked for a favour. Persistence was enough for him to get what he requested. God is not a reluctant giver. May we have the courage to ask and the persistence to continue as the Lord teaches.
- God is the giver of every good gift. We are invited to name what we want and to pray with confidence. As a parent will grant good gifts that are helpful, we ask you, Lord, to give us your Spirit to guide us in our searching and asking.

Friday 11 October
Luke 11:15–26
But some of them said, 'He casts out demons by Beelzebul, the ruler of the demons.' Others, to test him, kept demanding from him a sign

from heaven. But he knew what they were thinking and said to them, 'Every kingdom divided against itself becomes a desert, and house falls on house. If Satan also is divided against himself, how will his kingdom stand? – for you say that I cast out the demons by Beelzebul. Now if I cast out the demons by Beelzebul, by whom do your exorcists cast them out? Therefore they will be your judges. But if it is by the finger of God that I cast out the demons, then the kingdom of God has come to you. When a strong man, fully armed, guards his castle, his property is safe. But when one stronger than he attacks him and overpowers him, he takes away his armour in which he trusted and divides his plunder. Whoever is not with me is against me, and whoever does not gather with me scatters.

'When the unclean spirit has gone out of a person, it wanders through waterless regions looking for a resting-place, but not finding any, it says, "I will return to my house from which I came." When it comes, it finds it swept and put in order. Then it goes and brings seven other spirits more evil than itself, and they enter and live there; and the last state of that person is worse than the first.'

- People who are seen to do good can be labelled easily, in a negative way. Their motivation may be called into question. Jesus, you did good deeds in casting out demons. May we continue to clarify our intentions in serving in your name and not be put off by the opinions of others.
- Jesus spoke about the power of evil and the need to be alert. He reminds us that he is with us and that, with him on our side, we can prevail. May we not presume upon our resources or become too casual in putting our house in order.

Saturday 12 October
Luke 11:27–28
While he was saying this, a woman in the crowd raised her voice and said to him, 'Blessed is the womb that bore you and the breasts that nursed you!' But he said, 'Blessed rather are those who hear the word of God and obey it!'

- Motherhood and bearing children is cherished in scripture. It was seen as a sign of God's favour (Psalms 127, 128). We pray for a greater appreciation of mothers, with their love for their children.
- Jesus was born of Mary, who nursed him as a child and continued to look out for him. Her obedience to the word was lived out in her following him. As children of the word, may we imitate her in bringing Jesus into the world of our time.

13–19 October 2024

Something to think and pray about each day this week:

We live in an age that is fascinated by identity. There is ongoing debate on gender identity.

To understand who we are is a deep and healthy human need. So many people are not at home in their own skins and the application of labels can be deeply unhelpful. All of this sounds like serious inner work – and it is! But the Christian believes we need to turn outwards, not gaze inwards at the self. In the age of the selfie this is quite a challenge.

We start from a basic belief that every human being is made in the image of God; in this case, a relational God who is Father, Son and Holy Spirit (Trinity). At the very heart of God are mutual relations between the three. From what I gather neuroscience also holds that the brain is deeply social. Babies' brains take shape when they sense and experience loving interaction. They are intensely social little people. Their journey to self-discovery is always made in the company of others.

Often we hear people talking about 'my other half', or somebody who is or was 'a part of me'. The way we speak about love is always relational. Unconsciously we use the language of the Trinity; we sense that somebody else makes us complete. Two people together are exclusive, but add a third, equal love and what do we have? A community, a communion of love that is inclusive. You will have many glimpses of the Trinity in your life … just be open to them.

Tom Cox, *The Sacred Heart Messenger*, December 2021

The Presence of God

'Come to me, all you who are weary and are carrying heavy burdens, and I will give you rest.' Here I am, Lord. I come to seek your presence. I long for your healing power.

Freedom

God is not foreign to my freedom. The Spirit breathes life into my most intimate desires, gently nudging me towards all that is good. I ask for the grace to let myself be enfolded by the Spirit.

Consciousness

I remind myself that I am in the presence of the Lord. I will take refuge in his loving heart. He is my strength in times of weakness. He is my comforter in times of sorrow.

The Word

I take my time to read the word of God slowly, a few times, allowing myself to dwell on anything that strikes me. *(Please turn to the Scripture on the following pages. Inspiration points are there, should you need them. When you are ready, return here to continue.)*

Conversation

Jesus, you always welcomed little children when you walked on this earth. Teach me to have a childlike trust in you. Teach me to live in the knowledge that you will never abandon me.

Conclusion

Glory be to the Father, and to the Son, and to the Holy Spirit,
As it was in the beginning, is now and ever shall be,
World without end. Amen.

Sunday 13 October
Twenty-eighth Sunday in Ordinary Time
Mark 10:17–30

As he was setting out on a journey, a man ran up and knelt before him, and asked him, 'Good Teacher, what must I do to inherit eternal life?' Jesus said to him, 'Why do you call me good? No one is good but God alone. You know the commandments: "You shall not murder; You shall not commit adultery; You shall not steal; You shall not bear false witness; You shall not defraud; Honour your father and mother."' He said to him, 'Teacher, I have kept all these since my youth.' Jesus, looking at him, loved him and said, 'You lack one thing; go, sell what you own, and give the money to the poor, and you will have treasure in heaven; then come, follow me.' When he heard this, he was shocked and went away grieving, for he had many possessions.

Then Jesus looked around and said to his disciples, 'How hard it will be for those who have wealth to enter the kingdom of God!' And the disciples were perplexed at these words. But Jesus said to them again, 'Children, how hard it is to enter the kingdom of God! It is easier for a camel to go through the eye of a needle than for someone who is rich to enter the kingdom of God.' They were greatly astounded and said to one another, 'Then who can be saved?' Jesus looked at them and said, 'For mortals it is impossible, but not for God; for God all things are possible.'

Peter began to say to him, 'Look, we have left everything and followed you.' Jesus said, 'Truly I tell you, there is no one who has left house or brothers or sisters or mother or father or children or fields, for my sake and for the sake of the good news, who will not receive a hundredfold now in this age – houses, brothers and sisters, mothers and children, and fields, with persecutions – and in the age to come eternal life.'

- A generous, law-abiding man ran up to Jesus desiring to inherit eternal life. His external riches, his possessions, held him bound. Lord, may we hear your message and allow you to be the true riches that hold our hearts.
- We can dominate what we have or let it dominate us. Letting go of control does not come easily. May we let the Lord bring us to inner freedom so that we can do what seems impossible otherwise.

Monday 14 October
Luke 11:29–32

When the crowds were increasing, he began to say, 'This generation is an evil generation; it asks for a sign, but no sign will be given to it except the sign of Jonah. For just as Jonah became a sign to the people of Nineveh, so the Son of Man will be to this generation. The queen of the South will rise at the judgement with the people of this generation and condemn them, because she came from the ends of the earth to listen to the wisdom of Solomon, and see, something greater than Solomon is here! The people of Nineveh will rise up at the judgement with this generation and condemn it, because they repented at the proclamation of Jonah, and see, something greater than Jonah is here!'

- Coming to a true spirit of repentance can be challenging. The evil people of Nineveh were able to respond to the preaching of the prophet Jonah. Lord, you are greater than Jonah, so we pray to hear and respond to your call to conversion.
- The Queen of the South came a long distance to hear the wisdom of Solomon and was impressed by it. May we have the wisdom to hear the words of Jesus and be guided by them in our lives and relationships.

Tuesday 15 October
Luke 11:37–41

While he was speaking, a Pharisee invited him to dine with him; so he went in and took his place at the table. The Pharisee was amazed to see that he did not first wash before dinner. Then the Lord said to him, 'Now you Pharisees clean the outside of the cup and of the dish, but inside you are full of greed and wickedness. You fools! Did not the one who made the outside make the inside also? So give for alms those things that are within; and see, everything will be clean for you.'

- Another table situation, where a Pharisee invited Jesus to dine with him. The Pharisee was overly concerned about ritual cleanliness and washing beforehand. Lord, while we value external cleanliness, we pray that we may be blessed in having clean hearts.

- Jesus drew attention to the internal, giving examples of the cup and dish. What they contained was more significant. May we be wise enough to know what to value and keep our focus on that while giving alms in the name of Jesus.

Wednesday 16 October
Luke 11:42–46

Jesus said, 'But woe to you Pharisees! For you tithe mint and rue and herbs of all kinds, and neglect justice and the love of God; it is these you ought to have practised, without neglecting the others. Woe to you Pharisees! For you love to have the seat of honour in the synagogues and to be greeted with respect in the market-places. Woe to you! For you are like unmarked graves, and people walk over them without realising it.'

One of the lawyers answered him, 'Teacher, when you say these things, you insult us too.' And he said, 'Woe also to you lawyers! For you load people with burdens hard to bear, and you yourselves do not lift a finger to ease them.'

- When too much attention is given to details, the bigger picture can be obscured. This is true in a particular way when too much self-interest is involved. Lord, help us to retain a sense of perspective so that you can be the centre of our attention.
- Those who were focused on the law, in this case the religious laws, were caught in the external application without appreciating what they would lead to. May we have clarity on the end goal so that we can lighten the burdens of people and not impose undue obligations on them.

Thursday 17 October
Luke 11:47–54

Jesus said: 'Woe to you! For you build the tombs of the prophets whom your ancestors killed. So you are witnesses and approve of the deeds of your ancestors; for they killed them, and you build their tombs. Therefore also the Wisdom of God said, "I will send them prophets and apostles, some of whom they will kill and persecute," so that this generation may be charged with the blood of all the prophets shed since the foundation of the world, from the blood of Abel to the blood of Zechariah, who perished between the altar and the sanctuary. Yes, I tell you, it will be charged against this generation. Woe to you lawyers! For you have taken away the key of knowledge; you did not enter yourselves, and you hindered those who were entering.' When he went outside, the scribes and the Pharisees began to be very hostile toward him and to cross-examine him about many things, lying in wait for him, to catch him in something he might say.

- Failure to appreciate the true purpose of the law led to misguided decisions as well as the inability to hear the message of the prophets and apostles. We pray to see the law as a guide in life and help others to live it.
- Jesus' proclamation of the truth revealed the blindness of the Pharisees, who became hostile to Jesus and wanted to catch him out. Lord, help us to understand your message better so that it can be a rule of life that shows us the way.

Friday 18 October
St Luke, Evangelist
Luke 10:1–9

After this the Lord appointed seventy others and sent them on ahead of him in pairs to every town and place where he himself intended to go. He said to them, 'The harvest is plentiful, but the labourers are few; therefore ask the Lord of the harvest to send out labourers into his harvest. Go on your way. See, I am sending you out like lambs into the midst of wolves. Carry no purse, no bag, no sandals; and greet no one on the road. Whatever house you enter, first say, "Peace to this house!" And if anyone is there who shares in peace, your peace will rest on that person; but if not, it will return to you. Remain in the same house, eating and drinking whatever they provide, for the labourer deserves to be paid. Do not move about from house to house. Whenever you enter a town and its people welcome you, eat what is set before you; cure the sick who are there, and say to them, "The kingdom of God has come near to you."'

- Luke has given us a gospel of compassion and mercy. The Father who sent Jesus among us calls us and sends us with good news to others. We pray that we may share God's caring love with the many people who need it.
- The poor are prominent in the teaching of Jesus as portrayed by Luke. There are many poor people now who need a message of comfort and consolation. May we be messengers of hope who proclaim God's kingdom of justice, love and peace.

Saturday 19 October
Luke 12:8–12

Jesus said to his disciples, 'And I tell you, everyone who acknowledges me before others, the Son of Man also will acknowledge before the angels of God; but whoever denies me before others will be denied before the angels of God. And everyone who speaks a word against the Son of Man will be forgiven; but whoever blasphemes against the Holy Spirit will not be forgiven. When they bring you before the synagogues, the rulers, and the authorities, do not worry about how you are to defend yourselves or what you are to say; for the Holy Spirit will teach you at that very hour what you ought to say.'

- Our relationship with the Lord is central to life. It means acknowledging the Lord who acknowledges us as his own. We pray for a deeper faith that enables us to know and make the Lord known to the people of this age.
- Loyalty and fidelity are important qualities in life and in relationships. Jesus displays those gifts and is faithful to us. May we rely on the Lord in the challenges we encounter as he has promised us the Holy Spirit to help us.

The Twenty-ninth Week in Ordinary Time

20–26 October 2024

Something to think and pray about each day this week:

Pope Francis observed that 'every "yes" to God gives rise to stories of salvation for us and for others. Like Mary with her own "yes"' (8 December 2016). Humble as Mary's 'yes' to the angel Gabriel was, it gave rise to a huge story of freedom for us. What's more, the daring and confidence of Mary's 'yes' mirrored God's massive 'yes' in creating us. The first 'yes' was God's, God's 'Let there be light' (Genesis 1:3). The whole of creation poured forth from these powerful words, galaxy upon galaxy, countless stars scattered across the vast reaches of space like necklaces of pearls, then plan- et after planet, and finally human life itself. And when the fullness of time came, Mary echoed God's 'yes' in her 'Let it be done unto me according to thy Word' (Luke 1:38). Because of Mary's 'yes', God was able to take on human flesh. God becoming one of us: that's the most amazing thing that has ever happened in the history of the world. God became one of us so that through the miracle of grace we could partake in his divine nature.

Thomas Casey SJ, *Smile of Joy: Mary of Nazareth*

The Presence of God

'I am standing at the door, knocking,' says the Lord. What a wonderful privilege that the Lord of all creation desires to come to me. I welcome his presence.

Freedom

I will ask God's help
to be free from my own preoccupations,
to be open to God in this time of prayer,
to come to know, love and serve God more.

Consciousness

In God's loving presence I unwind the past day,
starting from now and looking back, moment by moment.
I gather in all the goodness and light, in gratitude.
I attend to the shadows and what they say to me,
seeking healing, courage, forgiveness.

The Word

Now I turn to the Scripture set out for me this day. I read slowly over the words and see if any sentence or sentiment appeals to me. *(Please turn to the Scripture on the following pages. Inspiration points are there, should you need them. When you are ready, return here to continue.)*

Conversation

Sometimes I wonder what I might say if I were to meet you in person, Lord.
I think I might say, 'Thank you', because you are always there for me.

Conclusion

I thank God for these moments we have spent together and for any insights I have been given concerning the text.

Sunday 20 October
Twenty-ninth Sunday in Ordinary Time
Mark 10:35–45

James and John, the sons of Zebedee, came forward to him and said to him, 'Teacher, we want you to do for us whatever we ask of you.' And he said to them, 'What is it you want me to do for you?' And they said to him, 'Grant us to sit, one at your right hand and one at your left, in your glory.' But Jesus said to them, 'You do not know what you are asking. Are you able to drink the cup that I drink, or be baptised with the baptism that I am baptised with?' They replied, 'We are able.' Then Jesus said to them, 'The cup that I drink you will drink; and with the baptism with which I am baptised, you will be baptised; but to sit at my right hand or at my left is not mine to grant, but it is for those for whom it has been prepared.'

When the ten heard this, they began to be angry with James and John. So Jesus called them and said to them, 'You know that among the Gentiles those whom they recognize as their rulers lord it over them, and their great ones are tyrants over them. But it is not so among you; but whoever wishes to become great among you must be your servant, and whoever wishes to be first among you must be slave of all. For the Son of Man came not to be served but to serve, and to give his life a ransom for many.'

- Mothers interceding for their children is not new. Bathsheba interceded with David for her son, Solomon, to succeed David as king (1 Kings 1). Jesus heard the ambition for James and John but he challenged them to redirect it. May our ambitions, which give us energy, be channelled to the glory of God.
- All the apostles struggled with following Jesus, as their own issues remained prominent. Jesus sought to bring them beyond self-interest to be people for others. Lord, may we imitate you who came to serve and who offered your life for us.

Monday 21 October
Luke 12:13–21

Someone in the crowd said to him, 'Teacher, tell my brother to divide the family inheritance with me.' But he said to him, 'Friend, who set me to be a judge or arbitrator over you?' And he said to them, 'Take care! Be on your guard against all kinds of greed; for one's life does not consist in the abundance of possessions.' Then he told them a parable: 'The land of a rich man produced abundantly. And he thought to himself, "What should I do, for I have no place to store my crops?" Then he said, "I will do this: I will pull down my barns and build larger ones, and there I will store all my grain and my goods. And I will say to my soul, Soul, you have ample goods laid up for many years; relax, eat, drink, be merry." But God said to him, "You fool! This very night your life is being demanded of you. And the things you have prepared, whose will they be?" So it is with those who store up treasures for themselves but are not rich towards God.'

- Property and inheritance are prominent issues in life and give rise to many conflicts. Security can be sought in possessions and property. May we have the freedom to see all as gift so that we find our true security in the Lord.

- Building, accumulating and storing up take on great prominence for many. Jesus spoke of being free and not to be worrying about passing things, like food and clothing (Luke 12:22–34). Lord, help us to know what is of lasting value, for you are our treasure.

Tuesday 22 October
Luke 12:35–38

Jesus said to his disciples, 'Be dressed for action and have your lamps lit; be like those who are waiting for their master to return from the wedding banquet, so that they may open the door for him as soon as he comes and knocks. Blessed are those slaves whom the master finds alert when he comes; truly I tell you, he will fasten his belt and have them sit down to eat, and he will come and serve them. If he comes during the middle of the night, or near dawn, and finds them so, blessed are those slaves.'

- Readiness and watchfulness are important features of waiting as they portray care, concern and being responsible. May we have that attitude in being ready for your coming to us, Lord, where we can offer comfort and hospitality.

- Generally, servants waited on their masters and offered them welcome, be it washing their feet or providing a meal. Jesus gave a different message, making himself the servant who 'will come and wait on them'. Lord, may we have the freedom to let you serve us and to let us be your servants, too.

Wednesday 23 October
Luke 12:39–48

Jesus said to his disciples, 'But know this: if the owner of the house had known at what hour the thief was coming, he would not have let his house be broken into. You also must be ready, for the Son of Man is coming at an unexpected hour.'

Peter said, 'Lord, are you telling this parable for us or for everyone?' And the Lord said, 'Who then is the faithful and prudent manager whom his master will put in charge of his slaves, to give them their allowance of food at the proper time? Blessed is that slave whom his master will find at work when he arrives. Truly I tell you, he will put that one in charge of all his possessions. But if that slave says to himself, "My master is delayed in coming", and if he begins to beat the other slaves, men and women, and to eat and drink and get drunk, the master of that slave will come on a day when he does not expect him and at an hour that he does not know, and will cut him in pieces, and put him with the unfaithful. That slave who knew what his master wanted, but did not prepare himself or do what was wanted, will receive a severe beating. But one who did not know and did what deserved a beating will receive a light beating. From everyone to whom much has been given, much will be required; and from one to whom much has been entrusted, even more will be demanded.'

- There is a time for everything (Ecclesiastes 3:1). Jesus gave practical advice about time, about being alert, reminding us to prepare for his coming again. Lord, you came as a friend, not a thief in the night, and desire us to be ready when you come to us.
- Peter questioned Jesus, who replied indicating what a faithful and prudent manager would do. The servant is to be responsible in carrying out his duties and in his relationships with others. We have

been entrusted with much so we pray that we may be responsible in its use.

Thursday 24 October
Luke 12:49–53

Jesus said to his disciples, 'I came to bring fire to the earth, and how I wish it were already kindled! I have a baptism with which to be baptised, and what stress I am under until it is completed! Do you think that I have come to bring peace to the earth? No, I tell you, but rather division! From now on, five in one household will be divided, three against two and two against three; they will be divided:

father against son
    and son against father,
mother against daughter
    and daughter against mother,
mother-in-law against her daughter-in-law
    and daughter-in-law against mother-in-law.'

- We are immersed into Christ in Baptism and share his mission. He had energy and conviction for what he came to be and do. May that fire be alight in us to complete what he wants for us and from us.
- The messages of the prophets brought divided opinions. Jesus' good news of peace did not find a ready response from many. We pray for union in a divided world, for a genuine hearing of his word of peace.

Friday 25 October
Luke 12:54–59

He also said to the crowds, 'When you see a cloud rising in the west, you immediately say, "It is going to rain"; and so it happens. And when you see the south wind blowing, you say, "There will be scorching heat"; and it happens. You hypocrites! You know how to interpret the appearance of earth and sky, but why do you not know how to interpret the present time?

'And why do you not judge for yourselves what is right? Thus, when you go with your accuser before a magistrate, on the way make an effort to settle the case, or you may be dragged before the judge, and the judge

hand you over to the officer, and the officer throw you in prison. I tell you, you will never get out until you have paid the very last penny.'
- People are able to interpret signs in the sky to predict the weather, be it rain or warmth. Lord, you gave many signs in your life. May we have the wisdom to read and interpret them and to live by them.
- Petty conflicts can get out of proportion and lead to lawsuits. They could be settled in a simpler and more amicable way. Lord, help us to be guided by your wisdom in finding peace and agreement with others.

Saturday 26 October
Luke 13:1–9
At that very time there were some present who told him about the Galileans whose blood Pilate had mingled with their sacrifices. He asked them, 'Do you think that because these Galileans suffered in this way they were worse sinners than all other Galileans? No, I tell you; but unless you repent, you will all perish as they did. Or those eighteen who were killed when the tower of Siloam fell on them – do you think that they were worse offenders than all the others living in Jerusalem? No, I tell you; but unless you repent, you will all perish just as they did.'

Then he told this parable: 'A man had a fig tree planted in his vineyard; and he came looking for fruit on it and found none. So he said to the gardener, "See here! For three years I have come looking for fruit on this fig tree, and still I find none. Cut it down! Why should it be wasting the soil?" He replied, "Sir, let it alone for one more year, until I dig round it and put manure on it. If it bears fruit next year, well and good; but if not, you can cut it down."'
- Jesus drew on two rather obscure events to highlight a clear call to repentance. It required more than interpreting possible causes of external disasters. May we have the humility to look within for a change of heart that facilitates an authentic response to the Lord.
- The story of the fig tree provides a powerful message to a world that tends to look for instant results. We ask for the patience to do our part and to wait on the Lord's time for fruit to be borne.

27 October–2 November 2024

Something to think and pray about each day this week:

Dear Lord, recently I read of someone who felt that other people's profiles were drawn in strong black, or in colour with magic markers, but hers was sketched only in light pencil. I sometimes feel like that woman, almost invisible, unimportant. Maybe it goes with seniority!

Psychologists tell us that to be truly alive someone else's loving gaze is needed: otherwise we can never blossom to our full potential. I know you do your best to provide everyone with good parents, they're a great blessing to a child, but of course this doesn't always happen. You also send us good grandparents, relatives, friends who help us to believe we are worthwhile. They are escorts of your loving care. You want us to receive your great gift, the conviction that we are OK, that we are loved and that we matter.

May your word today convince me that I am good, worthwhile, lovable and wonderful; that I am your beloved, your unique creation, the apple of your eye. May I believe that, no matter what, you love me infinitely, that you embrace me tenderly and live within me and that you have dreams for me that go way beyond my own. For you, I will always be important! My core identity is that I am your beloved! You are, so to speak, part of my DNA.

If I could see myself as I am in your eyes everything would slip into place. Not only am I important to you but I am important for the world. What I am by your gift helps to draw the whole world nearer to God. Let me live out of this rich mystery and be happy about myself, and my low profile. You yourself seem to like a low profile too.

Brian Grogan SJ, *I Am Infinitely Loved*

The Presence of God
'Be still, and know that I am God!' Lord, your words lead us to the calmness and greatness of your presence.

Freedom
If God were trying to tell me something, would I know?
If God were reassuring me or challenging me, would I notice?
I ask for the grace to be free of my own preoccupations
and open to what God may be saying to me.

Consciousness
In the presence of my loving Creator, I look honestly at my feelings over the past day: the highs, the lows and the level ground. Can I see where the Lord has been present?

The Word
In this expectant state of mind, please turn to the text for the day with confidence. Believe that the Holy Spirit is present and may reveal whatever the passage has to say to you. Read reflectively, listening with a third ear to what may be going on in your heart. *(Please turn to the Scripture on the following pages. Inspiration points are there, should you need them. When you are ready, return here to continue.)*

Conversation
Remembering that I am still in God's presence,
I imagine Jesus standing or sitting beside me,
and I say whatever is on my mind, whatever is in my heart,
speaking as one friend to another.

Conclusion
Glory be to the Father, and to the Son, and to the Holy Spirit,
As it was in the beginning, is now and ever shall be,
World without end. Amen.

Sunday 27 October
Thirtieth Sunday in Ordinary Time
Mark 10:46–52

They came to Jericho. As he and his disciples and a large crowd were leaving Jericho, Bartimaeus son of Timaeus, a blind beggar, was sitting by the roadside. When he heard that it was Jesus of Nazareth, he began to shout out and say, 'Jesus, Son of David, have mercy on me!' Many sternly ordered him to be quiet, but he cried out even more loudly, 'Son of David, have mercy on me!' Jesus stood still and said, 'Call him here.' And they called the blind man, saying to him, 'Take heart; get up, he is calling you.' So throwing off his cloak, he sprang up and came to Jesus. Then Jesus said to him, 'What do you want me to do for you?' The blind man said to him, 'My teacher, let me see again.' Jesus said to him, 'Go; your faith has made you well.' Immediately he regained his sight and followed him on the way.

- A named, blind beggar on the side of the road had the faith to ask Jesus to have mercy on him. May we have that faith to recognise Jesus for who he is and the humility to ask him for what we need.

Monday 28 October
Ss Simon and Jude, Apostles
Luke 6:12–19

Now during those days he went out to the mountain to pray; and he spent the night in prayer to God. And when day came, he called his disciples and chose twelve of them, whom he also named apostles: Simon, whom he named Peter, and his brother Andrew, and James, and John, and Philip, and Bartholomew, and Matthew, and Thomas, and James son of Alphaeus, and Simon, who was called the Zealot, and Judas son of James, and Judas Iscariot, who became a traitor.

He came down with them and stood on a level place, with a great crowd of his disciples and a great multitude of people from all Judea, Jerusalem, and the coast of Tyre and Sidon. They had come to hear him and to be healed of their diseases; and those who were troubled with unclean spirits were cured. And all in the crowd were trying to touch him, for power came out from him and healed all of them.

- We remember two little-known apostles, Simon and Jude. They were called by name to be companions of Jesus for mission. We pray that, as their successors, we may respond to the Lord's call more fully and support others in his name.

Tuesday 29 October
Luke 13:18–21

He said therefore, 'What is the kingdom of God like? And to what should I compare it? It is like a mustard seed that someone took and sowed in the garden; it grew and became a tree, and the birds of the air made nests in its branches.'

And again he said, 'To what should I compare the kingdom of God? It is like yeast that a woman took and mixed in with three measures of flour until all of it was leavened.'

- Jesus used a household example of yeast that ferments dough. A small amount of yeast has the capacity to bring significant change. May we be yeast in our world to bring change for good and let the Lord work through the little we have.

Wednesday 30 October
Luke 13:22–30

Jesus went through one town and village after another, teaching as he made his way to Jerusalem. Someone asked him, 'Lord, will only a few be saved?' He said to them, 'Strive to enter through the narrow door; for many, I tell you, will try to enter and will not be able. When once the owner of the house has got up and shut the door, and you begin to stand outside and to knock at the door, saying, "Lord, open to us", then in reply he will say to you, "I do not know where you come from." Then you will begin to say, "We ate and drank with you, and you taught in our streets." But he will say, "I do not know where you come from; go away from me, all you evildoers!" There will be weeping and gnashing of teeth when you see Abraham and Isaac and Jacob and all the prophets in the kingdom of God, and you yourselves thrown out. Then people will come from east and west, from north and south, and will eat in the kingdom of God. Indeed, some are last who will be first, and some are first who will be last.'

- Jesus was on his way to Jerusalem to fulfil his mission. It would entail many challenges. We ask for help, as responsible disciples, to make that journey with him and to accept its cost.

Thursday 31 October
Luke 13:31–35

At that very hour some Pharisees came and said to him, 'Get away from here, for Herod wants to kill you.' He said to them, 'Go and tell that fox for me, "Listen, I am casting out demons and performing cures today and tomorrow, and on the third day I finish my work. Yet today, tomorrow, and the next day I must be on my way, because it is impossible for a prophet to be killed away from Jerusalem." Jerusalem, Jerusalem, the city that kills the prophets and stones those who are sent to it! How often have I desired to gather your children together as a hen gathers her brood under her wings, and you were not willing! See, your house is left to you. And I tell you, you will not see me until the time comes when you say, "Blessed is the one who comes in the name of the Lord."'

- Herod, the fox, was like a man with different masks, unsure of how to relate to Jesus, whose ministry revealed much about Jesus and about Herod. Lord, may we appreciate your prophetic message and respond to it in truth.

Friday 1 November
The Solemnity of All Saints
Matthew 5:1–12a

When Jesus saw the crowds, he went up the mountain; and after he sat down, his disciples came to him. Then he began to speak, and taught them, saying:

'Blessed are the poor in spirit, for theirs is the kingdom of heaven.

'Blessed are those who mourn, for they will be comforted.

'Blessed are the meek, for they will inherit the earth.

'Blessed are those who hunger and thirst for righteousness, for they will be filled.

'Blessed are the merciful, for they will receive mercy.
'Blessed are the pure in heart, for they will see God.
'Blessed are the peacemakers, for they will be called children of God.
'Blessed are those who are persecuted for righteousness' sake, for theirs is the kingdom of heaven.
'Blessed are you when people revile you and persecute you and utter all kinds of evil against you falsely on my account. Rejoice and be glad, for your reward is great in heaven, for in the same way they persecuted the prophets who were before you.'

- All saints reminds us that we belong to a large family, as we remember those who have gone before us and now enjoy life with God. They are the blessed ones who lived out the Beatitudes. May we draw strength from them and their intercession as we continue our journey to the fullness of life.
- These saints include our own loved ones who have completed the journey of this life. We pray that saints, known and unknown, will continue to support us to live that message of blessedness.

Saturday 2 November
The Commemoration of All the Faithful Departed (All Souls)
John 6:37–40
Jesus said, 'Everything that the Father gives me will come to me, and anyone who comes to me I will never drive away; for I have come down from heaven, not to do my own will, but the will of him who sent me. And this is the will of him who sent me, that I should lose nothing of all that he has given me, but raise it up on the last day. This is indeed the will of my Father, that all who see the Son and believe in him may have eternal life; and I will raise them up on the last day.'

- We remember all who have died, acknowledging human limitations and failings. God's desire for them is life to the full. Lord, we ask you to give to all the faithful departed a place of rest, light and peace.

The Thirty-first Week in Ordinary Time

3–9 November 2024

Something to think and pray about each day this week:

When is a good time to pray? In the Gospels, we learn that Jesus prayed in the morning and at night. He rose early in the morning to pray (Mark 1:35). Before choosing the apostles, he spent the whole night in prayer (Luke 6:12). But as well as praying at the opening of the day and during the night, Jesus was in communion with the Father throughout the day. In other words, although he chose certain moments for formal prayer, his prayer was in fact continuous. He was bathed in a continual awareness of the Father. He was totally in tune with the Father; so much so that the Father was always speaking through him. Jesus put it this way, 'I have not spoken on my own, but the Father who sent me has himself given me a commandment about what to say and what to speak' (John 12:49).

It would be great if you could make it your ultimate goal to imitate Jesus and 'pray without ceasing' (1 Thessalonians 5:17). You can start by imitating Jesus' rhythm of formal prayer and making sure to pray both morning and evening.

Thomas G. Casey SJ, *The Mindful Our Father*

The Presence of God
As I sit here, the beating of my heart, the ebb and flow of my breathing, the movements of my mind are all signs of God's ongoing creation of me. I pause for a moment and become aware of this presence of God within me.

Freedom
It is so easy to get caught up with the trappings of wealth in this life. Grant, O Lord, that I may be free from greed and selfishness. Remind me that the best things in life are free: Love, laughter, caring and sharing.

Consciousness
Knowing that God loves me unconditionally, I can afford to be honest about how I am. How has the day been, and how do I feel now? I share my feelings openly with the Lord.

The Word
Lord Jesus, you became human to communicate with me.
You walked and worked on this earth.
You endured the heat and struggled with the cold.
All your time on this earth was spent in caring for humanity.
You healed the sick, you raised the dead.
Most important of all, you saved me from death.
(*Please turn to the Scripture on the following pages. Inspiration points are there, should you need them. When you are ready, return here to continue.*)

Conversation
Sometimes I wonder what I might say if I were to meet you in person, Lord.
I think I might say, 'Thank you' because you are always there for me.

Conclusion
I thank God for these moments we have spent together and for any insights I have been given concerning the text.

Sunday 3 November
Thirty-first Sunday in Ordinary Time
Mark 12:28b–34

One of the scribes came near and heard them disputing with one another, and seeing that he answered them well, he asked him, 'Which commandment is the first of all?' Jesus answered, 'The first is, "Hear, O Israel: the Lord our God, the Lord is one; you shall love the Lord your God with all your heart, and with all your soul, and with all your mind, and with all your strength." The second is this, "You shall love your neighbour as yourself." There is no other commandment greater than these.' Then the scribe said to him, 'You are right, Teacher; you have truly said that "he is one, and besides him there is no other"; and "to love him with all the heart, and with all the understanding, and with all the strength", and "to love one's neighbour as oneself", – this is much more important than all whole burnt-offerings and sacrifices.' When Jesus saw that he answered wisely, he said to him, 'You are not far from the kingdom of God.' After that no one dared to ask him any question.

- Commandment sounds negative and a commandment to love seems ambiguous. However, in looking to Jesus, whose life was one of love, a new understanding is offered. May we draw strength from him whose food was to do the will of the Father who sent him in love to bring salvation.
- Love is the heart of life. External actions find their true meaning when they come from that foundation. Lord, may we further your kingdom by how we live our relationship with you and with one another in love.

Monday 4 November
Luke 14:12–14

He said also to the one who had invited him, 'When you give a luncheon or a dinner, do not invite your friends or your brothers or your relatives or rich neighbours, in case they may invite you in return, and you would be repaid. But when you give a banquet, invite the poor, the crippled, the lame, and the blind. And you will be blessed, because they cannot repay you, for you will be repaid at the resurrection of the righteous.'

- The Lord's invitations are inclusive. He could share table with the poor, the tax collectors and sinners. Lord, help us to move beyond our selective and comfortable invitations to reach out to others in your name.

Tuesday 5 November
Luke 14:15–24

One of the dinner guests, on hearing this, said to him, 'Blessed is anyone who will eat bread in the kingdom of God!' Then Jesus said to him, 'Someone gave a great dinner and invited many. At the time for the dinner he sent his slave to say to those who had been invited, "Come; for everything is ready now." But they all alike began to make excuses. The first said to him, "I have bought a piece of land, and I must go out and see it; please accept my apologies." Another said, "I have bought five yoke of oxen, and I am going to try them out; please accept my apologies." Another said, "I have just been married, and therefore I cannot come." So the slave returned and reported this to his master. Then the owner of the house became angry and said to his slave, "Go out at once into the streets and lanes of the town and bring in the poor, the crippled, the blind, and the lame." And the slave said, "Sir, what you ordered has been done, and there is still room." Then the master said to the slave, "Go out into the roads and lanes, and compel people to come in, so that my house may be filled. For I tell you, none of those who were invited will taste my dinner."'

- Jesus came to the lost sheep of the house of Israel. His own people did not respond very well to his invitations, finding excuses and justifying their stance. May we have the honesty to recognise the truth of our situation and to respond accordingly.
- Those who thought they were on the inside track did not respond, so the outsiders were invited in. As the outsiders, the crippled, the blind and the lame, may we cherish the invitations offered to us in being included in the Lord's list of guests.

Wednesday 6 November
Luke 14:25–33

Now large crowds were travelling with him; and he turned and said to them, 'Whoever comes to me and does not hate father and mother, wife and children, brothers and sisters, yes, and even life itself, cannot be my disciple. Whoever does not carry the cross and follow me cannot be my disciple. For which of you, intending to build a tower, does not first sit down and estimate the cost, to see whether he has enough to complete it? Otherwise, when he has laid a foundation and is not able to finish, all who see it will begin to ridicule him, saying, "This fellow began to build and was not able to finish." Or what king, going out to wage war against another king, will not sit down first and consider whether he is able with ten thousand to oppose the one who comes against him with twenty thousand? If he cannot, then, while the other is still far away, he sends a delegation and asks for the terms of peace. So therefore, none of you can become my disciple if you do not give up all your possessions.'

• A dedicated life of love requires some discipline. Living for others invites us to let go of selfish concerns that can be so influential. Lord, give us the wisdom to make good choices, knowing what to choose and what to forego so that we can live more fully for you.

Thursday 7 November
Luke 15:1–10

Now all the tax-collectors and sinners were coming near to listen to him. And the Pharisees and the scribes were grumbling and saying, 'This fellow welcomes sinners and eats with them.'

So he told them this parable: 'Which one of you, having a hundred sheep and losing one of them, does not leave the ninety-nine in the wilderness and go after the one that is lost until he finds it? When he has found it, he lays it on his shoulders and rejoices. And when he comes home, he calls together his friends and neighbours, saying to them, "Rejoice with me, for I have found my sheep that was lost." Just so, I tell you, there will be more joy in heaven over one sinner who repents than over ninety-nine righteous people who need no repentance.

'Or what woman having ten silver coins, if she loses one of them, does not light a lamp, sweep the house, and search carefully until she finds it? When she has found it, she calls together her friends and neighbours, saying, "Rejoice with me, for I have found the coin that I had lost." Just so, I tell you, there is joy in the presence of the angels of God over one sinner who repents.'

- The introduction to three parables of losing and finding is very revealing. Jesus' association with tax collectors and sinners and his eating with them led to the Pharisees and scribes grumbling. Lord, you reach out to us. May we welcome your acceptance and find joy in your forgiving love.
- These are stories of searching, finding and rejoicing. They tell of the Lord's merciful love, care and concern. As lost sheep, may we rejoice in the Lord finding us and carrying us back to his fold.

Friday 8 November
Luke 16:1–8

Then Jesus said to the disciples, 'There was a rich man who had a manager, and charges were brought to him that this man was squandering his property. So he summoned him and said to him, "What is this that I hear about you? Give me an account of your management, because you cannot be my manager any longer." Then the manager said to himself, "What will I do, now that my master is taking the position away from me? I am not strong enough to dig, and I am ashamed to beg. I have decided what to do so that, when I am dismissed as manager, people may welcome me into their homes." So, summoning his master's debtors one by one, he asked the first, "How much do you owe my master?" He answered, "A hundred jugs of olive oil." He said to him, "Take your bill, sit down quickly, and make it fifty." Then he asked another, "And how much do you owe?" He replied, "A hundred containers of wheat." He said to him, "Take your bill and make it eighty." And his master commended the dishonest manager because he had acted shrewdly; for the children of this age are more shrewd in dealing with their own generation than are the children of light.'

- God has entrusted much to us. We have been made stewards of God's property and creation. May we respond to that gift and be responsible managers of its use.
- A dishonest manager exploited his position to satisfy his own self-interest. He was called to account for what he did and was praised for his cleverness, not his dishonesty. In a world of bargaining and making deals, may we have the honesty to do what is right.

Saturday 9 November
The Dedication of the Lateran Basilica
John 2:13–22

The Passover of the Jews was near, and Jesus went up to Jerusalem. In the temple he found people selling cattle, sheep, and doves, and the money-changers seated at their tables. Making a whip of cords, he drove all of them out of the temple, both the sheep and the cattle. He also poured out the coins of the money-changers and overturned their tables. He told those who were selling the doves, 'Take these things out of here! Stop making my Father's house a market-place!' His disciples remembered that it was written, 'Zeal for your house will consume me.' The Jews then said to him, 'What sign can you show us for doing this?' Jesus answered them, 'Destroy this temple, and in three days I will raise it up.' The Jews then said, 'This temple has been under construction for forty-six years, and will you raise it up in three days?' But he was speaking of the temple of his body. After he was raised from the dead, his disciples remembered that he had said this; and they believed the scripture and the word that Jesus had spoken.

- The temple was a gathering place for God's people to worship. Jesus had respect for the temple and its place in the lives of the people. May our focus be on God's presence and our being called together to worship and give thanks.
- Jesus was pointing to a new era and a new temple. Ultimately, he wanted respect for God and having space for God in life. External buildings were not his main concern. We pray that as temples in whom God dwells that we may be at home with the presence of Jesus.

The Thirty-second Week in Ordinary Time

10–16 November 2024

Something to think and pray about each day this week:

Our screens are filled with frightening images of climate change, which is increasingly called the climate crisis, or even the climate catastrophe. This crisis is not something that is happening in other parts of the world; it is something that happens in the world, and there is only one world. The planet we share is not just our 'common home'; it is our only home. There is no Planet B.

Our future – and the future of the planet – depends on facing up to our responsibility both globally and locally. Conversion and faith, responding to the cry of the earth and the allied cry of the poor, demands significant changes in how we live, in our lifestyle. Changing our way of living merits being called a conversion, as real conversion is not only a change of practice, but requires a change of heart, a transformation from within. Change from within can only happen in a sustained way when it is nourished by the One who lives within every person. Meeting the Lord in the Word of God, in the life of the Church, and in each other is the food that transforms our lives. It is there that we discover the roots of ecological conversion. Of course, this can be expressed in different ways: some will name it as the discovery of the indwelling of the presence of the Holy Spirit in the rhythms of the natural world, in the beauty of creation and in each other that brings about conversion. Whatever names we use, the reality and the urgent call to change remain the same.

Paralysis and wishing the crisis away is no longer an option. Let us resolve to make one change, no matter how little, so that this earth, our common home, may be, for all, the gift God creates it to be.

Archbishop Dermot Farrell, *The Sacred Heart Messenger*, March 2022

The Presence of God

At any time of the day or night we can call on Jesus.
He is always waiting, listening for our call.
What a wonderful blessing.
No phone needed, no e-mails, just a whisper.

Freedom

Lord, grant me the grace to have freedom of the spirit. Cleanse my heart and soul so that I may live joyously in your love.

Consciousness

Knowing that God loves me unconditionally, I look honestly over the past day, its events and my feelings. Do I have something to be grateful for? Then I give thanks. Is there something I am sorry for? Then I ask forgiveness.

The Word

The word of God comes down to us through the Scriptures.
May the Holy Spirit enlighten my mind and my heart
to respond to the Gospel teachings:
to love my neighbour as myself,
to care for my sisters and brothers in Christ.
(Please turn to the Scripture on the following pages. Inspiration points are there, should you need them. When you are ready, return here to continue.)

Conversation

I know with certainty that there were times when you carried me, Lord. There were times when it was through your strength that I got through the dark times in my life.

Conclusion

Glory be to the Father, and to the Son, and to the Holy Spirit,
As it was in the beginning, is now and ever shall be,
World without end. Amen.

Sunday 10 November
Thirty-second Sunday in Ordinary Time
Mark 12:38–44

As he taught, he said, 'Beware of the scribes, who like to walk around in long robes, and to be greeted with respect in the market-places, and to have the best seats in the synagogues and places of honour at banquets! They devour widows' houses and for the sake of appearance say long prayers. They will receive the greater condemnation.'

He sat down opposite the treasury, and watched the crowd putting money into the treasury. Many rich people put in large sums. A poor widow came and put in two small copper coins, which are worth a penny. Then he called his disciples and said to them, 'Truly I tell you, this poor widow has put in more than all those who are contributing to the treasury. For all of them have contributed out of their abundance; but she out of her poverty has put in everything she had, all she had to live on.'

- The scribes were very concerned with externals, with their position and their importance. They were the ones to devour the houses of widows. Help us to see beyond our own importance to what is of true value.
- A poor widow was in marked contrast to the scribes. She was a model of generosity in giving everything she had, not just what she had over and above. Lord, the widow models you in giving all; may she inspire us to be generous in life.

Monday 11 November
Luke 17:1–6

Jesus said to his disciples, 'Occasions for stumbling are bound to come, but woe to anyone by whom they come! It would be better for you if a millstone were hung around your neck and you were thrown into the sea than for you to cause one of these little ones to stumble. Be on your guard! If another disciple sins, you must rebuke the offender, and if there is repentance, you must forgive. And if the same person sins against you seven times a day, and turns back to you seven times and says, "I repent", you must forgive.'

The apostles said to the Lord, 'Increase our faith!' The Lord replied, 'If you had faith the size of a mustard seed, you could say to this mulberry tree, "Be uprooted and planted in the sea", and it would obey you.'

- We are called to repentance and to rely on the Lord for what we need. We pray for the faith that will set us free and sustain us amid the challenges we encounter.

Tuesday 12 November
Luke 17:7–10

'Who among you would say to your slave who has just come in from ploughing or tending sheep in the field, "Come here at once and take your place at the table"? Would you not rather say to him, "Prepare supper for me, put on your apron and serve me while I eat and drink; later you may eat and drink"? Do you thank the slave for doing what was commanded? So you also, when you have done all that you were ordered to do, say, "We are worthless slaves; we have done only what we ought to have done!"'

- The role of slaves was clear as they were expected to be available for whatever their owner desired. Jesus, though you were Lord and Master, you made yourself a slave for us. May we imitate you in being available to serve others in your name.

Wednesday 13 November
Luke 17:11–19

On the way to Jerusalem Jesus was going through the region between Samaria and Galilee. As he entered a village, ten lepers approached him. Keeping their distance, they called out, saying, 'Jesus, Master, have mercy on us!' When he saw them, he said to them, 'Go and show yourselves to the priests.' And as they went, they were made clean. Then one of them, when he saw that he was healed, turned back, praising God with a loud voice. He prostrated himself at Jesus' feet and thanked him. And he was a Samaritan. Then Jesus asked, 'Were not ten made clean? But the other nine, where are they? Was none of them found to return and give praise to God except this foreigner?' Then he said to him, 'Get up and go on your way; your faith has made you well.'

- Lepers, who were supposed to remain isolated, approached Jesus, pleading for mercy. Please give us your healing so that we do not become isolated from you or others.
- It was an outsider, a Samaritan, who took time to come back and give thanks to Jesus for healing. Did the others forget or were they too busy celebrating? We pray that in our busy lives we do not take our blessings for granted but turn to God in gratitude.

Thursday 14 November
Luke 17:20–25

Once Jesus was asked by the Pharisees when the kingdom of God was coming, and he answered, 'The kingdom of God is not coming with things that can be observed; nor will they say, "Look, here it is!" or "There it is!" For, in fact, the kingdom of God is among you.'

Then he said to the disciples, 'The days are coming when you will long to see one of the days of the Son of Man, and you will not see it. They will say to you, "Look there!" or "Look here!" Do not go, do not set off in pursuit. For as the lightning flashes and lights up the sky from one side to the other, so will the Son of Man be in his day. But first he must endure much suffering and be rejected by this generation.'

- There are external kingdoms where privileges and rules of membership are defined for citizens. Lord, your kingdom is of a different kind, one where you desire to rule over our hearts in love. Help us to grow as members of your kingdom, where we are at home with you and your leadership.

Friday 15 November
Luke 17:26–37

Just as it was in the days of Noah, so too it will be in the days of the Son of Man. They were eating and drinking, and marrying and being given in marriage, until the day Noah entered the ark, and the flood came and destroyed all of them. Likewise, just as it was in the days of

Lot: they were eating and drinking, buying and selling, planting and building, but on the day that Lot left Sodom, it rained fire and sulphur from heaven and destroyed all of them – it will be like that on the day that the Son of Man is revealed. On that day, anyone on the housetop who has belongings in the house must not come down to take them away; and likewise anyone in the field must not turn back. Remember Lot's wife. Those who try to make their life secure will lose it, but those who lose their life will keep it. I tell you, on that night there will be two in one bed; one will be taken and the other left. There will be two women grinding meal together; one will be taken and the other left.' Then they asked him, 'Where, Lord?' He said to them, 'Where the corpse is, there the vultures will gather.'

- The message of the gospel is paradoxical. The lowly are raised, the poor are blessed and it is in losing life that we keep it. We pray to be guided by the Lord and to allow him to be our primary focus in how we live.

Saturday 16 November
Luke 18:1–8
Then Jesus told them a parable about their need to pray always and not to lose heart. He said, 'In a certain city there was a judge who neither feared God nor had respect for people. In that city there was a widow who kept coming to him and saying, "Grant me justice against my opponent." For a while he refused; but later he said to himself, "Though I have no fear of God and no respect for anyone, yet because this widow keeps bothering me, I will grant her justice, so that she may not wear me out by continually coming."' And the Lord said, 'Listen to what the unjust judge says. And will not God grant justice to his chosen ones who cry to him day and night? Will he delay long in helping them? I tell you, he will quickly grant justice to them. And yet, when the Son of Man comes, will he find faith on earth?'

- The widow knew the judge's weak point – she persisted and he gave in unwillingly for the sake of peace. Jesus, you reveal a God of justice who will respond to our prayers. May we have the courage and faith to persist in our asking.

The Thirty-third Week in Ordinary Time

17–23 November 2024

Something to think and pray about each day this week:

Lord, awareness of your love can slip away from my heart so easily, whenever there's a disaster I begin to doubt it. My small mind starts whirling, and I ask, 'How could you do this to me?' or 'How could you let that happen to someone else?' The dark side of things can so quickly eclipse the light. I say – excuse me for this! – 'Where the hell are you gone?' My demons then have a field day.

Let me instead watch out for your way of going about things. At the beginning, you tell us, darkness lay over the face of the earth then, first of all your works, you created light. Why did you let darkness have its place; why not obliterate it? But light and darkness *both* have their place in your scheme of things. This helps me! It makes me less surprised at the darkness that is around and focuses me on the fact that the light will come back. I should not expect a world without some darkness.

Because you come into the world as divine light, darkness is pushed back and can't eclipse it. I should focus on you as light, holding the darkness at bay, dealing resourcefully with suffering and evil. In another world perpetual light will shine on us all, but for now help me to live in the light myself and to battle the darkness as you do. After all I am infinitely loved and you need me to be 'the light of the world'. May I believe that patient endurance illuminates what is dark from the inside. So it was on Calvary and can be in my life too.

Brian Grogan SJ, *I Am Infinitely Loved*

The Presence of God

'Be still, and know that I am God!' Lord, may your spirit guide me to seek your loving presence more and more for it is there I find rest and refreshment from this busy world.

Freedom

By God's grace I was born to live in freedom. Free to enjoy the pleasures he created for me. Dear Lord, grant that I may live as you intended, with complete confidence in your loving care.

Consciousness

How am I today?
Where am I with God? With others?
Do I have something to be grateful for? Then I give thanks.
Is there something I am sorry for? Then I ask forgiveness.

The Word

God speaks to each of us individually. I need to listen, to hear what he is saying to me. Read the text a few times, then listen. *(Please turn to the Scripture on the following pages. Inspiration points are there, should you need them. When you are ready, return here to continue.)*

Conversation

How has God's word moved me? Has it left me cold?
Has it consoled me or moved me to act in a new way?
I imagine Jesus standing or sitting beside me.
I turn and share my feelings with him.

Conclusion

I thank God for these moments we have spent together and for any insights I have been given concerning the text.

Sunday 17 November
Thirty-third Sunday in Ordinary Time
Mark 13:24–32

Jesus said to his disciples, 'But in those days, after that suffering,
the sun will be darkened,
>and the moon will not give its light,
>and the stars will be falling from heaven,
>and the powers in the heavens will be shaken.

Then they will see "the Son of Man coming in clouds" with great power
and glory. Then he will send out the angels, and gather his elect from
the four winds, from the ends of the earth to the ends of heaven.

'From the fig tree learn its lesson: as soon as its branch becomes
tender and puts forth its leaves, you know that summer is near. So also,
when you see these things taking place, you know that he is near, at the
very gates. Truly I tell you, this generation will not pass away until all
these things have taken place. Heaven and earth will pass away, but my
words will not pass away.

'But about that day or hour no one knows, neither the angels in
heaven, nor the Son, but only the Father.'

- As we come near the end of the Church's year, we are reminded of
  end times, with the Son of Man coming on the clouds with great
  power and glory. Lord, help us to appreciate the deeper message of
  the hope you promise, in gathering the elect from the four winds.

Monday 18 November
Luke 18:35–43

As he approached Jericho, a blind man was sitting by the roadside
begging. When he heard a crowd going by, he asked what was
happening. They told him, 'Jesus of Nazareth is passing by.' Then he
shouted, 'Jesus, Son of David, have mercy on me!' Those who were in
front sternly ordered him to be quiet; but he shouted even more loudly,
'Son of David, have mercy on me!' Jesus stood still and ordered the man
to be brought to him; and when he came near, he asked him, 'What
do you want me to do for you?' He said, 'Lord, let me see again.' Jesus
said to him, 'Receive your sight; your faith has saved you.' Immediately

he regained his sight and followed him, glorifying God; and all the people, when they saw it, praised God.

- This is another account of a blind man who desired to have his sight restored. Lord, there are times when we lose our vision and are blinded by passing things; please give us the healing to return our focus to you when we have lost it.
- The blind man inquired and discovered Jesus was passing by and shouted out. Some ordered him to be quiet. Lord, your desire met that of the blind man. May you transform our desires and lead us to give praise to you for all you have done for us.

Tuesday 19 November
Luke 19:1–10

He entered Jericho and was passing through it. A man was there named Zacchaeus; he was a chief tax-collector and was rich. He was trying to see who Jesus was, but on account of the crowd he could not, because he was short in stature. So he ran ahead and climbed a sycamore tree to see him, because he was going to pass that way. When Jesus came to the place, he looked up and said to him, 'Zacchaeus, hurry and come down; for I must stay at your house today.' So he hurried down and was happy to welcome him. All who saw it began to grumble and said, 'He has gone to be the guest of one who is a sinner.' Zacchaeus stood there and said to the Lord, 'Look, half of my possessions, Lord, I will give to the poor; and if I have defrauded anyone of anything, I will pay back four times as much.' Then Jesus said to him, 'Today salvation has come to this house, because he too is a son of Abraham. For the Son of Man came to seek out and to save the lost.'

- Zacchaeus was short in stature, but he was a rich tax collector. His limitation became an asset, as in climbing a tree he made himself visible to Jesus, who called him. We pray that our limitations may make us available to you, Lord, in recognising our need of your ministry for us.
- Zacchaeus wanted to see Jesus, who desired to meet him. Jesus called him down to earth from his tree and invited himself to his house. Lord, you call us beyond our past, reminding us that today you are bringing salvation to our houses.

Wednesday 20 November
Luke 19:11–28

As they were listening to this, he went on to tell a parable, because he was near Jerusalem, and because they supposed that the kingdom of God was to appear immediately. So he said, 'A nobleman went to a distant country to get royal power for himself and then return. He summoned ten of his slaves, and gave them ten pounds, and said to them, "Do business with these until I come back." But the citizens of his country hated him and sent a delegation after him, saying, "We do not want this man to rule over us." When he returned, having received royal power, he ordered these slaves, to whom he had given the money, to be summoned so that he might find out what they had gained by trading. The first came forward and said, "Lord, your pound has made ten more pounds." He said to him, "Well done, good slave! Because you have been trustworthy in a very small thing, take charge of ten cities." Then the second came, saying, "Lord, your pound has made five pounds." He said to him, "And you, rule over five cities." Then the other came, saying, "Lord, here is your pound. I wrapped it up in a piece of cloth, for I was afraid of you, because you are a harsh man; you take what you did not deposit, and reap what you did not sow." He said to him, "I will judge you by your own words, you wicked slave! You knew, did you, that I was a harsh man, taking what I did not deposit and reaping what I did not sow? Why then did you not put my money into the bank? Then when I returned, I could have collected it with interest." He said to the bystanders, "Take the pound from him and give it to the one who has ten pounds." (And they said to him, "Lord, he has ten pounds!") "I tell you, to all those who have, more will be given; but from those who have nothing, even what they have will be taken away. But as for these enemies of mine who did not want me to be king over them – bring them here and slaughter them in my presence."'

- Jesus was near Jerusalem. His listeners did not understand the Kingdom of God and they did not want to have Jesus to rule over them. The parable highlights the different relationships and responses. Lord, give us a better understanding so that we can be more responsible members of your kingdom.

Thursday 21 November
Luke 19:41–44

As he came near and saw the city, he wept over it, saying, 'If you, even you, had only recognised on this day the things that make for peace! But now they are hidden from your eyes. Indeed, the days will come upon you, when your enemies will set up ramparts around you and surround you, and hem you in on every side. They will crush you to the ground, you and your children within you, and they will not leave within you one stone upon another; because you did not recognise the time of your visitation from God.'

- Jerusalem, the city of peace, did not understand Jesus. He desired the best for it and lamented over it. Lord, open our eyes to the depth of your concern for us so that we may take your message more fully to heart.
- This account can be seen as foretelling the destruction of Jerusalem, which would happen many years after Jesus' death. We pray that we may recognise the time of God's visitation so that we can be more in tune with Jesus' desire for us at this time.

Friday 22 November
Luke 19:45–48

Then he entered the temple and began to drive out those who were selling things there; and he said, 'It is written,
   "My house shall be a house of prayer";
      but you have made it a den of robbers.'
Every day he was teaching in the temple. The chief priests, the scribes, and the leaders of the people kept looking for a way to kill him; but they did not find anything they could do, for all the people were spellbound by what they heard.

- God's house was to be one of prayer and worship, not a place for a den of robbers. The sacred place was to offer sacred space for God in the people's lives. Lord, give us a deeper sense of the sacred and of your invitation to us.
- The leaders were looking for a way to kill Jesus, whereas the people were spellbound by his daily teaching in the temple. The contrasting

attitudes speak to the world of now. May we have the freedom to listen anew and have the strength to live the truth of Jesus.

Saturday 23 November
Luke 20:27–40
Some Sadducees, those who say there is no resurrection, came to him and asked him a question, 'Teacher, Moses wrote for us that if a man's brother dies, leaving a wife but no children, the man shall marry the widow and raise up children for his brother. Now there were seven brothers; the first married, and died childless; then the second and the third married her, and so in the same way all seven died childless. Finally the woman also died. In the resurrection, therefore, whose wife will the woman be? For the seven had married her.'

Jesus said to them, 'Those who belong to this age marry and are given in marriage; but those who are considered worthy of a place in that age and in the resurrection from the dead neither marry nor are given in marriage. Indeed they cannot die any more, because they are like angels and are children of God, being children of the resurrection. And the fact that the dead are raised Moses himself showed, in the story about the bush, where he speaks of the Lord as the God of Abraham, the God of Isaac, and the God of Jacob. Now he is God not of the dead, but of the living; for to him all of them are alive.' Then some of the scribes answered, 'Teacher, you have spoken well.' For they no longer dared to ask him another question.

- The Pharisees believed in the resurrection but the Sadducees did not. Each group had its own concerns about Jesus. Lord, may our questions be authentic and bring us to a deeper relationship with you.
- Jesus saw that the world had its rules and its limits, but he was leading to something beyond that. He drew attention to events such as the burning bush, which was not burnt up. May we appreciate the God of the living, who is more than the message of this passing world.

24–30 November 2024

Something to think and pray about each day this week:

Today, in our diverse world, we all come to faith from different places and from different backgrounds. Faith in Christ is sort of like the great equaliser. Prayer is one of the spiritual disciplines we all have to learn. We can ask several questions about prayer: How do you say a prayer? What is a personal prayer? How can I grow my prayer life?

Finding God in all things is integral to the Ignatian worldview. 'The world is charged with the grandeur of God' (Gerard Manley Hopkins). This God is present in our lives, 'labouring for us' in all things; he can be discovered, through faith, in all natural and human events, in history as a whole and, most especially, in the lived experience of each individual person.

Pope Francis exhorts us: 'Prayer unites us; it makes us brothers and sisters … and reminds us of a beautiful truth which we sometimes forget, that in prayer, we all learn to say "Father", "Dad". We learn to see one another as brothers and sisters. In prayer, there are no rich and poor people, there are sons and daughters, sisters and brothers. In prayer, there is no first or second class, there is brotherhood. It is in prayer that our hearts find the strength not to be cold and insensitive in the face of injustice. In prayer, God keeps calling us, opening our hearts to charity.'

In this way we can keep helping one another to experience the joy of knowing that God is in our midst and that God helps us to find solutions to the injustices that he himself has already experienced. Set a time for prayer to create a prayer lifestyle! Going deeper in prayer happens over time and with help.

Sunny Jacob SJ, *The Sacred Heart Messenger*, June 2022

The Presence of God
'Come to me, all you who are weary and are carrying heavy burdens, and I will give you rest.' Here I am, Lord. I come to seek your presence. I long for your healing power.

Freedom
By God's grace I was born to live in freedom. Free to enjoy the pleasures he created for me. Dear Lord, grant that I may live as you intended, with complete confidence in your loving care.

Consciousness
Knowing that God loves me unconditionally, I look honestly over the past day, its events and my feelings. Do I have something to be grateful for? Then I give thanks. Is there something I am sorry for? Then I ask forgiveness.

The Word
God speaks to each of us individually. I listen attentively to hear what he is saying to me. Read the text a few times, then listen. *(Please turn to the Scripture on the following pages. Inspiration points are there, should you need them. When you are ready, return here to continue.)*

Conversation
I know with certainty that there were times when you carried me, Lord. There were times when it was through your strength that I got through the dark times in my life.

Conclusion
Glory be to the Father, and to the Son, and to the Holy Spirit,
As it was in the beginning, is now and ever shall be,
World without end. Amen.

Sunday 24 November
Our Lord Jesus Christ, King of the Universe
John 18:33b–37
Then Pilate entered the headquarters again, summoned Jesus, and asked him, 'Are you the King of the Jews?' Jesus answered, 'Do you ask this on your own, or did others tell you about me?' Pilate replied, 'I am not a Jew, am I? Your own nation and the chief priests have handed you over to me. What have you done?' Jesus answered, 'My kingdom is not from this world. If my kingdom were from this world, my followers would be fighting to keep me from being handed over to the Jews. But as it is, my kingdom is not from here.' Pilate asked him, 'So you are a king?' Jesus answered, 'You say that I am a king. For this I was born, and for this I came into the world, to testify to the truth. Everyone who belongs to the truth listens to my voice.'

- Jesus was a king of a different kind, as was his kingdom, not being of this world. He was a spiritual leader who came to bring the fullness of life to his followers. Lord, you desired your way of love to rule our hearts so that we may be one in you and with you.
- Pilate's image of a king was of one of the earthly realm, with power and glory. Jesus' kingdom was where his way and word would find a home in the human heart and give direction to life. May that kingdom of Jesus come, one of love and peace that will transform our lives and relationships.

Monday 25 November
Luke 21:1–4
He looked up and saw rich people putting their gifts into the treasury; he also saw a poor widow put in two small copper coins. He said, 'Truly I tell you, this poor widow has put in more than all of them; for all of them have contributed out of their abundance, but she out of her poverty has put in all she had to live on.'

- We are familiar with wealthy people giving large donations and being recognised and honoured for doing so. We pray that we may be like the poor widow in being generous with the little we have to give honour to God in the poor.

- St Paul reminds us that all we have is gift (1 Corinthians 4:7). Possessiveness imprisons us and allows insecurity to have an undue influence. May we appreciate what we have in this passing life and not cling to it.

Tuesday 26 November
Luke 21:5–11
When some were speaking about the temple, how it was adorned with beautiful stones and gifts dedicated to God, he said, 'As for these things that you see, the days will come when not one stone will be left upon another; all will be thrown down.'

They asked him, 'Teacher, when will this be, and what will be the sign that this is about to take place?' And he said, 'Beware that you are not led astray; for many will come in my name and say, "I am he!" and, "The time is near!" Do not go after them.

'When you hear of wars and insurrections, do not be terrified; for these things must take place first, but the end will not follow immediately.' Then he said to them, 'Nation will rise against nation, and kingdom against kingdom; there will be great earthquakes, and in various places famines and plagues; and there will be dreadful portents and great signs from heaven.'

- The ornate temple is in marked contrast to the poor widow who offered two small copper coins. Her legacy would remain but this elaborate temple would be destroyed. Lord, help us to retain perspective in life so that our hearts are set on what is of lasting value.
- Jesus gave a warning about the end times. The destruction of the temple was like the end of the world. Jesus wanted to alert his listeners to what would endure. Lord, you spoke of the end, but you remind us not to be terrified, as you remain our security.

Wednesday 27 November
Luke 21:12–19
Jesus said, 'But before all this occurs, they will arrest you and persecute you; they will hand you over to synagogues and prisons, and you will be

brought before kings and governors because of my name. This will give you an opportunity to testify. So make up your minds not to prepare your defence in advance; for I will give you words and a wisdom that none of your opponents will be able to withstand or contradict. You will be betrayed even by parents and brothers, by relatives and friends; and they will put some of you to death. You will be hated by all because of my name. But not a hair of your head will perish. By your endurance you will gain your souls.'

- Those end times will bring struggles in relationships, with suffering, arrest and betrayal, even by one's own. Lord, give us the words of wisdom that we need in our time of testing.

- There was a clear call to trust God in the midst of all the difficulties that would arise because of the name of Jesus. May we have the endurance to stand firm, trusting in your presence and the promise of salvation.

Thursday 28 November
Luke 21:20–28

'When you see Jerusalem surrounded by armies, then know that its desolation has come near. Then those in Judea must flee to the mountains, and those inside the city must leave it, and those out in the country must not enter it; for these are days of vengeance, as a fulfilment of all that is written. Woe to those who are pregnant and to those who are nursing infants in those days! For there will be great distress on the earth and wrath against this people; they will fall by the edge of the sword and be taken away as captives among all nations; and Jerusalem will be trampled on by the Gentiles, until the times of the Gentiles are fulfilled.

'There will be signs in the sun, the moon, and the stars, and on the earth distress among nations confused by the roaring of the sea and the waves. People will faint from fear and foreboding of what is coming upon the world, for the powers of the heavens will be shaken. Then they will see "the Son of Man coming in a cloud" with power and great glory. Now when these things begin to take place, stand up and raise your heads, because your redemption is drawing near.'

- There is a picture of doom and gloom, of destruction and devastation. Jerusalem will be destroyed and the people scattered. We pray that in such difficult situations we may hold on to what endures, relying on the Lord to provide what we truly need.
- Many become concerned about the second coming of Jesus, but the real challenge is to accept his first coming and the reason for it. In the midst of the difficulties, we are invited to stand up, to raise our heads. Lord, may we draw assurance from you that our liberation is drawing near.

Friday 29 November
Luke 21:29–33

Then he told them a parable: 'Look at the fig tree and all the trees; as soon as they sprout leaves you can see for yourselves and know that summer is already near. So also, when you see these things taking place, you know that the kingdom of God is near. Truly I tell you, this generation will not pass away until all things have taken place. Heaven and earth will pass away, but my words will not pass away.'

- We note the change of season in nature. The presence of leaves and seeds indicates that new life is emerging, May we have the insight to note where God's life is sprouting so that we can facilitate the bearing of fruit in his name
- This life is transient. There is growth and bearing of fruit, just as there is change and decay. Lord, in noting what is passing, may we attend to what is enduring as you remind us that your world will not pass away.

Saturday 30 November
St Andrew, Apostle
Matthew 4:18–22

As he walked by the Sea of Galilee, he saw two brothers, Simon, who is called Peter, and Andrew his brother, casting a net into the lake – for they were fishermen. And he said to them, 'Follow me, and I will make you fish for people.' Immediately they left their nets and followed him. As he went from there, he saw two other brothers, James son of

Zebedee and his brother John, in the boat with their father Zebedee, mending their nets, and he called them. Immediately they left the boat and their father, and followed him.

- Andrew was somewhat overshadowed by his brother Simon Peter. He, too, was fisherman who left his nets to fish for people. Jesus and his way became the focus. May we have the freedom to hear the Lord's call anew and leave aside what is not needed in following him.

- We have arrived at the end of the Church year, but it is like a cycle that begins again with Advent, as we prepare to welcome Jesus anew. May we draw strength from Andrew to remain centred on the Lord, to welcome his call and the mission he shares with us.